'*Queer Theory Now* is an invaluable res
McCann and Monaghan define key ter
the work of theorists of colour and trans theorists, the authors uncover the
variegated histories that have converged on, and diverged from, queer theory.
Eminently teachable.'

— **Jean-Thomas Tremblay**, *New Mexico State University, USA*

'This is a rigorous and pedagogically designed introduction to queer theory
that covers not only the field's foundations but also more recent debates.
Moreover, the inclusion of case studies, definitions of key terms and film rec-
ommendations makes complex ideas accessible for students finding their way
in queer theory.'

— **Sam McBean**, *Queen Mary University of London, UK*

'Part disciplinary history, part field assessment, part critical reference, *Queer
Theory Now* is perhaps most importantly a primer for the queer work ahead.
It will be a welcome queer pedagogy text in both undergraduate and graduate
classrooms.'

— **Matt Brim**, *College of Staten Island, CUNY, USA*

'The last real primer for queer theory was Annemarie Jagose's *Queer
Theory* over 20 years ago. *Queer Theory Now* fills that enormous gap, covering
key areas such as intersectionality, the global dimensions of queerness,
and the history of the field, while remaining attentive to the difficulties of
defining the complex and ever-evolving perspectives on sexuality and gender.'

— **Ross G. Forman**, *University of Warwick, UK*

'The most concise yet comprehensive explanation of the past, present and
future of queer theory available today. This book traces queer theory's significant histories and locates its renewed relevance in contemporary times. It
makes queer theory's evolution and complexities easy to access and is a must-
have for any university library.'

— **Joanna McIntyre**, *Swinburne University of Technology, Australia*

'*Queer Theory Now* is a thorough synthesis of thirty years of queer theory and
its precursors. It should be required reading in classrooms around the world.
An essential primer!'

— **Don Romesburg**, *Sonoma State University, USA*

'An absolute must read! *Queer Theory Now*, carefully crafted by McCann and Monaghan, is an incredibly timely, necessary and rich resource. Undergraduates and post-graduate students interested in engaging with historical and contemporary debates in queer theories will find much to stimulate their thinking in this book.'

– Leanne Coll, *Deakin University, Australia*

'McCann and Monaghan have written one of the most insightful overviews of queer theory currently available. It is highly recommended for those seeking an accessible guide to key ideas, issues, developments, and controversies in this field. The writers deserve credit for their ample demonstration of queer theory's applicability to a range of disciplines, lives, and events.'

– Páraic Finnerty, *University of Portsmouth, UK*

QUEER THEORY NOW

From Foundations to Futures

Hannah McCann and
Whitney Monaghan

BLOOMSBURY ACADEMIC

LONDON • NEW YORK • OXFORD • NEW DELHI • SYDNEY

BLOOMSBURY ACADEMIC
Bloomsbury Publishing Plc
50 Bedford Square, London, WC1B 3DP, UK
1385 Broadway, New York, NY 10018, USA
29 Earlsfort Terrace, Dublin 2, Ireland

BLOOMSBURY, BLOOMSBURY ACADEMIC and the Diana logo
are trademarks of Bloomsbury Publishing Plc

First published 2020 by RED GLOBE PRESS
Reprinted by Bloomsbury Academic, 2022, 2023

Copyright © Hannah McCann and Whitney Monaghan, under exclusive licence
to Springer Nature Limited 2020

Hannah McCann and Whitney Monaghan have asserted their right under the Copyright,
Designs and Patents Act, 1988, to be identified as Authors of this work.

For legal purposes the Acknowledgements on p. xvii constitute
an extension of this copyright page.

A catalogue record for this book is available from the British Library.

A catalog record for this book is available from the Library of Congress.

ISBN: HB: 978-1-3520-0784-8
PB: 978-1-3520-0751-0
ePDF: 978-1-3520-0752-7
ePub: 978-1-3503-1453-5

Printed and bound in Great Britain

To find out more about our authors and books visit
www.bloomsbury.com and sign up for our newsletters.

To Tim, tireless crusader for queer

Contents

List of Figures and Tables

Figures

Tables

Key Terms/Concepts

Dedicated explanatory boxes for italicized terms.

Key Debates/Queer Theory in Practice

As appears in the order in the text.

Recommended Films

1. Defining Queer Theory	*But I'm a Cheerleader* *The Celluloid Closet* *Mulholland Drive*
2. From Pathology to Pride	*The Rejected* *Daughters of Bilitis Video Project* *When We Rise*
3. Sexuality and Feminism	*Born in Flames* *Inside Deep Throat* *Itty Bitty Titty Committee*
4. AIDS and Acting Up	*Chocolate Babies* *The Gift* *BPM (Beats Per Minute)*
5. Outing the Closet	*Orlando* *Paris is Burning*
6. Theory Meets Identity	*All About My Mother* *Hedwig and the Angry Inch* *The Miseducation of Cameron Post*
7. Negotiating Intersections	*Margarita with a Straw* *Futuro Beach* *Moonlight*
8. Temporality and Queer Utopias	*The Birds* *Butterfly* *Show Me Love*

Acknowledgements

First and foremost, we are indebted to the activists and thinkers that have come before us that have shaped "theories" of queer. We hope that this book sheds some light on key genealogies, terms and applied uses of queer theory, that trace multiple strands to bring in new and diverse perspectives to queer theory debates.

Thank you to our editor, Lloyd Langman, for taking a chance on the need for a new queer theory textbook, and for all of the helpful suggestions along the way. Thanks also to Helen Keane for providing the necessary advice to get this project started. Our gratitude is also to our students, who have both delighted in and troubled queer theory, and who have shaped our approach to this text more than anyone else.

Thank you also to those who read and provided comment on draft chapters – Sarah Baker, Jay Daniel Thompson and Sophie Pascoe. Thank you to our queer comrades for helping our intellectual development in queer theory and the many and varied discussions, in particular Shane Tas, Amy Thomas, Lucy Nicholas, Luara Karlson-Carp, Clare Southerton and Rosanne Kennedy. Thank you also to Kalissa Alexeyeff, Cathy Ayres, Briony Lipton, Nida Mollison, Nicola Menser Hearn, Kirsten Stevens and Janice Loreck for their endless encouragement.

To Hayley Summers and Geraldine Fela – thank you for supporting us through this process, and for enriching our queer lives.

1 Defining Queer Theory

KEY TERMS AND CONCEPTS	queer, queering, genealogy, the gender binary, LGBTIQ, norms, normalisation, normative, normativity, heteronormativity, anti-normativity, postqueer

DEFINING THE INDEFINABLE

How can theory be "queer"? What is the difference between queer identity, queer politics and queer theory? Is queer theory always related to sexuality in some way? The aim of this book is to help make sense of these questions by tracing queer theory across a range of historical contexts. As we find, though queer identity, politics and theory can be understood to offer separate and often conflicting approaches, a historical lens helps us understand how these tensions have come to be. We find that we cannot understand what queer theory "now" is, without looking backward, and at times, rethinking a few grand narratives.

It is often said that queer theory is difficult to define, or that it is antithetical to the spirit of the theory to tie it down to a single meaning. As we will see throughout this book, queer is a "deliberately ambiguous term" that is simultaneously a way of naming, describing, doing and being (Monaghan 2016, 7). This is where queer theory finds its radical potential as a term to challenge, interrogate, destabilise and subvert, but it also means there is difficulty in pinpointing queer theory's meaning. As Annamarie Jagose notes, it is "a concept that prominently insists on the radical unknowability of its future formations," that maintains a "strategically open-ended relational character" (2009, 158). Or, as Donald Hall has argued, we must understand queer theory in the plural: "there is no 'queer theory' in the singular, only many different voices and sometimes overlapping, sometimes divergent perspectives that can be loosely called 'queer theories'" (2003, 5). Queer theory is, it seems, mercurial (Dilley 1999).

While this avoidance of definability may seem unhelpful, we can also see that the persistently repeated idea of queer theory as "indefinable" works as

1

its own form of definition. The insistence on indefinability hints at queer theory as a lens that emphasises the slipperiness of meaning and the transgression of categories and boundaries. Although the idea of queer theory emerged explicitly in academia in the 1990s, it has lasting relevance precisely because of its ability to remain flexible and open to new directions and discussions.

Importantly, use of the term "queer" preceded its conjunction with "theory". Originally, "queer" was a term broadly used to refer to what was odd, strange, abnormal or sick, and along these lines employed as a colloquial slur for homosexuality (Halperin 2003). In the 1980s, queer was reclaimed by the LGBTIQ community as an umbrella term to designate resistant and non-normative sexuality, seemingly unburdened from the separatist strains that had emerged around gay and lesbian identities (discussed in Chapter 4). Maintaining a relation to its original meaning, reclaiming "queer" was about being *different*, but unapologetically so. As Heather Love notes, "When queer was adopted in the late 1980s it was chosen because it evoked a long history of insult and abuse – you could hear the hurt in it" (2007, 2). As Judith Butler has also argued, it is precisely queer's links to "accusation, pathologization, insult" that gives "queer" its discursive power when re-used and repeated as a self-identifier (1993, 18).

As we discuss at length in Chapter 4, the widespread recuperation of the term queer occurred in the 1980s alongside new forms of activism around HIV and AIDS. Despite conservative rhetoric, the virus was not a result of sexual "identity" but rather, was transmitted through sexual "practices". Here, the machinations of the virus itself, combined with the need for mass mobilisation against unresponsive governments and the pharmaceutical industry, led to a new kind of activism organised around coalitions rather than discrete identities. "Queer" took on a new profound meaning, intended to account for the coalitional thinking and organising in the LGBTIQ community at the time.

Even though the early use of the term queer in activism had a profound impact on the shape of theory to come, it was not until the 1990s that "queer" came to be explicitly connected to "theory". The term "queer theory" was coined by Teresa de Lauretis in 1990, at a conference of the same name held at The University of California, Santa Cruz (see de Lauretis 1991). Describing the language around "lesbian and gay" identity at the time, de Lauretis suggests:

> the term "Queer Theory" was arrived at in the effort to avoid all of these fine distinctions in our discursive protocols, not to adhere to any one of the given terms, not to assume their ideological liabilities, but instead to both transgress and transcend them – or at the very least problematize them. (1991, v)

As David Halperin argues, de Lauretis' use of the term was "deliberately disruptive", to challenge what was taken for granted as "theory" in the academy, and to contest the boundaries of lesbian and gay studies (2003, 340). Five years after de Lauretis coined the term queer theory, Lauren Berlant and Michael Warner explored some of the usages and potentials of the term "queer" in their essay "What Does Queer Theory Teach Us About X?" In this essay, Berlant and Warner refuse to pin queer theory to a single meaning, and argue that queer thinking "takes on varied shapes, risks, ambitions, and ambivalences in various contexts" (1995, 344). While "queer theory is not a theory *of* anything in particular", Berlant and Warner argue that it constituted from a range of academic and non-academic contexts and is animated by a desire to create publics that understand differences of privilege and struggle (1995, 344). They caution against solidifying this "queerness" into the label queer theory as they suggest it "makes queer and nonqueer audiences forget these differences and imagine a context (theory) in which queer has a stable referential content and pragmatic force" (1995, 344). As this illustrates, from its early use in theoretical terms, "queer" operated as a wish and a hope for a different kind of thinking and engagement with questions of sexuality, gender, identity, power and the politics of oppression.

Key term: Queer and queering

As Janet Jakobsen outlines, we can differentiate the uses of "queer" in three ways (1998, 516–517):

- As a noun (example: "this is the queer space").
- As an identity that resists traditional categories (example: "I identify as queer").
- As a verb (example: "let's queer gender!").

These ways of using "queer" are often in tension with one another. Jakobsen suggests that the last option – queer as a kind of *doing* rather than *being* – holds the most political potential because it focuses on resistance (rather than description) and practice (rather than identity).

To undertake "queering" is to deploy queer as a verb, to challenge and resist expectations or norms. For example, "queering femininity" might mean thinking about how femininity can be more than an oppressive gender ideal, and can be embodied in non-normative ways (McCann 2018).

QUEER THEORY BEYOND IDENTITY

Queer theory questions the foundations of sexual identity (Britzman 1995, 153). The fundamental idea of queer theory as resistant to fixed categorisations has meant that the theory has and continues to be applied far beyond questions of sexuality. In learning about queer theory for the first time, it might initially feel off-putting to apply the term "queer" to issues beyond sexuality, to try and see the "queer" in the "straight", and/or to push beyond the question identity itself (see Chapters 5 and 6). Queer theory now means much more than a focus on "same-sex" desire, pushing beyond the concept of identity itself. As Love identifies:

> These days, queer is not only also about race, class, gender, ethnicity, and nation, but is also about affect, citizenship, the death drive, diaspora, digitality, disability, empire, friendship, globalization, the impersonal, indirection, kinship, living underground, loss, marginality, melancholia, migration, neoliberalism, pedagogy, performativity, publicity, self-shattering, shame, shyness, sovereignty, subversion, temporality, and terrorism. (2011, 182)

Yet as Love also warns us, celebrating the expansive possibilities of queer theory comes with risks, not least of which is losing a sense of how discrete identities can be a help rather than a hindrance in terms of political resistance and working together (2011, 184). Love adds that while queer theory helps us to grapple with the messiness of life – the contingencies of lived experience – we may still feel attached to particular identity categories (see Chapter 6).

The concept of intersectionality has been used by queer thinkers to open queer theory to a multitude of new questions beyond sexuality. As we discuss in Chapter 3, intersectionality was first theorised by Kimberlé Crenshaw in 1989 but it has origins in much earlier writings of women of colour including Pauli Murray in the mid-1960s and 1970s, and the Black feminism of The Combahee River Collective in the later 1970s. Crenshaw sought to move beyond understanding identity through a single axis such as race or gender, and her theory of intersectionality functioned as a means of understanding how women's sexual oppression occurs at the intersection of different domains of oppression. While she originally focused on the intersection of race and gender, the concept of intersectionality can be used to better understand the interrelationality of various modes of identity difference such as race, gender, sexuality, ethnicity, nationality, age, ability or other facets of identity. As such, it offers a substantial means of expanding the purview of queer theory as it pushes beyond sexuality and the limits of identity more broadly (we discuss *and* critique the concept at length in Chapter 7).

Cathy Cohen was one of the first to take up this understanding of intersectionality to challenge queer theory's singular focus on sexuality. Her essay "Punks, Bulldaggers, and Welfare Queens" (1997) argued that an intersectional approach to queer theory could enable us to extend our thinking about identity, power and oppression. Numerous queer theorists have taken this up and applied an intersectional queer lens to their politics and analysis. As Martin F. Manalansan IV argues, what is now known as the queer(s) of colour critique is premised upon on this understanding of the "co-constitutive nature of social life and cultural categories" (2018, 1288).

Building on these perspectives, throughout this book we explore many instances where an intersectional focus can provide us with a means of challenging queer theory's seemingly singular focus on sexuality in order to think more broadly about the "queer" and the social. In Chapter 7 we also explore tensions between intersectionality and queer theory and consider the ambivalence that some theorists have towards queer theory when it is divorced from sexual identity. As Love remarks, "It's just that it's hard for me to imagine a form of queerness that does not maintain its ties to a specific form of sexual identity. Behind my work on affect, historiography, and the social, there is a lesbian in bed crying" (2011, 180). We note this here because although queer theory is often applied beyond questions of sexual categories, many of the thinkers who have been and continue to be influential in this field are concerned with sexuality.

There have also been some concerns raised about what has been lost in queer theory's move away from, or against, earlier ways of discussing identity. As Halperin argues, queer theory was readily and immediately absorbed by the academy, supplanting previous engagements around sexuality. He notes,

> Despite its implicit (and false) portrayal of lesbian and gay studies as liberal, assimilationist, and accommodating of the status quo, queer theory has proven to be much more congenial to established institutions of the liberal academy. (2003, 341)

We note this here to establish why and how the first chapters of this book labour on exploring the historical background to queer theory, even as some of the history that we outline may seem at first only opaquely related.

GENEALOGIES OF QUEER THEORY

While we acknowledge queer theory's academic genealogy, we also take an inter-sectional lens towards histories of activism, key debates, events and cultural productions that have contributed to queer theory as we understand it today. It is important to acknowledge these connections when we sketch out these genealogies of queer theory, keeping in mind as Altman (2018) notes, that queer theory's evolution has seen many activists become scholars and many scholars become activists. By doing so we can be attuned to the multiple paths from which the concept of "queer" has emerged, such as via Black feminist theory (Bliss 2015).

The first chapters of this book are dedicated specifically to thinking through these connections via historicising sexuality (Chapter 2), feminist debates around sex and sexuality (Chapter 3), and the role of the AIDS crisis and activism (Chapter 4). Though each of these chapters offers a chronology that attempts to set up a roadmap of ideas informing queer theory, this is not to suggest a linear progressive narrative of how the theory came to be. Rather, these chapters function as genealogies of queer theory, to show that queer theory has ushered in – *and been ushered in by* – a central guiding interest in troubling fixed notions.

Tracing the history of a theory that resists definition is no easy task, and the genealogies that we offer here may provide new ways of thinking but might also be limited in other ways. We can only hope that the ideas offered here are taken as contingent, and that these histories may be re-thought and re-written in future iterations of understanding queer theory *now*. As you travel through the genealogies of queer theory, it is important to keep in mind that queer theory emerged in reflection on/conversation with prior theories of sexuality and gender, as well as histories of thinking around race, embodiment, ability, affects and more. We could imagine this as a funnel through

---

Key term: Genealogy

Genealogy traditionally means "line of descent", and/or tracing this lineage. Drawing on Friedrich Nietzsche's *Genealogy of Morals*, Michel Foucault (see Chapter 2) suggested a new understanding of genealogy: a method for investigating the history of ideas. Following Foucault, to undertake a genealogical analysis means looking at how present ideas have been shaped by the past, and working against narratives that assume change or "progress" is inevitable.

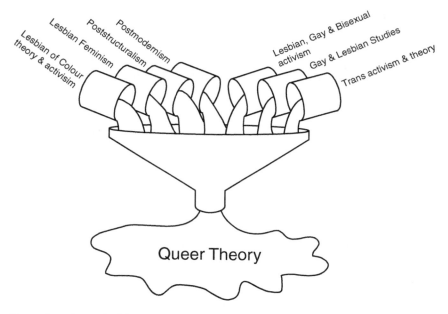

Figure 1.1   Several of the main areas of thinking and political action that have influenced queer theory

which several buckets of theory, activism and cultural texts are poured and which all contribute to the multivalent and polymorphous queer theory that we know today (Figure 1.1).

POSTMODERNISM, POSTSTRUCTURALISM AND QUEER THEORY

In addition to its development through the histories of activism, thinking and debate that we sketch out in Chapters 2, 3 and 4, queer theory has also been understood as emerging from a particular academic context. While we do not wish to suggest this is the only way to understand queer theory, it is worth considering this part of queer theory's intellectual genealogy. Queer theory first entered the academy during the so-called "postmodern turn", a period marked by an emphasis on language, deconstruction, difference, fragmentation, multiple truths, discourse and rethinking old grand narratives and ideas

of how power is structured (Walton 2012, 186–187). Highlighting the relationship between queer theory and the postmodern turn, Britzman suggests:

> Queer Theory occupies a difficult space between the signifier and the
> signified, where something queer happens to the signified – to history and
> to bodies – and something queer happens to the signifier – to language and
> to representation. (1995, 153)

In other words, queer theory, like postmodernism, "troubles" our ways of
talking about and understanding things.

To make matters more confusing, however, "poststructuralism" is sometimes used synonymously with postmodernism, or is understood as a subset
of postmodern theory. As David Walton defines, poststructuralists "share a
very similar attitude [as postmodernists] towards identity as fundamentally
fragmentary, endlessly multiple and constantly deferred" (2012, 186–187).
Key thinkers around poststructuralism include Michel Foucault, Jacques
Lacan and Jacques Derrida (Miller 1998).

We might wonder then: is queer theory the same as postmodernism,
which is the same as poststructuralism? Some scholars have argued that
this is indeed the case. Others have argued that queer theory's original ties
to questions of sexuality are the defining element that distinguishes it from
being simply another name for postmodernism (Green 2002). Regardless of
perspective, it is clear that there is significant overlap between these types of
thinking and theorising. Epitomising the blurring of lines between postmodernism, poststructuralism, feminist theory and queer theory, Butler, in her
book *Gender Trouble* (discussed in Chapter 5), famously challenges the way
we think and talk about the gender binary of "male" versus "female" (2008).
Butler points out that many feminists at the time inadvertently reinforced
sexuality as "naturally" heterosexual and thus understood gender as a fundamental binary. Butler questions both the signified (bodies as gendered) and
the signifier (the language of gender), to re-think what is taken for granted
as "natural". Given Butler's focus on politics, language and sexuality, her
approach has been described as postmodern feminism, poststructuralism and/or queer theory. It is also important to locate her writing within a
genealogy of lesbian feminism – within *Gender Trouble*, Butler challenges the
heterosexism of feminist theory and critiques lesbian feminist communities in
particular for upholding rigid categories of identity.

Blurring such as this may make it difficult to understand the boundaries of
queer theory with respect to postmodernism, poststructuralism and even some
strands of feminism. However, it is necessary to remember, as Cohen reminds

us, the field that was "later ... recategorized as queer theory" (1997, 439) actually emerged from postmodern theory *in interaction with* lesbian, gay, bisexual and transgender activists, especially those from the margins of race, class and gender. When we situate queer theory within a particular academic genealogy, we must acknowledge that it has always also been inflected by histories of activism and resistance to oppressions. Because of this we do not simply equate queer theory to postmodernism and poststructuralism even though it may share many overlaps with these ways of theorising. Focusing on other genealogies (as we do in Chapters 2, 3 and 4) provides us with insight into many other intellectual, political and cultural threads from which queer theory has developed.

While some have claimed that "queer theory is an exercise in discourse analysis" (Giffney 2018, 7), queer theory now has arguably shifted away from

---

Key concept: The gender binary

The gender binary is the idea that gender can be understood in terms of the categories male versus female. Feminist theorists have long critiqued this simplification, arguing that "sex" (biology), ought to be understood as distinct from "gender" (cultural interpretations of biology). This is known as the "sex/gender distinction". As Jane Pilcher and Imelda Whelehan explain:

> The purpose of affirming a sex/gender distinction was to argue that the actual physical or mental effects of a biological difference had been exaggerated to maintain a patriarchal system of power and to create a consciousness among women that they were naturally better suited to "domestic" and nurturant roles. (2017, 57)

Butler famously questioned the distinction in *Gender Trouble*, suggesting that biology is always given cultural meaning and therefore "perhaps [sex] was always already gender" (2008, 9).

Butler argues that sex operates within a "heterosexual matrix" whereby male/female is to man/woman is to masculine/feminine is to desires women/desires men. In other words, the gender binary does not simply refer to male versus female, but an entire set of normative expectations that also encompasses embodiment and desire. Much of queer theory is not simply concerned with sexuality, but the entire gender system that underpins it.

---

the earlier linguistic emphasis of poststructuralist writing. Indeed, as we out-line in Chapter 5, Butler's *Gender Trouble* has been critiqued extensively for its focus on language to the detriment of bodies/materiality (though this was a critique which she attempted to address in her subsequent book *Bodies That Matter*). Indeed, calls to both postmodern and poststructuralist paradigms appear to have waned, surpassed by other "turns" in theory such as affect theory, new materialism and non-representational theory, which have re-focused on the bodily and sensate, displacing the centrality of the linguistic and cognitive. Despite these changes, queer theory persists, and continues to be invoked in conversation and integration with other theoretical develop-ments (see Chapter 7).

Key term: LGBTIQ

The acronym LGBTIQ refers to "Lesbian, Gay, Bisexual, Transgender, Intersex, Queer", and is often used as an umbrella term to describe or imagine a community of sexually and gender diverse persons. Others use "queer" in the same way (that is, as an umbrella noun/identity). Umbrella terms are necessarily and problematically homogenising. As Gloria Anzaldúa describes, "Queer is used as a false unifying umbrella which all 'queers' of all races, ethnicities and classes are shoved under. At times we need this umbrella to solidify our ranks against outsid-ers. But even when we seek shelter under it we must not forget that it homogenizes, erases our differences" (2009, 164).

Before the acronym LGBTIQ was in common use, "gay" or "gay and lesbian" were predominantly used as umbrella terms. Variants of the acro-nym include the addition of questioning, allies, pansexual and a plus-sign to indicate other identities not otherwise accounted for (LGBTQQIAAP+). The term QUILTBAG has also been particularly popular in online commu-nities (queer/questioning, undecided, intersex, lesbian, trans, bisexual, asexual, and/or gay/genderqueer). Gender and sexual minorities (GSM) and diverse sexualities and genders (DSG) are also sometimes used.

The term LGBTIQ has been critiqued for misrepresenting the cohe-siveness of diverse gender and sexual groups as a "community". For example, it is often argued that the use of the term "LGBTIQ" distracts from the disproportionate focus given to L and G (lesbians and gay men) compared to BTIQ (bisexuals, transgender persons, intersex persons and queer identifying people). As Altman suggests, the acronym also "conflates both biological and cultural understandings of sexuality and gender" and flattens difference, distorting "the ways in which these are understood in many non-western societies" (2018, 1252).

Keeping in mind these issues, we use the term LGBTIQ throughout this book in the same way that some people might use queer, to avoid confusion between *identity* and *theory*. We acknowledge the limitations of the term to capture the diversity of sexual and gendered life (though we might note that this is where queer *theory* can step in to help!).

QUEER THEORY AGAINST NORMATIVITY

For much of its history, queer theory has situated itself as challenging normativity – particularly heteronormativity – in society (Gamson and Moon 2004, 49). As Michael Warner most famously notes: "The task of queer social theory ... must be to confront the default heteronormativity of modern culture with its worst nightmare, a queer planet" (1991, 16). Warner coined the term "heteronormativity" to describe the pervasive and largely invisible heterosexual norms that underpin society. An example of heteronormativity in practice is the representation of "ordinary" family units as comprising a "mother" and a "father", and where alternative family arrangements are either not represented, or are depicted as a deviation from this norm.

As many have suggested, the concept of heteronormativity is influenced by the earlier feminist theorisation of "compulsory heterosexuality" offered by Adrienne Rich (1980). Contributing to debates in the arena of lesbian feminism that we explore further in Chapter 3, Rich argues that society is organised in such a way that lesbian identity is considered a deviation from the "normal" baseline of heterosexuality. As Stevi Jackson suggests, Rich offers an early conceptualisation of heteronormativity that reminds us that it is not only homosexual-identifying persons who are marginalised by this system, but that *everyone* is affected negatively by the regulation of sexuality and gender (2006b, 105). Importantly, heteronormativity is not equivalent to heterosexuality itself, as Jackson explains:

[H]eterosexuality, while depending on the exclusion or marginalization of other sexualities for its legitimacy, is not precisely coterminous with heterosexual sexuality. Heteronormativity defines not only a normative sexual practice but also a normal way of life. (2006b, 107)

Engaging with this problematic of heteronormativity, queer theory has often sought to illuminate queer identities and formations that would otherwise be erased or invisible under heteronormative arrangements of the social. Queer theory has also focused in part on making room for queerness to exist through writing and queering the heteronormative through re-reading the "straight" (see Chapter 5).

While the concept of heteronormativity has been productive for queer theory, along these lines critique has also shifted to understanding the "homonormative" elements of LGBTIQ culture (discussed in Chapter 6). The concept of homonormativity has origins in transgender activism. As Stryker argues, homonormativity was used in the 1990s to "articulate the double sense of marginalization and displacement experienced within transgender political and cultural activism" (2008, 145). Stryker notes that the term was first used as a "back-formation from the ubiquitous *heteronormative*, suitable for use where homosexual community norms marginalized other kinds of sex/gender/sexuality difference" (2008, 147). In the early 2000s, the concept was popularised by Lisa Duggan, who used it to describe a new trend towards "mainstreaming" in LGBTIQ politics in the 1990s that sought to distance itself from more "radical" left organising (2002). Duggan describes this new direction as a "highly visible and influential center-libertarian-conservative-classic liberal formation in gay politics" (2002, 177). Today, homonormativity is often used to describe a tendency in the LGBTIQ community to defend homosexuality as no different from heterosexuality (Robinson 2016). An example of this is the frequent catch cry of marriage equality campaigns, that "love is love". Queer theory involves challenging this drive towards mainstreaming, or what is often referred to as "assimilation" (Seidman 2009, 19). As Deborah Britzman suggests, "In its positivity, Queer Theory offers methods of imagining difference on its own terms: as eros, as desire, as the grounds of politicality" (1995, 154). In other words, queer theory has often strived towards emphasising difference and the margins, rather than sameness.

Key concepts: Norms, normalisation, normative, normativity

Norms

A key aspect of queer theory is resisting dominant norms, so what exactly is a "norm"? Norms generally refer to standards, rules or expectations. Norms are associated with the "normal" and opposed from the "abnormal". Queer theory is particularly concerned with resisting norms around gender and sexuality, and questioning what is considered "normal" versus "abnormal" in these contexts.

Normalisation

In addition to resisting norms, queer theory seeks to interrogate processes of normalisation. Normalisation is a term that was introduced by Foucault to explain how norms function as a form of social control within modern societies. As Stephen Valocchi argues, "The process of normalisation ... is done by the constitution of persons who reiterate norms in order to become knowing and knowable, recognized and recognizable to others. In this way, the work of social control is accomplished" (2016, 1). By analysing this process, queer theory is thus concerned with the question of how norms are regulated and connected to social power.

Normative

Queer theory is also interested in understanding and often resisting the normative. While the term normative is related to the idea of norms, it is important to differentiate between the two terms. Norm simply describes a dominant rule, standard or expectation, but normative refers to the context surrounding how these things are established, perpetuated and often morally endorsed. As Butler describes:

> the word is one I use often, mainly to describe the mundane violence performed by certain kinds of gender ideals. I usually use 'normative' in a way that is synonymous with 'pertaining to the norms that govern gender'. But the term 'normative' also pertains to ethical justification, how it is established, and what concrete consequences proceed therefrom. (2008, xxi)

Normativity

More broadly, queer theory is interested in critiquing, destabilising, subverting and challenging normativity. The term normativity refers to the system through which norms, normalisation and the normative are naturalised and made to seem ideal. Many queer thinkers focus their critiques on both heteronormativity and homonormativity.

QUEER THEORY WITHOUT ANTI-NORMATIVITY

In recent times, some queer theorists have questioned the reliance of queer theory on "anti-normativity", that is, always focusing on what is *not* normative as most resistant. As Jagose contends, "Queer theory's antinormativity, we can say, is evident in its anti-assimilationist, anticommunitarian or antisocial, anti-identitarian, antiseparatist, and antiteleological impulses" (2015, 27). Jagose points out that despite the desire to escape a focus on discrete sexual identities, much queer theory writing has tended to focus solely on "subaltern sexual protagonists", as she suggests, "certain sexual actors and orientations, certain sexual practices and venues, have proved good to think with" (2010, 519). The trouble with this approach, however, is that it has tended to over-emphasise certain sexual practices and identities as the key sites of radical transformative possibility, rather than seeing the rupturing potential of sites assumed to be "straight".

Jagose's exemplar of a sexual practice that would *not* ordinarily be considered queer, is women faking orgasms (discussed further in Chapter 8). She argues that this practice demonstrates a kind of queer resistance, and though it might not be transformative it could be seen as, "an erotic invention that emerges from a set of culturally specific circumstances as a widespread sexual observance, a new disposition or way of managing one's self in sexual relations" (2010, 535). Jagose's point is not that we should champion fake orgasms per se, but rather, that we should extend our lens of queer theory analysis beyond narrow definitions of the margins. Jack Halberstam has raised similar concerns around who we do/do not attend to in queer theory. As he suggests:

> [L]et's turn our attention to the heterosexual woman, who, after all, so often has been forced to function as a model of conformity, a symbol of subjugation and the whipping girl for anything that goes wrong with sexual morality. (2012, 82)

Halberstam, like Jagose, suggests that there might be a way to engage with questions of gender and sexuality that do not leave out ostensibly "straight" characters from analysis.

One of the issues at stake in valorising anti-normativity in queer theory, is that it risks queer theory becoming synonymous with the "anti-normative". In doing so, queer theory might lose its critical edge in deconstructing identities/boundaries. Indeed, anti-normativity as a centralising force might involve drawing sharper boundaries, and lose the anti-identarian coalitional

Queer theory in practice: The hetero/homo binary

Queer theorists have often questioned the binary terms within which sexuality is often understood, that is, the distinction between the heterosexual and the homosexual. The category heterosexual rejects any association with the homosexual, and vice versa. But as Diana Fuss suggests:

> Heterosexuality can never fully ignore the close psychical proximity of its terrifying (homo)sexual other, any more than homosexuality can entirely escape the equally insistent social pressures of (hetero)sexual conformity. Each is haunted by the other. (1991, 3)

We frequently see this boundary-drawing in practice from the playground to popular culture. For example, the catchphrase "no homo" is used to reinforce the boundaries of heterosexuality against homosexuality.

Similarly, arguments in popular culture about which celebrities should be allowed to represent gay or lesbian characters also often reinforce the category of homosexuality against heterosexuality. While such debates rightly reflect broader issues around the policing of sexuality in mainstream media, they also rely on the idea that sexuality always needs to be disclosed and is a fixed characteristic of a person – a position that queer theory resists. As Calvin Thomas argues, "Queer theory ultimately asks: who the f*** knows who or what one is in relation to the question of whom or how or what or when or even if one f***s?" (2018, 23).

focus of queer's earlier incarnations. As Cohen points out, "queer politics" has sometimes failed to live up to its radical promises because of the blunt binary distinction often made between the "queer" and the "straight" (1997, 438). Such divisions often fail to do justice to the intersections of marginalisation such as those of race and class, where oppression or exclusion cannot simply be understood along the lines of sexuality. Cohen also reminds us of the possibilities of queer, as she writes,

> At the intersection of oppression and resistance lies the radical potential of queerness to challenge and bring together all those deemed marginal and all those committed to liberatory politics. (1997, 440)

Similarly Robyn Wiegman warns against: "[T]he limitations of configuring any dualistic account of the political as a transgressive ideal" (2015, 66). In other words, we should be wary of prescribing anti-normativity as the source of the political, because this does not account for what the content of these "norms" might be (Wiegman 2015, 49). Further, Manalansan highlights that relations between queerness and normativity are never static, arguing that we need to understand:

> [H]ow queerness and queers are awash in the flow of the everyday – where norm and queer are not easily indexed or separable but are constantly colliding, clashing, intersecting and reconstituting. (2018, 1288)

Whether we take up Jagose or Halberstam's suggestions to take the "normative" as a serious focus, or look to Cohen, Wiegman and Manalansan's suggestions that we cannot simply reject the "normative", the point here is to be careful how we deploy queer theory. While critiquing heteronormativity/homonormativity might be a central focus of many queer theory approaches, we should always be attentive to the dangers of prescribing anti-normativity as *the* solution.

THE DEATH OF QUEER THEORY?

Around a decade after the establishment of queer theory within the academy, theorists began to question its relevance and efficacy. Sharon Marcus suggests that the term queer had been taken up too speedily and without critical awareness of its limits. She writes:

> *[Q]ueer* has been the victim of its own popularity, proliferating to the point of uselessness as a neologism for the transgression of any norm (queering history, or queering the sonnet). Used in this sense, the term becomes confusing, since it always connotes a homosexuality that may not be at stake when the term is used so broadly. *Queerness* also refers to the multiple ways that sexual practice, sexual fantasy, and sexual identity fail to line up consistently. That definition expresses an important insight about the complexity of sexuality, but it also describes a state experienced by everyone. If everyone is queer, then no one is – and while this is exactly the point queer theorists want to make, reducing the term's pejorative sting by universalizing the meaning of *queer* also depletes its explanatory power. (2005, 196)

Marcus is just one of many theorists who have argued that the term queer may have an expiration date. As O'Rourke suggests, "there is a certain discourse which propagates the idea that queer theory ... is always already dead, buried, over, finished" (2011, 103). Hence, in 2002, Stephen Barber and David Clarke noted that "it is not especially surprising to hear that the survival of queer theory has been questioned or its possible 'death' bruited" (2002, 4). A year later, in 2003, Halberstam reflected on the value of queer studies by observing that "some say that queer theory is no longer in vogue; others characterize it as fatigued or exhausted of energy and lacking in keen debates; still others wax nostalgic for an earlier moment" (2003, 361). This sentiment is emphasised by Janet Halley and Andrew Parker who, in 2011, reflect on how they had heard "from some quarters that queer theory, if not already passé, was rapidly approaching its expiration date" (2011, 1).

In 2009, David Ruffolo's book *Postqueer Politics* was published. Ruffolo argues that "Queer has reached a political peak" and critiques queer theory for valorising a dualism between queer and heteronormativity (2009, 1). Ruffolo imagines how we may use the work of philosophers such as Gilles Deleuze to expand the remit of queer to enhance its relevance to contemporary political questions. Rather than reject queer theory, Ruffolo links queer with concepts such as "becoming" (in Deleuze's terms) – postqueer ultimately seeks to *renew* queer as a powerful and vibrant concept. Hence, even in an era of (so-called) postqueer politics, queer theory has a future (O'Rourke 2011, 104). As Michael O'Rourke suggests:

> With each new book, conference, seminar series, each new masters program, we hear (yet again) that Queer Theory is over. Some argue that the unstoppable train of queer theory came to a halt in the late nineties having been swallowed up by its own fashionability. It had become, contrary to its own anti-assimilationist rhetoric, fashionable, very much included, rather than being the outlaw, it wanted to be. But the books and articles still continue to appear, the conferences continue to be held. And, if it were true that Queer Theory has been assimilated completely, become sedimented, completely domesticated (or at least capable of being domesticated) then it really would be over. Nobody would be reading any more for we would already know what was to come. (2011, 104)

As we explore throughout this book, queer theory has certainly not reached an expiration date. The pliant nature of queer theory has enabled it to maintain relevance by insisting on its own "radical unknowability" (Jagose 2009, 158) and it continues to be taken up, experimented with and pushed in new directions. We trace some of the ways in which queer theory has evolved, outline its new shapes and gesture to places within and beyond the academy where queer theory is thriving. In doing so, we seek to demonstrate the value of queer theory *now*, and point to some of the ways that students, activists, artists and scholars may continue the project of testing queer theory's limits, shaping it anew for themselves.

ROADMAP FOR *QUEER THEORY NOW*

In the following chapters you will notice that the discussion moves between different periods of time, but each considers the implications for the present (the "now"), as well as how the "now" might lead us to re-read the past. *Queering* our memories of the past is a move that has been encouraged by theorists such as Michael Hames-García (2011b). As Hames-García contends, genealogies of queer theory have often occluded the role that whiteness plays in the construction of these accounts. He also suggests, "[T]he most prominent queer theorists have too often justified their scholarship and argued for its originality based on claims that it could be better than other, competing approaches" (2011b, 43). For us, Hames-García's important critique of the way that queer theory is often done, leaves us questioning how best to "do" the story of queer theory here. Following Hames-García's critique, we hope that our work offered attends to shifts in theory and rethinking queer genealogies. Yet we also wish to give a grounding in queer theory that does attend to the "typical" story of queer theory even as we problematise this, and bring new insights, to offer a foundation for understanding some of the oft-discussed queer theorists and their writings to help make sense of the field to be undone. In taking this approach, the genealogies that we offer in *Queer Theory Now* might help us to see how our narratives of the past inform our present-day politics and theory.

In the first chapters, we offer groundwork for thinking about how queer theory came to be, starting much earlier than the emergence of the term "queer theory" itself. These chapters all consider the radical importance of earlier social movements around sexuality, gender and race, in shaping queer theory. In Chapter 2, we begin by tracing the influence of Foucault's writing on later queer theory to come, and the problems and limits of Foucault's genealogy. We also consider shifts in thinking about sexuality from the sexologists, to the homophile movement, Gay Liberation and later LGBTIQ movements. In Chapter 3, we trace key ideas in queer theory in relation to the history of feminist activism, considering in particular women's liberation movements, lesbian organising, questions of race and difference, and debates around sex and pleasure. Chapter 4 turns to the specific role that the AIDS crisis played in shaping the use of the term "queer", and in turn, queer theory in the academy.

The chapters following this constitute the so-called "beginning" of the explicit articulation of queer theory. In Chapter 5, we focus on the work of Butler and Sedgwick specifically, who would both become central figures in the field of queer theory, yet who offer different forms of queer critical enquiry. Chapter 6 investigates the conundrum of identity politics and queer theory that emerged in the 1990s, in more depth, looking at debates around identity, attachments and lived experience. Here we give time to the role of transgender studies in shaping queer theory. We consider the problems and paradoxes of queer theory's insistence on permanent openness, versus the lived realities of sexual and gendered life.

In the final chapters, we look at how queer theory is (and has always been) unfolding in a plurality of directions, and the orientations of queer theory to come. Chapter 7 gives greater attention to the question of intersectional considerations in influencing (yet sometimes being excluded from) queer theory thinking. Here we look at both the importance of intersectional approaches in queer theory, as well as the intersections in applications of queer theory as it has emerged in different academic contexts. The final chapter, Chapter 8, concerns the question of temporality and queer futures. Here we consider the role of "hope" in queer theory thinking, and the tension between thinking of the past, present and future in terms of queer theory orientations. Across this book as a whole, we make a case for the enduring relevance and potential of queer theory. In each chapter we explore the intellectual and political developments that queer theory has contributed to and, in the final chapter, we gesture to the worth of queer theory for a new generation writing, fighting, thinking and dreaming of queer futures. Each chapter provides a list of further readings, questions and films that you might like to watch to think through the ideas in greater depth.

This book hopes to offer a sense of the grounding of queer theory in activism, and to illustrate the theoretical and practical uses of queer theory historically, today and into the future. We hope to make some sense of queer theory's past, present and future, even as we maintain queer uncertainty, for as Noreen Giffney describes: "queer discourses touch us, move us and leave us unsettled, troubled, confused" (2018, 9). Despite the continuing relevance of queer theory, we may also wish to heed critical readings of this theory as too-readily absorbed into the existing systems of thought, rather than always achieving the aspirational vision of its initial provocation. We hope that however "useful" queer theory might be for your theoretical toolkit, you continue to question its relationship with the status quo. Indeed, we ought to remain vigilant about what queer theory "does", and for whom, even as we might seek to re-shape the boundaries of what queer theory is now, and what it might become.

Further reading

Henry Abelove, Michèle Aina Barale, and David M. Halperin (eds.). (1993). *The Lesbian and Gay Studies Reader*. New York: Routledge.

This collection draws together the critical texts in lesbian and gay studies that preceded the articulation of queer theory, including Rich's essay on "Compulsory Heterosexuality".

Nikki Sullivan. (2003). *A Critical Introduction to Queer Theory*. New York: New York University Press.

Sullivan offers an overview of queer theory and its origins, including discussions of "queer race" and transgender theory.

Meg-John Barker, and Julia Scheele. (2016). *Queer: A Graphic History*. London: Icon Books.

This graphic reader from Barker and Scheele offers a basic introduction to many key ideas in queer theory in an easy to engage with format.

Noreen Giffney, and Michael O'Rourke (eds.). (2018). *The Ashgate Research Companion to Queer Theory*. New York: Routledge.

This diverse collection of reflections and analyses includes extensive discussion of identity, discourse, normativity and relationality, by leading queer theorists.

QUESTIONS TO CONSIDER

- How does queer "theory" compare to queer "politics" and "identity"? Do these uses involve different ideas of what queer means, or do they share common goals?
- Do you think it is most useful to think of "queer" as a "doing"? Why?
- What are some examples of how heteronormativity shapes everyday life?

Recommended films

But I'm a Cheerleader (**Jamie Babbit 1999**) is a comedy that follows the plight of a young woman, Megan, who is sent by her conservative parents to a gay conversion therapy camp. The film takes a satirical look at the norms and expectations of sexuality and gender, and suggests that there is a certain "queerness" to heteronormative logics.

The Celluloid Closet (**Rob Epstein and Jeffrey Friedman 1995**) is a documentary film that charts the representation of lesbian, gay, bisexual and transgender identity throughout the history of film. Directors Rob Epstein and Jeffrey Friedman take us on a journey through the heteronormative and homophobic lenses through which queer life has often been represented.

Mulholland Drive (**David Lynch 2001**). This surreal noir-thriller follows the plight of a young woman in Hollywood following a car crash. The film experiments with identity, sexuality, dreams and multiple "truths" and realities, making it a postmodern classic that resonates with queer theory.

2 From Pathology to Pride

KEY TERMS AND CONCEPTS	discourse, power, bio-power, repressive hypothesis, pathologise, asexuality, polymorphous perversity, sexology, homophile movement, sexual script theory, assimilation, Gay Liberation, bisexuality, pride

QUEER THEORY AND THE HISTORY OF SEXUALITY

Is queer theory always about sexuality? To answer this question, it is crucial that we first ask: what is sexuality? In this chapter we focus on discussions of the history of sexuality that have influenced queer theorists, including the role of medicine and psychiatry in shaping the sexual subject. This chapter considers how the pathologisation of homosexuality at once "legitimised" discrimination but also provided a basis for a discourse of homosexual rights and homosexual organisations (the homophile movement) to emerge. The relationship and contrasts between the homophile and later Gay Liberation movement illustrates the ideological basis of the "assimilation" versus "transgression" debate still unfolding in discussion of queer theory and politics today. Moving to a more contemporary context, we also consider the globalised LGBTIQ pride movement, and the increasing debate around the corporatisation of pride parades. This history has been traced by many scholars and has often been refracted through popular culture, yet revisiting this history suggests that neat narratives of "progress" ought to be questioned.

Importantly, as flagged in our introduction, adopting an intersectional lens when examining queer history is crucial, which in this chapter means attending to the intersecting issues of race, class, ability and gender in discussing sexuality. For example, as we explore, the pathologisation of homosexuality is intimately connected to projects of colonialism, racialisation and the invention of whiteness. Similarly, early gay and lesbian activism has strong connections to the civil rights movement, a point sometimes overlooked in genealogies of queer theory. These intersections need to be highlighted in order to counter the whitewashing and erasure that is so prevalent in earlier accounts and that continues to function in representations of these LGBTIQ histories.

HISTORY ACCORDING TO FOUCAULT?

Foucault published many influential works throughout his life, though it is his *History of Sexuality: Volume 1*, first published in French in 1976 (and translated into English 1978), that is perhaps most significant for understanding queer theory. Foucault influenced many later key queer theorists such as Gayle Rubin, Butler and Sedgwick, though has often been critiqued for some of his lack of attention to the specificity of gender, and women's issues specifically (Huffer 2010, 5). Foucault introduces many key ideas within *History of Sexuality: Volume 1*, coining the term "repressive hypothesis" and highlighting mechanisms of confession, and practices of psychiatry and medicine that relate to the production of sexuality. Through all of this, he foregrounds speech and language as key to the formation of sexuality.

However, while many genealogies of queer theory begin with Foucault, there have also been attempts to reframe the history of sexuality that he offers, specifically in terms of decolonial approaches. For example, Scott Lauria Morgensen suggests modifying Foucault's reading of history to specifically attend to the settler-colonial dynamics underpinning "modern sexuality" (2011, 23). Following Indigenous feminist calls to decolonise theorisations of gender and sexuality (explored in detail in Chapter 7), Morgensen (2011) argues that queer theory must attend to the way that Indigenous populations were marked as "queer" in relation to settler sexuality, and forcibly governed by colonial "civilizing" logics on this basis. As Ann Stoler (1995) has also argued, Foucault's concepts can be productively adapted to better account for

---

Biography: Michel Foucault

Foucault was a poststructuralist philosopher, literary critic, historian, social theorist and activist, born in Poitiers, France on 15 October 1926. Foucault graduated from the École Normale Supérieure in 1952, and taught in universities across Europe in the following decade. In 1969, Foucault became a Professor of the History of Systems of Thought at the Collège de France, and gave lectures across the world. Foucault was also active in various leftist political protest movements – including the student uprising in 1968 – up to his death in Paris on 25 June 1984 (Gutting 2005).

colonial logics. Stoler argues that the history Foucault traces should be understood in the context of a broader, imperial, racialised context and history, as she suggests, "We are in the felicitous position to draw on Foucault's insights and go beyond them" (1995, 94).

Key concept: Discourse

The term "discourse" is used across multiple disciplines and means different things in different contexts. In linguistics and some social sciences, discourse often refers to structures that are larger than sentences, or, language in use (Cameron and Panovic 2014). However, many in the social sciences and humanities draw upon Foucault's definition, which understands discourse as a form of social *practice*. Foucault describes discourse in the plural as, "practices that systematically form the objects of which they speak" (Foucault 1972). In other words, discourses are *ways of talking* that shape how we think about and understand the world.

In *History of Sexuality: Volume 1* Foucault argues that, "the society that emerged in the nineteenth century ... put into operation an entire machinery for producing true discourses concerning [sex]" (1976, 69). This scientific approach (which Foucault termed "scientia sexualis") was not about pleasure, but about the production of knowledge, the "truth" of sex.

For example, when thinking about sexuality we could compare:

- medical discourse that might focus on questions of sexual "dysfunction" and sexual "health", using scientific data and statistics; versus
- religious discourse that might focus on sexual practices that are "morally" permissible versus those which are "sinful", using theological dictates.

Understanding that different discursive lenses shape what can be "known" to be "true" is a key aspect of Foucauldian thinking. This has shaped queer theory approaches to questioning discourses of sexuality.

The repressive hypothesis

Foucault begins *History of Sexuality: Volume 1* by negating what he calls the "repressive hypothesis". Foucault draws attention to a widespread belief in thinking about sexuality: that by the 1800s any prior openness had been supplanted by Victorian bourgeois attitudes towards sex, through which "sexuality was carefully confined" or repressed (1978, 3). As Foucault outlines, there is a commonly held belief that *prior* to the Victorian era, "a certain frankness" around sexual behaviours permeated public life:

> Sexual practices had little need of secrecy; words were said without undue reticence, and things were done without too much concealment; one had a tolerant familiarity with the illicit. Codes regulating the course, the obscene, and the indecent were quite lax ... It was a time of direct gestures, shameless discourse, and open transgressions, when anatomies were shown and intermingled at will, and knowing children hung about amid the laughter of adults. (1978, 3)

However, "so the story goes", following this period there was a grand silencing and repression of sexuality. Foucault explicitly challenges this story and questions the implicit benefit of re-telling the history of sexuality along these lines. As he suggests:

> Why do we say, with so much passion and so much resentment against our most recent past, against our present, and against ourselves that we are repressed? By what spiral did we come to affirm that sex is negated? What led us to show, ostentatiously, that sex is something we hide, to say it is something we silence? (1978, 8–9)

Foucault puts assumptions about the history of sexual repression into context to argue that sexuality was not truly "repressed" during the Victorian era. He raises historical, theoretical and political doubts about the repressive hypothesis (see Table 2.1).

The discursive explosion

Foucault challenges the myth of repression by suggesting that this so-called period of silence was actually part of a "veritable discursive explosion" around sex and sexuality (1978, 17). Some may identify policing of language and

Table 2.1   The various doubts about the "repressive hypothesis" that Foucault
raises in *The History of Sexuality: Volume 1*

	Historical accuracy	*Historico-theoretical*	*Historico-political*
Doubt raised	Foucault questions whether popular assumptions about the period of repression are historically accurate.	Foucault questions the theoretical assumptions made about the relationship between knowledge and power in understanding the history of sexuality.	Foucault questions whether we are more liberated now than in the past, and the political motives of making such claims.
Resulting questions	What can be found in revisiting archives from this era of supposed repression?	Does power primarily operate to *repress* sexuality? Can power have other effects?	What is the benefit to speakers in making the claim that we are more liberated *now* than in the past?

speech around sexuality that occurred throughout the period as evidence of "repression". However, Foucault suggests that if we look closely at the mechanisms of regulation, and the scientific, psychiatric and medical discourses that were in operation, we can actually see a "steady proliferation of discourses concerned with sex" and indeed a "transforming of sex [itself] into discourse" (1978, 20). Foucault traces an emerging confessional imperative, for example via psychiatric practice, through which subjects were compelled to confess to sexual acts that broke the law (such as sodomy), thus transforming their desires "into discourse" by talking about sex and sexuality as much as possible (1978, 21).

Drawing out links between discourse, knowledge and power, Foucault argues that this was actually part of a bigger transformation in the organisation of power, through which human bodies, sex and sexuality had come to be "managed, inserted into systems of utility, regulated for the greater good of all, [and] made to function according to an optimum" (1978, 24). During the industrial revolution bodily norms around ability, gender, race, sexuality and sexual development had emerged. Deviations were described in detail through both legal and medical texts and while some "irregularities" or "perversions" came to be thought of as illnesses and were treated as such, others bore the brunt of legal sanctions (Davis 2006; D'Emilio 1998).

The establishment of these norms – and the classification of specific deviations – was motivated by a set of basic concerns, as Foucault describes: "to ensure population, to reproduce labor capacity, to perpetuate the form of social relations" (1978, 37). In other words, the emergence of sexuality as a discourse in the Victorian era was governed by the need to constitute normative (heterosexually reproductive) bodies that would be "economically useful and politically conservative" (Foucault 1978, 37). Foucault claims that specifically the emergent discourse of sexuality hinged around four specific mechanisms (Table 2.2).

Similarly to Foucault's ideas around the development of sexuality, scholars and historians have traced the emergence of the concept of whiteness and the extension of the racialisation of non-white others. As Allen argues, whiteness was invented to scientifically legitimise social control over labour through

Table 2.2   Foucault's descriptions of the different ways that knowledge was produced around sex and how it was managed

Mechanism	What/How	Subject produced
"Hysterization of women's bodies"	Sexualisation and medical management of women's bodies for reproductive purposes.	"The hysterical woman"
"Pedagogization of children's sex"	Panic around children's sexual impulses and implementation of various mechanisms to control it.	"The masturbating child"
"Socialization of procreative behaviour"	Focus on the economic necessity of the family unit, hinged around the reproductive heterosexual couple.	"The Malthusian couple"
"Psychiatrization of perverse pleasure"	Distinction of sexual inclinations such that normal versus perverse pleasures (such as heterosexual drives versus homosexual ones) could be determined and treated.	"The perverse adult"

projects of colonialisation, enslavement and the genocide of Indigenous peoples (Allen 1994a, 1994b; Almaguer 1994; Jacobson 1999; O'Brien 2010). However, as Stoler (1995) suggests, though many have drawn out the links between the discursive construction of sexuality and the construction of racialised subjects under colonial rule, it is also possible to refigure Foucault's formulations via a deeper understanding of the imperial colonial context of the Victorian era which he does not explicitly consider. Stoler raises several key questions (1995, 6):

- Was the demand for the "truth of sex" a result of the confessional imperative or were "truth" claims emerging more directly because of imperial theorisations of race at the time?
- Should racialised subjects be specifically included in the subjects produced and targeted by the emergent discourse of sexuality?
- Could any of the sexual subjects that Foucault describes even function without a "racially erotic counterpoint"?

Stoler concludes that "In short-circuiting empire, Foucault's history of European sexuality misses key sites in the production of that discourse, discounts the practices that racialized bodies, and thus elides a field of knowledge that provided the contrasts for what a 'healthy, vigorous, bourgeois body' was all about" (1995, 7).

Key concept: Power

In *History of Sexuality: Volume 1* Foucault offers two distinct ways of theorising power and suggests that there has been a contemporary shift in how power is arranged, shifting from sovereign to disciplinary:

- **Sovereign/juridical power:** power in a hierarchy from above. That is, the power of the law or state enforced by the king or judge. This power is fundamentally repressive.
- **Disciplinary power:** power dispersed in a grid, from below. That is, the power that filters through all social life and the disciplinary regimes that are enforced by one another. This power crystallises in institutions such as schools, clinics and so on, and the dynamics of norms and surveillance of one another leads to "docile bodies" (compliant bodies). This power is fundamentally productive.

As Foucault describes: "Power is everywhere; not because it embraces everything, but because it comes from everywhere. And 'Power', insofar as it is permanent, repetitious, inert, and self-reproducing, is simply the over-all effect that emerges from all these mobilities ... power is not an institution, and not a structure; neither is it a certain strength we are endowed with; it is the name that one attributes to a complex strategical situation in a particular society" (1978, 93).

In the final part of *History of Sexuality: Volume 1* Foucault develops his notion of power to include **"bio-power"** (1978, 140). He explains this as a regime of power which involves the measurement, discipline and management of bodies – a crucial element supporting the development of capitalism. Many have since expanded Foucault's discussion of bio-power. For example, Stoler (1995) suggests adapting bio-politics to account for settler colonialism, to understand the way that Indigenous populations were (and continue to be) governed by racist bodily logics.

The "invention" of homosexuality

It may seem strange to think of homosexuality as something that was "invented". However, many theorists following Foucault's line of thought suggest that with the emergence of a discourse of sexuality, sexual *acts* were transformed into sexual *identities*. Most historians of sexuality highlight that "same-sex" relationships have always existed in some form or other across all cultures, but that the identity categories through which we understand sexuality today (including heterosexuality) have not always existed. As Jonathan Katz highlights, both "homosexuality" and "heterosexuality" are historically and culturally specific terms for categorising sexuality (2014, 12).

Recently, this popular reading of Foucault's contribution to queer theory being the invention of "identity" has been troubled. As Lynne Huffer suggests, Foucault was primarily concerned with subject formation:

With the rise of positivism, that inner life has been frozen into the attributes of a character to be viewed under a microscope and dissected into the elements that constitute a "case history". This ethical alteration describes not so much the constitution of the modern "identity" of identity politics – again, Foucault does not use the word here – than it does a process of rationalist, positivist objectification through the production of an ethico-moral double. (2010, 72–73)

This rendering of Foucault is important to keep in mind, to understand how his notion of sexual subjectivation differs from contemporary renderings of identity as discrete and personal self "truths".

Focusing on European medical and juridical constructions of sexuality, Foucault argues that homosexuality first emerged in 1870 when German psychiatrist Karl Westphal (also known as Carl von Westphal) published an article in which he argued that certain "contrary sexual sensations" (which we would likely now understand as "homosexual") were congenital rather than acquired vices. For Foucault, this article marked the emergence of homosexuality as an identity, as it was the moment in which homosexuality was characterised as "a certain quality of sexual sensibility" rather than a type of sexual relation (1978, 43). Prior to this, the term "sodomy" had been used to refer to certain sexual acts (especially anal intercourse) which were historically forbidden because they were linked to sin – and notably not tied to an identity, meaning that anyone could be accused of them. It was not until the nineteenth century that homosexuality began to solidify as an identity. Rather than talking about acts or behaviours, homosexuality became, particularly within medical discourse and the law, "a personage, a past, a case history, and a childhood, in addition to being a type of life, a life form, and a morphology" (Foucault 1978, 43). Foucault highlights this transition, suggesting: "The sodomite had been a temporary aberration, the homosexual was now a species" (1978, 43).

Historians have noted several key figures in this emergent scientific discourse on sexuality. In most cases, their works began to appear in English language medical journals in the 1880s and 1890s. In each case, "same-sex" desire, which was once thought of in terms of sin and criminality, was re-classified in medical terms. Early European sexologists described same-sex desire as a disease, a congenital defect or a form of perversity. For instance, Karl Heinrich Ulrichs published a series of brochures between 1864 and 1879, in which he described "same-sex" desire as a mismatch between body and soul (Oosterhuis 1992, 13). Ulrichs coined the terms "Urnings" and "Uranism" to describe patients whose soul did not match their anatomy. Similarly, German sexologist and psychologist Richard von Krafft-Ebing published *Psychopathia Sexualis* in 1886, in which he described "same-sex" desire along with necrophilia, sadism, masochism, paedophilia (and others) as pathologies, or aberrations (Oosterhuis 1992, 13).

Around the same time, Westphal's work on "contrary sexual feeling", which had been published several years earlier in 1870, and which Foucault identifies as the dawn of homosexuality, began to appear in medical journals across Europe. Though these early studies used different language to describe same-sex desire, they suggested that medicine should be the key site for responding

Key term: Pathologise

To "pathologise" means to designate or categorise something as "abnormal". In turn, this requires a designation of what is "normal". Historically, sexuality and gender have been pathologised, particularly within medical, psychiatric and psychological discourses. For example, up until 1973 homosexuality was understood as a mental disorder in the American Psychiatric Association's Diagnostic and Statistical Manual of Mental Disorders (DSM) (De Block and Adriaens 2013). It was only removed following pressure from gay rights activists (Drescher 2015). However, gender has continued to be included in various iterations of the DSM, through classifications such as "Gender identity disorder" (GID) introduced in 1980 (more recently reclassified as "Gender dysphoria").

While pathologizing discourse is problematic, historically it has also been productive for individuals and groups to reclaim that which is marked out as "abnormal". For example, in the novel *The Well of Loneliness* by Radclyffe Hall (1928) (which would come to circulate as an infamous text exploring lesbian and/or transgender themes), the main character uses the language of "inversion" to describe their identity. As Lisa Walker suggests, "Hall's depiction of her protagonist, Stephen Gordon, owes its theory about sexual 'inversion' to nineteenth-century sexologists, and it is largely this medical model that defined the figure of the butch for the prefeminist lesbian community" (Walker 1993, 881). Sexual and gender categories have historically provided a framework for self-identification with previously unidentified subject positions, as well as legitimisation for organisations advocating for LGBTIQ rights.

However, as Stryker notes, designations such as GID have been received in mixed ways by transgender communities: "Some people resent having their sense of gender labelled as a sickness, while others take great comfort from believing they have a condition that can be cured with proper treatment" (2008, 13). This highlights the tension that pathologizing discourses poses: simultaneously offering a point of collective identification for rights-based claims, and promoting stigmatising and narrow classifications that gate-keep access to resources.

to deviant sexual behaviours, rather than response via legal or religious frameworks (Somerville 2000, 18).

A key influential figure in this scholarship is British physician Havelock Ellis, who published *Studies in the Psychology of Sex* throughout the late 1890s and early 1900s. In *Volume Two: Sexual Inversion*, he explored "sexual inversion", which he conceived of in both congenital (permanent) and situational (temporary) forms:

> In the girl who is congenitally predisposed to homosexuality it will continue and develop; in the majority it will be forgotten as quickly as possible, not without shame, in the presence of the normal object of sexual love. (1927, 122)

For Ellis, situational homosexuality was a "precocious play of natural instinct", a passing phase of "passionate friendships, of a more or less unconsciously sexual character" that developed in the absence of opposite-sex partners (1927, 132). Though he did write about men, Ellis considered this type of relationship far more prevalent for women and he argued that it was fostered within settings where women were in constant association without the company of men. Ellis considered situational homosexuality to be "found in all countries", and in an appendix on "the school-friendships of girls", Ellis highlighted what he saw as a remarkable similarity between schoolgirl romances in Italian, English and American high schools. In each of these accounts, same-sex desire was described as a "tenderness natural to this age and sex" (Ellis 1927, 250).

Queer theory in practice: Transnational sexology?

Histories of sexology have been produced in various contexts. For example, Fang Fu Ruan's work *Sex in China: Studies in Sexology in Chinese Culture* (1991) outlines a very long history of sexological work in the region. In China this history is bound up with philosophical and religious convictions of different dynasties. Ruan claims that "The world's oldest sex handbooks are Chinese" (1991, 1). Similarly, Sanjay Srivastava's *Passionate Modernity: Sexuality, Class and Consumption in India* (2007) considers the history of sexology in India, and the gender and class dynamics bound up with the study of sex.

However, aside from simply tracking and tracing different ways of thinking about sex in different contexts, Gargi Bhattacharyya (2002) suggests that the way we imagine sexuality (or "queerness" as the case may be) can influence, and obscure, what is to be found. Bhattacharyya points out that the hetero/homo divide used in Western accounts presumes that sexuality:

1. can be understood as an identity;
2. is used about a self-narrating individual;
3. is a specific historical concept in relation to sex acts. (2002, 42)

These assumptions mean that "sexuality" as it is often deployed in the West, is distinctly Western.

RACISM IN WESTERN SEXOLOGY

It is important to note that these early ideas about sexuality stemmed from previous studies of racial difference. In theorising inversion Ellis (a passionate eugenicist) borrowed heavily from nineteenth-century racial "science", which used a methodology of comparative anatomy to categorise bodies according to visual markers of difference. As Somerville highlights, Ellis "echoed earlier anatomical catalogs of African women" (2000, 28). Consider, for instance, the language that Ellis uses to describe the anatomy of the female "invert" in relation to a "normal" woman:

> *Sexual Organs* – (a) Internal: Uterus and ovaries appear normal. (b) External: Small clitoris, with this irregularity, that the lower folds of the labia minora, instead of uniting one with the other and forming the frenum, are extended upward along the sides of the clitoris, while the upper folds are poorly developed, furnishing the clitoris with a scant hood. The labia majora depart from normal conformation in being fuller in their posterior half than in their anterior part, so that when the subject is in the supine position they sag, as it were, presenting a slight resemblance to fleshy sacs, but in substance and structure they feel normal. (1927, 136)

While rarely mentioning race in explicit terms, scholars such as Ellis borrowed methodologies and conclusions from the project of racial definition, and in doing so, deeply entwined (racist and sexist) discourses of race and sexuality. Hence, in *Queering the Color Line* (2000), Siobhan Somerville highlights that in the USA the classification of bodies as either "homosexual" or "heterosexual" actually emerged at the same time as boundaries between "Black" and "white" bodies were being aggressively constructed and policed (2000, 3). Kobena Mercer and Isaac Julien similarly argue that racism has long underpinned all Western constructions of sexuality:

> The prevailing Western concept of sexuality ... already contains racism. Historically, the European construction of sexuality coincides with the epoch of imperialism and the two interconnect. (1988, 106)

Though the history of Western sexuality has often been relayed in deracialised terms in Foucault's work, and in the work of historians who trace similar ideas, this is a history that cannot be disentangled from questions and histories of race.

While it is not possible to trace a linear cross-cultural transmission of ideas around sexuality, some scholars have elucidated the proliferation of ideas of sexuality transnationally. For instance, Tze-lan D. Sang's *The Emerging Lesbian: Female Same-Sex Desire in Modern China* (2003) and Fran Martin's *Backward Glances: Contemporary Chinese Cultures and the Female Homoerotic Imaginary* (2010), trace ideas around sexuality in modern Chinese culture, which have often been through Japanese interpretations (Martin 2010; Sang 2003). What is at stake in all of these accounts, as Foucault describes, is, "the very production of sexuality" within and across cultures (1978, 105). Foucault proclaims that:

> Sexuality must not be thought of as a kind of natural given which power tries to hold in check, or as an obscure domain which knowledge tries gradually to uncover. It is the name that can be given to a historical construct: not a furtive reality that is difficult to grasp, but a great surface network in which the stimulation of bodies, the intensification of pleasures, the incitement to discourse, the formation of special knowledges, the strengthening of controls and resistances, are linked to one another, in accordance with a few major strategies of knowledge and power. (1978, 105–106)

This is significant for queer theory because Foucault asserts that sexuality is not "natural"; it is part of a web of knowledge and power, a network of discourse. It should also be noted that for Foucault, while power and knowledge are discursively transmitted, produced and reinforced, discourse also "undermines and exposes" power; it "renders it fragile and makes it possible to thwart it" (Foucault 1978, 101). This is an important suggestion: that multiple and even contradictory discourses can circulate simultaneously.

Later psychoanalytic discourse moved away from physiological models to consider sexuality as a function of psychological development, however, the physiological models proposed by Ellis and others persisted (in the USA at least) because they "resonated with and reinforced prevailing American models of racialized bodies" (Somerville 2000, 21). The most influential voice in this new area of psychoanalysis was Sigmund Freud, who laid out a developmental model of sexuality in *Three Essays* in 1905. Locating sexuality as drive, Freud considered it to be culturally and historically specific, yet "saw homosexuality as a developmental arrest, a fixation, or a sign of immaturity" (Drescher 2001, 52). Freud's psychoanalytic perspective became incredibly popular, though notably did not completely supersede earlier models. Sedgwick (2008) would later describe these as "universalising" and "minoritising" models (see Chapter 5), and highlight how they continue to coexist in our understandings of sexuality.

Key concept: Polymorphous perversity

Freud used the term "polymorphous-perverse disposition" to describe the "perversions" in sexual desire that may be acquired during development (Freud and Strachey 2000). Freud argued that such perversions occurred as a result of fixations during the development of libidinal drives, which should normally unfold in the following stages:

1. Oral (0–1): the mouth as a site of pleasure and exploration.
2. Anal (1–3): experimentation with bodily functions.
3. Phallic (3–6): awareness of genitalia.
4. Latency (6–12): development of conscience.
5. Genital (12+): emergence of sexual urges.

Freud argued that as children go through these stages they experience bisexual desires, however, in order to develop mature gender identity homosexual attachments had to be rejected. Freud's ideas would later be taken up and challenged by feminist and queer theorists such as Butler (Chapter 5).

An important critique of Freud's understanding of sexuality is also offered by Steven Angelides' *A History of Bisexuality* (2001). According to Angelides, even though Freud understood dispositions as "polymorphous", his theory of healthy sexual development also rendered bisexuality impossible in adult life. Freud's insistence on oppositional gender as determining sexuality, and the notion that desire could only ever be singularly directed (not simultaneous), positioned bisexuality as unobtainable in "the present tense" (2001, 70).

FIGHTING FOR HOMOSEXUAL RIGHTS

The emergence of medical, psychiatric and psychoanalytic research that sought to categorise sexuality in the nineteenth century worked to pathologise those who did not conform to the heterosexual norms of the era. However, while this was the basis for social control of "perversity", it also made possible new discursive formations. As Foucault highlights, around the same time "homosexuality began to speak in its own behalf, to demand that its legitimacy or 'naturality' be acknowledged, often in the same vocabulary, using the same categories by which it was medically disqualified" (1978, 101). Despite the problematic and pathologised construction of sexuality offered by sexologists like Ellis, the language used in these accounts would come to be recuperated and utilised in activism around sexuality in the decades that followed.

As homosexuality began to solidify as an identity, so too did homosexual rights organisations emerge in Europe in the late 1800s. In 1869, writer and human rights campaigner Karl Maria Benkert (later known as Karoly-Maria Kertbeny) wrote an open letter in opposition to anti-sodomy legislation that would criminalise sex between men (Steakley 1975). While this legislation was introduced in 1871, Benkert's letter sparked the beginnings of a movement defending homosexuality. German neurologist Magnus Hirschfeld similarly opposed this aspect of the penal code, and in 1897 he founded the first homophile organisation: the Scientific Humanitarian Committee (Lauritsen and Thorstad 1995). Building upon Karl Ulrich's models of sexuality (as a mismatch between body and soul), Hirschfeld understood homosexuality as an abnormality of co-mingled femininity and masculinity. With this understanding of homosexuality as congenital, he established the Scientific Humanitarian Committee to persuade judicial bodies to abolish the anti-sodomy legislation. The Scientific Humanitarian Committee worked towards legislative reform by highlighting the suffering caused by anti-sodomy legislation and emphasising the harmlessness of homosexuals. In 1903, Benedict Friedlander founded the Community of the Special, an organisation that supported the Scientific Humanitarian Committee but opposed Hirschfeld's conservative position, describing it as "degrading and a beggarly ... pleading for sympathy" (Lauritsen and Thorstad 1995, 50). Hirschfeld later founded the Institute for Sexual Science, which housed a significant archive of materials on gay cultural history and which was burnt down by the Nazis in 1933.

Taking some of Hirschfeld's ideas to England, sexologists Ellis and Edward Carpenter established the British Society for the Study of Sex Psychology in 1914. The British Society for the Study of Sex Psychology also had connections with the Scientific Humanitarian Committee. However, this group had an educational rather than legislative focus, arguing that "We do not think the time has arrived in England for a similar demand to be made" (Lauritsen and Thorstad 1995, 50). Through the British Society for the Study of Sex Psychology, Ellis and Carpenter founded a library and made connections with like-minded researchers in the USA.

Around the same time as Simone de Beauvoir was publishing *The Second Sex* in France, in the USA, Dr Alfred Kinsey's reports on *Sexual Behavior in the Human Male* (1948) and *Sexual Behavior of the Human Female* (1953) were released. Kinsey and his team collected data from 5,300 white men and 5,940 white women respectively, with the aim being to "discover what people do sexually, what factors may account for their patterns of sexual behaviour, how their sexual experiences have affected their lives, and what social significance there may be in each type of behaviour" (Kinsey et al. 1988, 3). The reports detailed activities such as masturbation, pre-marital sex, homosexual sex, orgasm and more. The first report also included a scale, which captured a range of sexual behaviours beyond and in-between homosexual and heterosexual (see Figure 2.1). Kinsey also noted a score of "X" that referred to no sexual behaviour (Kinsey Institute 2018). Despite the many methodological concerns raised about the work, Kinsey's findings revealed a diversity of sexual desires and proclivities to a wide audience.

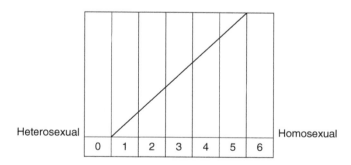

Figure 2.1   The Kinsey Scale, where 0 = exclusively heterosexual and 6 = exclusively homosexual

Key term: Asexuality

Though Kinsey identified an "X" on his scale to reflect no sexual behaviour, it is only in recent decades that there has been growing awareness and discussion of asexuality. Asexuality in its broadest sense refers to identifying as someone who does not experience sexual desire (Cerankowski and Milks 2010, 651). Karli June Cerankowski and Megan Milks suggest that although some asexual identifying people live otherwise "normative" lives, on a theoretical level asexuality can be understood as queer as it goes against dominant expectations of sexual desire. They write, "[W]e suggest that asexuality as a practice and a politics radically challenges the prevailing sex-normative culture" (2010, 661).

As Jacinthe Flore (2014) suggests (drawing on Foucault), asexuality also has a history that can be tracked through sexology. Examining the early emphasis on sexual "dysfunction", and the assumption that sexual activity is core to human identity, Flore writes, "historically, research into human sexuality has turned existence into *sexistence*, embalmed in the possibilities and threats of sexuality" (2014, 18, emphasis in original). Flore suggests that rather than defining asexuality by what it is not, asexuality might instead be thought of as a position resistant to a normative sexualised subject positioning.

The homophile movement

Early homosexual rights groups and publications often used the term "homophile" as a descriptor. This term was coined in the 1920s to refer to same-sex attracted people and it meant "same love". For a time, it was used interchangeably with "homosexual", but fell out of popularity in the late 1960s. Groups were often named in a covert manner to protect members from exposure, and frequently sought opinions of psychological experts, often inviting them to their meetings. In order to naturalise and justify homosexuality, "homophile anthropology" also emerged in Western homophile groups as a way to evidence homosexuality as both global and timeless, though often involved positioning Western sexuality as more developed (Churchill 2008, 48).

In Europe, organising began in the early 1910s in the Netherlands with the Dutch Scientific Humanitarian Committee, but many other European homophile groups did not emerge until the late 1940s, after the Second World War. In 1946, the Cultuur en Ontspannings Centrum (COC) formed in Amsterdam, whose publications included reflections on homophile activities across the world. Historians have noted that COC, like many other homophile groups, regarded emerging gay nightlife subcultures with apprehension, instead advocating for respectability in more normative cultural terms (Churchill 2008). However, others suggest that this relationship was mixed, with some crossover between the commercial subcultural and homophile organising worlds (Rupp 2011).

The earliest record of a North American homophile organisation is the Chicago Society of Human Rights, which was founded in 1924, and favoured the approach taken by Ellis and Carpenter (Katz 1992). The Chicago Society of Human Rights appealed to rationality, desired to uphold existing laws and emphasised homosexuals as sympathetic figures. The organisation was established to:

> promote and to protect the interests of people who by reasons of mental and psychic abnormalities are abused and hindered in the legal pursuit of happiness which is guaranteed them by the Declaration of Independence, and to combat the public prejudices against them by dissemination of facts according to modern science among intellectuals of mature age. The Society stands only for law and order; it is in harmony with any and all general laws insofar as they protect the rights of others, and does in no manner recommend any acts in violation of recent laws nor advocate any matter inimical to the public welfare. (Katz 1992, 385)

In 1925, key members of the Society were arrested without warrants and with little evidence – a powder puff was found in the secretary's bedroom – and this particular organisation was disbanded (Katz 1992, 391).

Other homophile groups emerged and continued, working towards increasing tolerance of homosexuality through educational programmes and political reform. Into the 1950s the movement was increasingly transnational, as reflected in a key slogan, "We are everywhere!" (Churchill 2008, 32). In 1951, the first International Congress for Sexual Equality was held in Amsterdam (Rupp 2011). From this came the International Committee for Sexual Equality (ICSE), connecting homophile groups across Europe and the USA. Annual conferences attracted around 100 to 500 participants (Loftin 2012, 71). As Leila Rupp argues, this network was built on a shared sense of homophile identity:

> This identity, very much in sync with the ideas developing in national homophile movements, built on the rejection of homosexuals as sinful, criminal, or pathological, mobilizing experts in the fields of science, medicine, religion, and law to support claims of normality. (2011, 1026)

Furthermore, periodicals published by various homophile groups had wide international reach, connecting individuals up, across and beyond the West. As David Churchill (2008) suggests, despite the transnational nature of organising, popular histories of homophile groups have skewed towards the North American context, particularly focusing on The Mattachine Society and Daughters of Bilitis (DOB). Churchill suggests that we must understand these groups within an international rather than purely local framework, given the internationally connected outlook of much of the organising.

In 1951, a small group of Los Angeles-based activists, including Harry Hay and Chuck Rowland, founded the Mattachine Society. Several founding members had been active within the Communist party and they advocated for homosexual rights with a decisively Marxist tone. Early discussion papers circulated by the Society emphasised homosexuals as a population unaware of their status as "a social minority imprisoned within a dominant culture" (D'Emilio 1998, 65). Through the 1950s, the Mattachine Society expanded, forming cell groups in other parts of the USA, including New York, Chicago and Washington. During this period, ties to other international homophile groups began, and indeed the Cold War fears of the period also meant that US-based groups looked to Western European allies for inspiration (Churchill 2008). This expansion occurred during the era of McCarthyism – during this period both homosexuals and Communists were viewed as subversive threats to US values. As a result, new members of the Mattachine Society increasingly opposed the organisation's association with the Communist party. In 1953, the Society was restructured, which split the organisation into groups loosely aligned with liberation and assimilation. The emerging homophile political mode of the period 1950s to 1960s has been described as "integrationist" (Esterberg 1994, 430) and "accommodationist rather than an oppositional" (Churchill 2008, 33).

A key ongoing critique of the Mattachine Society was that it ignored issues faced by women: it was an organisation founded by men, with a largely male membership and it dominantly focused on the concerns of men (such as police entrapment of gay men). While the Mattachine Society did not actively and explicitly exclude women, as D'Emilio argues, "in numerous, often unconscious ways, male homosexuals defined gayness in terms that negated the experience of lesbians and conspired to keep them out" (1998, 92–93). In response, in 1955, eight women including Del Martin and Phyllis Lyon established DOB in San Francisco, to counter the masculinist approach of the Mattachine Society and to advocate for homosexual women. This group was originally founded as an alternative social space to the predominantly working-class lesbian bars of the era, and early on emphasised a politics of respectability in order to destigmatise understandings of lesbian identity (Gallo 2007). Into the 1960s, despite difficulties for lesbians within some strands of feminism (discussed in Chapter 3), DOB became more closely affiliated with women's liberation organising and increasingly focused on "all" women (Esterberg 1994, 437).

The cultural conditions of the era shaped the focus of, and created political barriers for, homophile groups. As Churchill (2008) explains, the postwar period of the 1950s heralded a rise in human rights discourse, as well as civil rights organising and anti-colonial independence movements. Into the 1950s, this human rights discourse became more oriented towards articulating the rights of citizens in nationalist terms, and homophile organising aimed to distance homosexuality away from "perversion" towards notions of liberal democracy (Churchill 2008, 34). In aiming for respectable citizenship, many homophile groups distanced themselves from transgender individuals, often in highly classed terms. Churchill reflects that "Anecdotally, we know that the US-based homophile groups were middle class and that homophile publications reflected middle-class values of respectability, social aspiration, and normalcy" (2008, 46). Others have complicated the story of homophile respectability: as Martin Meekr argues through a focus on Mattachine, the "respectable public face" was merely a mask that obscured diverse activities undertaken by the group (2001, 81).

In the US context, fear of persecution meant that both the Mattachine Society and the DOB faced difficulty organising politically, with heavy government crackdowns on homosexuals in the 1950s and 1960s (Seidman 2002). During this period, it was considered deviant behaviour for women to dress in masculine attire, so women were required to be wearing at least three pieces of traditionally feminine clothing at all times. As historian Allan Bérubé also highlights:

> [Gays came] under heavy attack ... When arrested in gay bar raids, most people pleaded guilty, fretful of publicly exposing their homosexuality during a trial ... Legally barred from many forms of private and government employment, from serving their country, from expressing their opinions in newspapers and magazines, from gathering in bars and other public places as homosexuals, and from leading sexual lives, gay men and women were denied civil liberties ... Such conditions led to stifled anger, fear, isolation and helplessness. (2010, 181)

Seidman writes that in the USA, in popular culture and psychiatric discourse of this era, homosexuality "came to symbolize a threat to marriage, the family, and civilization itself" and homosexuals were "imagined as preda-tory, seductive, corrupting, promiscuous and ... gender deviant" (2002, 27). This issue was not confined to the USA. Indeed internationally, as Churchill explains, "Cutting across ideological boundaries, restrictions on homosexual-ity were part of modern state formation and the moral and physical regula-tion of citizens throughout North America and Europe" (Churchill 2008, 36). As sexuality was discursively constructed as sin, sickness and/or criminal, and therefore linked to the personal realm, many saw sexuality as a personal prob-lem rather than a political issue which sometimes limited activity and take-up (Armstrong 2002).

Gay Liberation

Homosexual activist groups that emerged in the 1960s and 1970s departed from the homophile focus on respectability (see Table 2.3). In the USA, the

---

Key concept: Sexual script theory

In 1973, John Gagnon and William Simon published *Sexual Conduct: The Social Sources of Human Sexuality*, which outlines their concept of "sexual script theory", about the social scripts that inform sexual behaviour. Gagnon and Simon were concerned with processes by which norms of appropriate sexual behaviour arise and take shape. They suggest that there are three scripts involved:

1. **Sexual cultural scripts** – scripts that determine what is socially undesirable versus culturally valorised.
2. **Interpersonal scripts** – the personal adaptation of individuals to cultural scripts.
3. **Intrapsychic scripts** – the internalised aspects of individual sexuality that may not take narrative form. (Wiederman 2015, 7–8)

Gagnon and Simon's work continues to be influential in studies of sexu-ality and suggests the importance of attending to social contexts for understanding sexual behaviour.

Table 2.3   Comparison of homophile and Gay Liberation goals and strategies

	Homophile	*Gay Liberation*
Goals	Assimilation, integration of homosexuals into society, constitutional rights, respectability, tolerance, safety, end to police violence, building transnational homosexual communities.	Visibility, liberation, pride, repeal anti-gay laws, advocate for anti-discrimination legislation, end to police violence, challenge the homo/hetero binary, challenge gender roles, critique the family, build radical gay cultures, sexual/gender revolution.
Strategies	Lobbying, writing letters, small coordinated public demonstrations (often in "respectable" attire), DIY publications including newsletters and magazines, TV advertising, providing legal and other advice and support, lesbian homophile groups affiliating with women's liberation.	Coming out, mass demonstrations, pride marches, DIY publications including pamphlets and posters, working with the women's movement/Black rights movements/trade unions.

Gay Liberation movement emerged as part of a "New Left", taking a radical approach to advocate for civil rights and democracy. The Black Power movement, Women's Liberation, and the Anti-War movement informed the context for the emergence of liberationist discourses. Gay Liberation was indebted to these movements, even borrowing their slogans – the famous "Gay Power" rallying cry came directly from "Black Power". Unlike the homophile movements, which obscured their purpose with coded language, Gay Liberation groups/organisations were named proudly and defiantly. This is because, as Dennis Altman highlights, "gay liberation ... is concerned with the assertion and creation of a new sense of identity, one based on pride in being gay" (1972, 109).

Popular imaginings of Gay Liberation in the USA often understand the Stonewall riots of June 1969 as a crucial moment, if not turning point (detailed below) (Stein 2019). However, it is worth noting that a shift from conformity to confrontation was perceptible in gay rights activism in the early 1960s. For instance, in 1963, the regional homophile group East Coast Homophile Organizations (ECHO) was formed. Members discussed openly protesting legislation discriminating against homosexuals in the federal workforce; in 1965, a satellite group of the Mattachine Society began an annual fourth of July protest outside Philadelphia's Independence Hall (Stein 2019). Furthermore, in 1966, a small riot followed a police assault of a trans person at a San Francisco eatery, Compton's Cafeteria – the venue had been a haunt for homeless youth and sexually and gender diverse people (Table 2.3) (Stryker 2008).

The Stonewall riots

The Stonewall Inn was one of only a few gay bars in New York City that permitted dancing; it had a diverse LGBTIQ patronage and was described by activist and author Vito Russo as a space for "people who were too young, too poor or just too much to get in anywhere else" (quoted in Carter 2004, 74). Police regularly raided the venue, and in the early hours of 28 June 1969 (with a warrant regarding illegal alcohol sales), five to six officers arrested various workers and patrons and demanded that the crowd of 200 leave the venue. On this occasion, the community fought back, and a riot broke out with the local LGBTIQ community battling police in the streets. The details of what happened that night are contested, but as Marc Stein outlines:

> According to some accounts, a lesbian was the first to fight back; multiple accounts emphasize the distinctively aggressive defiance of trans people and street youth. Soon the crowd, which included straight allies, was shouting at the police and throwing coins at the building ... over the next several hours, thousands of people rioted in the streets with campy courage and fierce fury. (2019, 5)

Though contested, many mainstream representations of Stonewall have whitewashed the events that followed, despite these historical accounts of people of colour and gender diverse folks as central to the uprising. Accounts suggests that Marsha P. Johnson, Jackie Hormona, Zazu Nova and Sylvia Rivera were at the front line. Johnson and Rivera would go on to become key activists for trans liberation in the USA, which we discuss further in Chapter 6. Rivera later recalled her animosity towards police on the night of the first riot: "You've been treating us like shit all these years? Uh-uh. Now it's our turn! ... It was one of the greatest moments in my life" (quoted in

Deitcher 1995, 67). There was only one photograph taken on the night of the first riot, which showed a group of homeless, largely white youth fighting with police. It appeared on the front page of *The New York Daily News* on Sunday, 29 June 1969.

Thousands of rioters came back the following night, and the night after that. Meetings were called and activists began distributing leaflets that read: "Do You Think Homosexuals are Revolting? You Bet Your Sweet Ass We Are" (Teal 1971). The Mattachine Society – still operating at the time – called for peace within the gay community. They posted a sign on the front of the bar that read: "We homosexuals plead with our people to please help maintain peaceful and quiet conduct on the streets of the Village" (Duberman 2013, 99). David Carter's *Stonewall: The Riots that Sparked the Revolution* (2004), includes an interview with Michael Fader, who was at the riots:

> We all had a collective feeling like we'd had enough of this kind of shit. It wasn't anything tangible anybody said to anyone else, it was just kind of like everything over the years had come to a head on that one particular night in the one particular place, and it was not an organized demonstra-tion. (Carter 2004, 160)

However, there are competing theories of why Stonewall happened when it did. As Stein (2019) argues, there are multiple explanatory frameworks gener-ally offered, all of which suggest Stonewall was just one part of a larger frame-work of political resistance where the riots:

- were the climax of/built on earlier homophile organising and resistance;
- were influenced by earlier resistance specifically around bars and police violence;
- emerged within the context of a diversity of social movements active at the time, including the anti-war movement, civil rights and women's liberation;
- happened within a broader context of pessimism and a violent downturn following some earlier gains for homosexual rights.

A year later, on 28 June 1970, the first gay pride marches took place in New York, Los Angeles, San Francisco and Chicago. Within two years there were gay rights groups in every major city in the USA, as well as Canada, Western Europe and Australia.

Queer theory in practice: The problem of bisexual exclusion

The "B" of LGBTIQ is often silent in histories of sexuality, with greater focus on gay and lesbian, and, more recently, trans identity. Self-identified bisexual activists have been a central part of LGBTIQ political history, active though rarely acknowledged, in key events such as the Sydney Mardi Gras. As Angelides argues, "the category of bisexuality seems to have been spared the rigors of [the] 'never-ending demand for truth'" (2001, 2). Despite queer theory's interest in deconstructing binaries, bisexuality has not always been well recognised or theorised. Today, the use of bisexuality even sometimes faces scrutiny for seemingly reinstating the gender binary through the prefix "bi", in comparison to terms such as "pansexuality".

Ellis recognised a unique bisexual orientation that involved attraction to both men and women. Furthermore, as noted above, the Kinsey Scale clearly demarcated a huge range of sexual behaviours that could not be classified as purely heterosexual or homosexual. However, much of the theory that has informed queer theory has derided, ignored or bracketed discussion of bisexuality. Though Freud pointed to an originary bisexual potential in all persons, he saw homosexuality as a problematic form of sexual development. Further, as Angelides argues, though some Gay Liberationists imagined bisexuality as a utopian goal of sexual liberation, it was something marked as a future possibility, rather than something that might be realised in the present.

Despite these early discussions, and some suggestions that bisexual identified persons might make up more than half of LGBTIQ communities, in general "B" in LGBTIQ has been historically forgotten, erased or excluded, in favour of centring on the homo/hetero binary in activism. For example, in 1996, the Sydney Gay and Lesbian Mardi Gras (as it was known then), following an increase in homophobic street violence, initiated membership rules that made it difficult for people to join unless they explicitly identified as gay, lesbian or transgender (McLean 2008). Applicants identifying as bisexual were made to include further justification for their membership, effectively excluding bisexual members. These membership rules were not changed until the early 2000s.

Angelides suggests that both gay and straight discourses mark bisexuality as impossible in order to maintain the firm boundaries of gender (man/woman) and sexuality (hetero/homo) upon which they rely. This has led some to suggest that a "bisexual theory" approach may be needed to *queer* queer theory (Erickson-Schroth and Mitchell 2009, 298). Here imagining bisexuality's radical queer potential is central; as Marjorie Garber writes, "The more borders to patrol, the more border crossings" (2000, 22).

The Sydney Mardi Gras

Australia has been a key locus of gay and lesbian liberationist politics in the Western world, with the key touchpoint being the Sydney Gay and Lesbian Mardi Gras, an event best described as part memorial, part protest and part celebration, which first started in 1978. Prior to this, Campaign Against Moral Persecution (CAMP) was Australia's first national homosexual rights lobby group, established in 1970 at a time when LGBTIQ people had few rights in Australia. At this time, homosexuality was criminalised in all states and territories, and discrimination and persecution were rampant. Homosexuality would eventually be decriminalised, but not until much later (Tasmania was the last state to decriminalise sex between men in 1997). In April 1978, Sydney-based activists Anne Talvé and Ken Davis received a letter from the San Francisco Gay Freedom Day Committee. It was sent to political groups around the world and it called upon them to organise events in the last week of June to mark the ninth anniversary of Stonewall (Carbery 1995). This sparked the emergence of a radical liberation organisation called the Gay Solidarity Group (GSG), which organised the first Gay and Lesbian Mardi Gras. The group aimed to use celebration to "arouse interest in gay political activism ... [and] mobilise protest action against" a forthcoming visit from Mary Whitehouse, a well-known British "morals" campaigner (Carbery 1995, 7).

The idea for a celebration rather than a traditional march was suggested by Ron Austin, a member of the New South Wales branch of CAMP in Australia. The idea was to create an event that "would be a celebration of gay and lesbian pride and freedom, a real celebration; something that would link up the politics of gay freedom in Oxford Street in a commercial sense" (Carbery

1995, 10). So, on Saturday, 24 June 1978, the city celebrated International Gay Solidarity Day with a march, followed by a public meeting and a celebratory parade at 10pm. The parade ended in a riot and 53 people were arrested. Protesters clashed with police in the days and months that followed, and demonstrations were organised in other parts of the country to drop the charges. Gay activist Larry Galbraith suggests, "The events of the first International Gay Solidarity Day had sparked off a fight for basic civil rights which no one had foreseen. But the battle for the right to march had been won. It was to be used with even greater effect in the years that followed" (cited in Carbery 1995, 17). The first Mardi Gras had effects far beyond the initial riot. As a result of Mardi Gras and the subsequent related protests, anti-protest laws in NSW were repealed. The gay community won the right to march for everyone (Ross 2013).

The Sydney Gay and Lesbian Mardi Gras began as a small political protest in 1978 and quickly became linked to the emerging pride movement, which sought to celebrate LGBTIQ identity around the world. By the 1990s, the Gay and Lesbian Mardi Gras had transformed into a glitzy televised cultural event with international significance. More recent iterations of Mardi Gras may appear to be all about colourful floats and glitter, though the event remains important for both participants and organisers, functioning as a form of

---

Queer theory in practice: Commercialisation of pride

With the proliferation and institutionalisation of pride marches around the world, so too have these spaces become increasingly commercialised. Big businesses often sponsor pride events and take centre stage in marches to promote their brands to an LGBTIQ market. The lucrative commercial value of LGBTIQ marketing is sometimes referred to as "the pink dollar".

Because of this dynamic, pride marches are frequently disrupted by LGBTIQ groups who seek to protest the capitalist recuperation of this LGBTIQ space. As Sandra Jeppesen explains: "Anti-capitalist queer organizing assumes a critical relation to the new power hierarchies that have been established within queer culture, to unlink queer culture from consumerism, offering critiques of gay villages steeped in commerce, the 'pink dollar', the gay niche market, and corporate sponsorship of Pride marches" (2010, 470).

entertainment but also as a memorial to Gay Liberation "affirming the rights of homosexuals to take their place in society openly and without apology" (Carbery 1995, 5).

From liberation to pride

Across the liberation movement, gay activists and organisations were united by their focus on pride and liberation. This movement viewed the public declaration of identity (or "coming out") as a meaningful political act. For activists in the movement, coming out was not just about publicly declaring your identity but rather a battle cry for LGBTIQ people to join the fight for equality, not just by coming "out of the closet", but out of the bars and onto the streets.

While the act of coming out politicised identity, the movement's focus on pride and liberation sought to reject associations between homosexuality, shame, repression and persecution. Each of these concerns responded in particular ways to earlier discourses and understandings of sexuality. Responding to (and ultimately rejecting) earlier movements, Gay Liberation suggested that sexuality was something to be affirmed. At the time, this affirmation was thought to be the best way to break free from traditional understandings of sex, gender and sexuality and, most importantly, to achieve political and sexual freedom. These concerns are reflected in activists' publications from the early 1970s and later interviews with key figures, along with most popular culture texts that represent their efforts. However, as we have mentioned, the historical accuracy of these representations must always be interrogated, as they have tended to simplify the key events and have consistently failed to represent the diversity of protesters involved in the movement.

Ideas from Gay Liberation are echoed in the modern pride movement, which celebrates LGBTIQ identity in parades, festivals and marches around the world. The first pride marches occurred in the USA in 1970 to commemorate the Stonewall riots. While LGBTIQ pride events occur globally, we must stress that participation in the pride movement is not a sign of a nation's "progressive" politics. In part this relates to the fact that the understandings of sex, gender and sexuality from which the pride movement has emerged are largely Western constructs.

Queer theory in practice: The globalisation of pride

Significant LGBTIQ pride events outside of North America and Australia have been organised in the following places:

Asia

The first pride-related event to be organised in Asia was the 1994 Manila Pride March in the Philippines. LGBTIQ pride events are now regularly held across Asia. For instance, India's Kolkata Rainbow Pride Walk was first held in 1999 and is the longest running LGBTIQ event in South Asia. Parades and marches have been held in Indian cities including Delhi, Bangalore, Pondicherry and Mumbai. However, India has a complex relation to LGBTIQ rights, having decriminalised homosexuality in 2009 and then later re-criminalised it in 2013. Japan also has hosted pride events annually since the mid-1990s with parades and festivals occurring in cities including Tokyo (Tokyo Rainbow Festival), Osaka (Kansai Rainbow Parade) and Sapporo (Sapporo Rainbow March) among others. South Korea has hosted the Korea Queer Culture Festival annually since 2000. This event includes LGBTIQ pride-related activities and a film festival. In the mid-2000s, Shanghai Pride was Mainland China's first pride event in 2009, while earlier events had been organised in Taiwan in 2003 and Hong Kong in 2005. Vietnam's LGBT Viet Pride has also been held annually since 2012.

Africa

South Africa hosts many LGBTIQ events with Johannesburg Pride the first of these in 1990. Annual pride parades have been held in Cape Town since 1993, and the country also hosts a Mr Gay South Africa pageant as well as a Johannesburg pride parade. Activists at the original pride parade in Johannesburg noted the relationship between their activism around sexuality, and the fight against apartheid. In recent years, LGBTIQ pride events have been organised in Mauritius and Tunisia, the latter of which recognises International Day Against Homophobia each year.

Europe

LGBTIQ groups in Europe have been organising events since the mid-1970s. Europe also hosts Europride, a major festival hosted by a different European city every year. In addition to this, LGBTIQ festivals and parades are organised annually in many major cities across Western Europe. Events include England's Pride in London, which originated in protests in the 1970s, Finland's Helsinki Pride (held annually since 1975), France's Marche des Fiertés LGBT (held annually since 1981) and Germany's two major pride events, Berlin Pride and Cologne Pride (both started in 1979). In Eastern Europe, LGBTIQ pride events have been met with protests and violence. For instance, Moscow held pride events from 2006 to 2010 that were met with increasing hostility from anti-LGBTIQ groups. In 2012, Russia placed a 100-year ban on gay pride-related activities.

South America
Brazil's São Paulo Gay Pride Parade is South America's best-known LGBTIQ event and is often reported to be the biggest LGBTIQ pride parade in the world. Smaller events are held annually in Brazilian cities and townships. Argentina also hosts the popular Buenos Aires Gay Pride Parade.

CONCLUSION: A HISTORY OF KNOWLEDGE AND POWER

Considering the history of sexuality sketched in this chapter, we can see that knowledge, power and sexuality are inextricably linked. The construction of knowledge around sexuality has worked to legitimise violence and discrimination against the LGBTIQ community, but has also influenced the articulation of identities available and the foundation for organising collectively to fight back. Foucault referred to this double-edged sword as "reverse discourse": where articulation of and demands on behalf of identities are made possible via the very language used to subjugate those identities (1978, 101). The key resistance movements traced throughout this book have attempted to shift terms around gender and sexuality with varying degrees of success.

While retrospectively considering the knowledge, understanding and political strategies presented by each of the periods we have discussed, it is tempting to attempt to offer a clear narrative of political progress. However, looking closely at these shifts in discourse about sexuality it becomes clear that any such narratives would not only be false, but insufficiently "global". Furthermore, the Gay Liberation movement in the West that many saw as a step towards radical iterations of gender and sexuality, has been critiqued as "usurpation by white, middle-class, gay men, and ... their sexist and misogynist agendas" (Sullivan 2003). Here we must note that for marginal groups, the terms of political debate are often set by those with the most power.

Further reading

Marc Stein. (2019). *The Stonewall Riots: A Documentary History*. New York: New York University Press.

Stein provides a detailed documentary account of the Stonewall riots and their influence on later politics, including much reflection on the competing versions of Stonewall history.

John D'Emilio. (1998). *Sexual Politics, Sexual Communities: The Making of a Homosexual Minority in the United States, 1940–1970*. 2nd ed., Chicago: University of Chicago Press.

D'Emilio's work continues to be the most comprehensive account of the homophile movement in the USA.

Graham Willett. (2000). *Living Out Loud: A History of Gay and Lesbian Activism in Australia*. Melbourne: Allen & Unwin.

This in-depth look at gay and lesbian activism in Australia will prove useful for those looking to see how ideas from Gay Liberation travelled "down under".

QUESTIONS TO CONSIDER

- What were Foucault's key problems with the way that Victorian sexuality had been imagined?
- Why is it important to complicate the history of sexuality offered by Foucault? What does Foucault miss?
- Did Gay Liberation differ from the earlier homophile movement?
- Have pride parades today left their political origins behind?

Recommended films

The Rejected **(John W. Reavis 1961).** This film was the first documentary on homosexuality that was broadcast on US television. It consists of short segments of experts explaining homosexuality (with a focus on men) from different perspectives. It provides a key insight into how homosexuality was represented and understood at the time.

Daughters of Bilitis Video Project **(1987).** This is an online archive of interviews with members of Daughters of Bilitis, focusing on the formation and impact of the organisation. Digitised by Lesbian Herstory Archives: http://herstories.prattinfoschool.nyc/omeka/exhibits/show/daughters-of-bilitis-video-pro

When We Rise **(Dustin Lance Black 2017).** A television mini-series that traces the lives of three key activists from the Gay Liberation movement. It provides fictional depictions of key historical events during the time.

3 Sexuality and Feminism

KEY TERMS AND CONCEPTS	Western feminist "waves", the sex/gender distinction, liberal feminism, radical feminism, socialist feminism, Marxist feminism, the personal is political, separatism, psychoanalysis, intersectional feminism, Black feminism, the erotic, anti-pornography feminism, pro-sex/sex radical feminism

QUEER THEORY'S FEMINIST FOUNDATIONS

What is the relationship between feminist and queer perspectives, and how did feminist ideas shape the queer thinking to come? How do these theoretical fields differ in their accounts of gender and sexuality, and in what ways do their agendas intersect? In this chapter, we explore the complex relations between feminism and queer theory. You might assume that you cannot adopt a queer theory position *without* feminism, and vice versa. As Mimi Marinucci argues,

> Precisely what it is that constitutes the subject matter of feminism varies from one form of feminism to the next. Despite this diversity, however, almost every form of feminism addresses at least gender and sex, and sometimes sexuality as well. There is thus an implicit connection between queer theory and feminist theory. (2010, 105)

Similarly, Lynne Huffer points to the inextricability of the fields by alluding to "queer theory's feminist birth" (2010, 45). However, while some readers may be attached to "queer" and "feminist" as intimately bound together, these theoretical strands have not always gelled so easily. As Janet McLaughlin, Mark E. Casey and Diane Richardson note, a lot of scholarly writing asserts "feminist and queer writers think differently about how to engage with issues around gender and sexuality" (2006, 2). They suggest the concepts of queer and feminism have even been viewed as "theoretically incompatible" based on their modes of reference, priorities and political agendas. From this perspective, queer attention to issues of discursive construction, local activity and cultural representation can clash with feminist attention to structural analysis, global struggle and issues of materiality. Indeed, as Pilcher and Whelehan argue, "Radical feminists are among those most sceptical of queer theory" (2017, 128). This chapter offers a way to think through the historical tensions between queer theory and *different forms* of feminism – what Jagose describes as "Thinking of feminist theory and queer theory as braided together in ongoing relations" (2009, 164). We attempt to unknot some of this braid in this chapter as we address key sites of feminist theorising and their queer intersections. In the latter part of the chapter we attend to synergies between feminism and queer theory today that draw upon a broader global context (explored in more detail in Chapter 7).

FEMINISM(S)

Though many feminist analyses share concerns around gender and (frequently) what is called "the woman question", feminism has always been in tension. Because of this, we ought not to speak of *feminism*, but rather, *feminisms*. Unpacking these various feminisms helps us to understand the interdependence of feminist and queer thought, beyond those strands that have focused on sexuality specifically (such as lesbian feminism) to feminism more broadly. Identifying the specifics of different feminisms is not always easy, particularly in terms of drawing out the implications of these ideas for queer theory.

We can begin to tease out the braid of feminist theory and queer theory by focusing on feminist approaches to gender, sex and sexuality that played a role in shaping queer thinking – whether directly or indirectly – and acknowledging that the feminisms rejected by queer theorists also shaped the field. It is crucial to recognise that many of the ideas that would later come to be interrogated by key queer theorists such as Sedgwick and Butler – who we discuss in detail in Chapter 5 – had their origins in the work of earlier Western feminist thinkers, particularly centred on a US context.

Key concept: Western feminist "waves"

The waves metaphor that is often used to describe eras of Western feminism first emerged in the 1960s. Activist Marsha Lear came up with the term "second wave feminism" as a rhetorical way to connect to earlier fights for women's rights marked by the suffrage movement (Kinser 2004, 129). Thus, it was also during this period that the definition of "first wave feminism" emerged. It is also essential to keep in mind that the idea of feminist "waves" often presents feminist history through a distinctly Western lens. While this wave metaphor can be useful to tell the story of feminisms past, the tensions and diversity of perspectives from different eras and locations must also be taken into account.

The different waves of Western feminism often discussed today are popularly summarised in *broad* terms as being concerned with:

- **Second wave:** women's liberation from the domestic sphere, equality in all aspects of life.
- **Third wave:** the politics of difference, with a focus on women's individual agency.
- **Fourth/fifth/new waves:** interconnectedness via the Internet, alternative forms of activism, highlighting diverse identifications.

However, as Linda Nicholson suggests, reliance on the idea of feminist "waves" can produce a sense of feminist history as a straightforward progress narrative (2016, 44). Clare Hemmings (2011) also asserts that progress narratives are damaging because they tend to flatten difference within each "wave". Hemmings shows how popular histories of feminist organising tend to separate Black lesbians from lesbian feminism and posit lesbian activism as inattentive to racial exclusion in a way that encourages contemporary readers to ignore the materialities of the past.

QUEER THEORY'S GENDER PROBLEM

A considerable number of feminist theorists posed lesbian feminist critiques of queer theory throughout the 1990s. While not the first to assert a divide between queer feminist thinking, Suzanna Danuta Walters' essay "From Here to Queer", published in 1996, is exemplary of this. Walters argues that queer theory often "erases lesbian specificity and the enormous difference that gender makes, evacuates the importance of feminism, and rewrites the history of lesbian feminism and feminism generally" (1996, 843). Walters suggests that queer theory positions itself as beyond gender, yet "man" remains a universal referent and "homosexual" is often understood purely in terms of gay men. As such, while queer theory may claim to denaturalise identity categories, it also risks ignoring the specificities of women's experiences (1996, 845).

That queer theory in the early 1990s began to be articulated as an area of thought *distinct* from feminism only furthered this problem. Taking the central text produced in 1993, *The Lesbian and Gay Studies Reader*, as her basis, Butler suggests:

> [T]he very formulation of lesbian and gay studies depends upon the evacuation of a sexual discourse from feminism. And what passes as a benign, even respectful, analogy with feminism is the means by which the fields are separated, where that separation requires the desexualization of the feminist project and the appropriation of sexuality as the "proper" object of lesbian/gay studies. (1994, 6)

Butler warns against differentiating these areas of inquiry, and strongly suggests that feminism has been mischaracterised without acknowledging the multiplicity of feminisms past that have engaged with questions of sexuality, race and class in complex ways. Furthermore, queer theory has synergies with feminisms past, relying on concepts that distinctly echo theoretical contributions from feminism that are not always recognised as such. As Linda Garber argues:

> Queer gender-fuck echoes lesbian-feminist androgyny. Post-structuralist "phallogocentrism" reframes an earlier feminism's "patriarchy". Queers' disruption of "heteronormativity" extends lesbian feminists' political choice of lesbianism. (2006, 79)

To further understand the role of feminist debates in shaping queer theory, we must turn to the different strands of feminism that emerged in the West during the so-called second wave.

FEMINISMS IN TENSION

First and foremost, the mid-twentieth-century civil rights movement – which had its political basis in the long struggle against segregation and systematic marginalisation in the USA – was central to influencing a generation of feminist activists in the West. This, along with protests against the Vietnam War, student organising and workers' strikes during the 1960s, brought a feeling that collective resistance was possible. A mass movement that became known as the "New Left" emerged from this wave of activism (Siegel 2007, 26). Understanding this historical basis is important for unpacking the shared history of various feminisms, but also the political differences that would take on significance in later debates around feminism's relationship to queer theory.

Within the context of this new period of activism, debates arose around the lack of specific focus on women's issues in some activist groups. As Deborah Siegel (2007) outlines, a split emerged in the late 1960s between those New Left women who wanted to remain within the broader movement who believed capitalism was the central target (the "politicos") and those who wanted to leave and organise separately against sexism (the "feminists", also known as early radical feminists). As Alison Jaggar (1983) describes, while earlier activism around women's rights (the so-called first wave) was based around issues of rights and equality, a new feminist language of oppression and liberation arose during the 1960s.

Key concept: The sex/gender distinction

As noted in Chapter 1, the sex/gender distinction is central to many feminist theories of gender. It was first explicitly theorised in 1972, by sociologist Ann Oakley in her book *Sex, Gender and Society*. The idea also arguably has its origins in the work of French philosopher Simone de Beauvoir, who claimed, "One is not born, but rather becomes, a woman" (1953, 295). De Beauvoir argued that one's biology or "sex" ought not be the determining factor of one's life. Originally published in 1949, de Beauvoir's text *The Second Sex* was translated into English in 1953, and became widely read, influencing the generation of feminists to come.

Many feminist thinkers in the 1960s and 1970s would come to take up the distinction between "sex" and "gender" offered by de Beauvoir, though there have since been many critiques of the sex/gender distinction. De Beauvoir's key idea of "becoming" (that one "becomes" a woman through social processes) was also echoed in the 1990s by Butler, via the concept of gender performativity. Yet, as we explore in more detail in Chapter 5, Butler also questioned whether a split between gender and sex is possible, or whether sex is always already gendered.

Alongside the radical strands of feminism that started at this time, a liberal women's rights agenda had emerged. Betty Friedan, from the USA, was a key figure in this strand of the women's movement, which was focused on legislative reforms and equal rights rather than revolutionary left activism. A journalist by training, Friedan's germinal book *The Feminine Mystique* was published in 1963, and detailed "the problem that has no name": the dissatisfaction many women felt in being condemned to marriage and the domestic sphere (1963, 15). Friedan was particularly scathing of Freud's accounts of women's dissatisfaction as based in psychosexual dynamics such as "penis envy". For Friedan, sex was a distraction from the root cause of women's dissatisfaction: inequality. As she argued, "The kind of sexual orgasm which Kinsey found in statistical plenitude in the recent generations of American women does not seem to make this problem go away" (1963, 29).

In contrast to Friedan, several key feminists articulated the case for a revolutionary feminist politics that specifically placed sexuality at the centre of their theory. For example, the *SCUM Manifesto* was written by Valerie Solanas in 1967, which allegedly stood for "Society for Cutting Up Men". Solanas' infamous piece opens,

> Life in this society being, at best, an utter bore and no aspect of society being at all relevant to women, there remains to civic-minded, responsible, thrill-seeking females only to overthrow the government, eliminate the money system, institute complete automation and destroy the male sex. (2004, 35)

Solanas' (perhaps satirical) text would later influence lesbian separatism, and unlike Friedan focused directly on questions of reproduction and the control of women's bodies. Shulamith Firestone's 1970 *The Dialectic of Sex* drew from Marxist and Freudian theory to argue that the basis of women's oppression was founded in reproductive dynamics. Kate Millett's 1970 *Sexual Politics* also looked at the power structures involved in sexual dynamics that entrench women's oppression (Millett 2016). Similarly Germaine Greer's *The Female Eunuch*, also published in 1970, argued that women had become "castrated" by a sexual culture which did not see women as anything more than sexual objects. Greer writes:

> What happens is that the female is considered as a sexual object for the use and appreciation of other sexual beings, men. Her sexuality is both denied and misrepresented by being identified as passivity. The vagina is obliterated from the imagery of femininity in the same way that the signs of

independence and vigour in the rest of her body are suppressed. The characteristics that are praised and rewarded are that of the castrate. (1970, 15)

Critiquing the methods and manner of activists like Friedan, Greer's work aimed to present the case for overthrowing the system rather than arguing for assimilation into it.

While there was broad agreement within the women's movement of the 1960s that women were oppressed, the question remained: by whom? Alison Jaggar has helpfully delineated four key strands of feminism often identifiable in the history of feminist thought: liberal, socialist, Marxist and radical (1983). While the first two branches were concerned with state-based reform efforts, the latter were focused on radical social transformation, namely revolution (see Table 3.1). Within radical feminism in particular "patriarchy theory" emerged, that is, the idea that the fabric of society was underpinned by "systematic male dominance of women" (Hines 2015). Borrowing from Marxist conceptions of class struggle, patriarchy theory understands women as a class (a "sisterhood") dominated by men who occupy a more privileged position in a gender hierarchy. As Ti-Grace Atkinson claims in her 1969 discussion of radical feminist theory, "Women were the first political class and the beginning of the class system" (Atkinson 2000). In contrast, as Jaggar describes, Marxists argued that "women are oppressed primarily because their oppression benefits capital" (1983, 70).

Table 3.1 builds upon Jaggar's work by identifying two additional strands of feminism of the second wave era, both of which centred on race. Articulating Black civil rights-based feminism in 1960s, Pauli Murray used the expression "Jane Crow" – a term that gestured to the Jim Crow laws that enforced racial segregation in the USA – to refer to the way that racism and sexism combined to oppress Black women. She famously wrote that Black women "have been doubly victimized by the twin immoralities of Jim Crow and Jane Crow" (1970, 87), and argued for legal reform to end discrimination based on both race and gender. Taking a more specifically revolutionary focus, Black feminism led by the Combahee River Collective sought to challenge and overthrow the simultaneous oppressions faced by women of colour. As Keeanga-Yamahtta Taylor notes, the Combahee River Collective understood that "experiences of oppression, humiliations, and the indignities created by poverty, racism, and sexism opened Black women up to the possibility of radical and revolutionary politics" (2017, 9). Both of these feminisms would later inform the concept of intersectionality (a term that understands how dimensions of oppression are intimately interconnected) and be taken up within queer(s) of colour theory, which interrogates questions of sexuality and gender in relation to ethnicity, race, racialisation and nation (discussed in Chapter 7).

Table 3.1   Some strands of "second wave" feminism and views on sexual oppression/freedom

	REFORM FOCUS	*REVOLUTION FOCUS*
GENDER-CENTRED	**Liberal feminism** Sexual freedom has wrongly been seen as the source of women's dissatisfaction in the domestic sphere, and is largely a distraction from other women's issues. Reforms of women's access to work, pay, childcare and general life choices is needed to achieve women's equality.	**Radical feminism** Women's sexual desires are oppressed by men: women are seen as passive to men's active sexuality, and women's pleasure and sexual interest is secondary. A gender revolution led by "the sisterhood" to overthrow the patriarchy is required.
CLASS-CENTRED	**Socialist feminism** Women lack sexual freedom due to social *and* economic oppression, particularly their relegation to the domestic sphere and unrecognised emotional work in this domain. Wide-scale social reform is needed to create a better world for all.	**Marxist feminism** Reproduction is key to women's sexual oppression – capitalism requires that men are producers/labourers (the working class), and women are reproducers (of the future working class). Economic revolution is required to achieve true equality.
RACE-CENTRED	**Black feminism (civil rights-based)** Gender *and* racial-based oppressions combine to limit Black women's freedoms. Racism and sexism must be addressed in tandem via civil rights reform in order to end discrimination.	**Black feminism (revolutionary)** It is essential to focus on the politics of identity when attempting to understand the workings of oppression. To guarantee liberation and equality, the revolution must be anti-racist, anti-capitalist, ant-imperialist and feminist.

Though delineating only six strands of feminism simplifies the different feminist approaches of the time (which were not necessarily so neatly "distinct"), it is nonetheless helpful for understanding the political ideas and aims that shaped various feminist responses to questions around sex and sexuality. The contribution of all feminisms of this period was to question the naturalness of the difference between men and women, which would later inform the feminist critique of heterosexuality and, in turn, queer theory (Jackson 2006a, 46). However, with radical feminism founded on the notion that women are oppressed by men as a class and that gender should be abolished, this laid the foundation for inevitable rifts with later queer perspectives that would argue for a greater focus on questions of sexuality and the deconstruction and proliferation (rather than obliteration) of gender categories.

Key concept: The personal is political

During the 1970s the idea that "The personal is political" became an important slogan. This was particularly taken up by radical feminists to highlight the "personal" ways in which men's systemic domination of women played out. The slogan was coined following Carol Hanisch's 1969 essay of the same name, created for a women's liberation publication edited by radical feminists. As Siegel suggests,

> "The Personal Is Political" meant that – suddenly! – sex, family life, household chores, and, indeed, everyday interactions between men and women were not simply private matters of individual choice but involved the exercise of institutional power. It meant that a refusal to fetch your male boss coffee might be part of a collective movement based on the human right to fulfillment. (2007, 32)

Along these lines, a key tactic employed at this time was consciousness raising. Consciousness raising involved women getting together to discuss their everyday lives, promoting a sense of solidarity of experience.

While the intention of "the personal is political" was to draw attention to the connection between the structural and the individual, this distinction was sometimes collapsed. As Koedt suggests, some lesbian groups claimed to be the "vanguard" of women's liberation and that such a claim involved "a confusion of a personal with a political solution" (1973, 250).

While queer theorists continue to be informed by the idea of "the personal is political", we may wish to take stock of Koedt's critique of lesbian feminism: to what extent do queer accounts sometimes collapse the personal and the political such that "queerness" is understood as a politically "superior" position? And to what extent would such a claim work against the aspirations of queer theory to deconstruct hierarchies?

Lesbians and feminism

Fragmentation also occurred around the question of lesbians within the women's movement in the 1960s and 1970s. As Anne Koedt describes, the growing awareness of lesbian sexuality was made possible by crossovers between the Gay Liberation and women's movements of the time: many feminists had a "heightened consciousness about lesbianism" (Koedt 1973). However, liberal feminists like Friedan argued that the association between homosexuality and deviancy meant that focusing on lesbian issues was not only a distraction; it was also dangerous for the women's movement (Calhoun 1994). Friedan referred to those fighting for lesbian issues to be canvassed as a "lavender menace".

In response to the derision of lesbians within the movement, on 1 May 1970 at the Second Congress to Unite Women in New York, a group of women sporting "Lavender Menace" t-shirts interrupted conference proceedings to protest the exclusion of lesbian issues from discussions. They distributed a manifesto titled *The Woman Identified Woman*, and identified themselves as the "Radicalesbians" (Radicalesbians 1970). In this manifesto the group suggested that lesbian sexuality ought not be seen merely as an "alternative" to sex with men, and indeed that lesbianism was about a deeper relationality and way of being in the world, beyond questions of sexuality. They write: "Until women see in each other the possibility of a primal commitment which includes sexual love, they will be denying themselves the love and value they readily accord to men, thus affirming their second-class status" (Radicalesbians 1970).

This articulation marked the beginning of a new strand of feminist organising that understood the domination of women by men as an ideology that had been *internalised* by women and that needed to be rectified (Gill 2008, 45). One of the phrases that became popular at this time, "feminism is the theory; lesbianism is the practice", is attributed to Ti-Grace Atkinson (Koedt 1973). Within this form of lesbian feminism, given the radical emphasis on critiquing gender roles, any so-called role-playing (such as butch and femme) or role-maintenance within homosexual relationships was seen by radical feminists as deeply problematic. Such critical views on butch/femme embodiment would later be critiqued by queer theorists such as Butler (1991).

As we have loosely sketched out here, the emergence of lesbian feminism was in many ways linked to the marginalisation of lesbian women within the women's movement. However, it was also, equally, a disavowal of earlier homophile and Gay Liberationist thought and action (detailed in Chapter 2), both of which were sometimes perceived to marginalise women's experience. For example, some lesbian separatists critiqued the sexism of the Gay Liberation movement and called for gay men to take action: "the discussion of homosexuality and feminism is the opportunity ... to confront your role as men in a patriarchal society and recognize the ways in which your sexism oppresses us, as lesbians" (Bebbington and Lyons 1975, 27). Lesbian feminism developed out of the desire to focus on issues directly pertaining to lesbian women. Some women felt that the Gay Liberation movement spoke largely for issues that related to men, and that liberationist writing, and action, had no interest in challenging the patriarchal power structures that oppressed them; however, the inevitability of this gendered "split" has been sometimes overstated (Fela and McCann 2017).

In the year following their emergence, the Radicalesbians split and various new groups formed with different ideas regarding how best to address the social and psychological dynamics of women's sexual oppression. One such group that formed, The Furies, advocated specifically for lesbian separatism organised around communal living (Kulpa 2009). As Jeanne Cordova distinguishes, in the 1970s separatism took on different forms – at times it was simply an organising principle, but at other times it was a political direction that argued for a completely separate world order (2000, 358). When Jill Johnson published *The Lesbian Nation: The Feminist Solution* in 1974, she strongly argued for lesbian separatism as a political tactic. While not all separatism was about lesbianism, and not all lesbians were separatist, much separatist organising was focused on questions of lesbianism as a key political strategy (Krieger 1996, 203). Diane Richardson argues that we might see synergies between the category of "political lesbian" with "queer" given that neither rely on explicit identification as lesbian/gay (2006, 32). In other words, both political lesbian and queer might be understood as *political* orientations that aim to challenge norms of sexuality and gender.

Yet, unlike queer theory, the politics of separatism sometimes led to reinforcing borders of gender and sexuality, and a reiteration of essentialist biological ideas. Bisexuality, for one, was treated as illegitimate. As Sharon Dale Stone highlights, many lesbian feminists rejected bisexuality, considering it a dilution of the lesbian feminist movement and a threat to the vision of a lesbian nation (1996, 108). Some lesbian feminist groups thought that bisexual women enjoyed the pleasures of lesbian culture but were unwilling to give up their heterosexual privilege. As Shane Phelan notes, one anti-bi idea that circulated was that "By sleeping with women, lesbians express their commitment to a world that values women" while sleeping with men revealed women to be "torn, half-hearted victims not entirely to be trusted" (1989, 49). In the face of this biphobic rhetoric, bisexual women played a significant role in the development of the different strands of feminism (and developed strands of critique especially focused on bisexual issues) and bisexual activists refused to be delegitimised and erased. Bisexual women began to organise politically in the

1980s through the formation of groups such as the Boston Bisexual Women's Network in 1983, the Chicago Action Bi-Women in 1983 and the Seattle Bisexual Women's Network in 1986 in the USA, all of which were built on the principles of feminism. These bisexual feminist organisations engaged in activism, published newsletters and provided support to bisexual women (see Beemyn 2004, 144). Beth Elliot argued, in 1992, that "Many [bisexual women] came of age and/or came out in time to help create the 'women's community' groundswell of the 1970s" (235). As such, she argued that: "We cherish our place in the women's community, a community many of us have worked strenuously to build, and we care passionately about maintaining our connection with it" (1992, 233–234) and "[T]oo many bisexual feminists do too much for the lesbian community to be regarded as separate from that community" (1992, 251). Later bisexual theorists would critique biphobic rhetoric and monosexism, engaging in debates about bisexuality that would enable the dominant binary of heterosexuality and homosexuality to be questioned (Erikson-Schroth and Mitchell 2009).

In addition, anti-trans viewpoints were expressed by radical feminists such as Greer (1970), Janice Raymond (1980) and, later, Sheila Jeffreys (1997). The 1970s had seen the emergence of women's music festivals and women's conferences, and it was in these arenas that transphobia was used to shore up boundaries of women-only space. For example, at the West Coast Lesbian Conference held in 1973, Elliot, one of the organisers and a transgender woman, was driven out after being attacked by several women in attendance (Cordova 2000; Heaney 2016). Transgender theorist and historian Susan Stryker suggests the event that sparked this was an accusation of sexual harassment, which she sees as part of an emerging discourse viewing transgender women as violators that represented an "unwanted penetration" into women's spaces (Stryker 2017). While there was resistance to this discourse (Heaney 2016), most histories of this event focus on the much publicized keynote speaker at the conference, Robin Morgan, who used her platform to publicly criticize Elliot and other transgender women, condemning them as men who "deliberately re-emphasize gender roles, and who parody female oppression and suffering" (Stryker 2017). However, while echoing separatist ideas, Morgan also spoke *against* lesbian separatism, claiming that it falsely divided women from one another (Samek 2016). She suggested that sexual orientation was irrelevant to the overall revolution required. Such views collapsed understandings of lesbian oppression (related to sexuality *and* gender) into sexism (related to gender alone) (Calhoun 1994).

As such, despite separatist politics emerging, lesbian issues remained marginal in feminist theory and organising. Adrienne Rich's essay "Compulsory Heterosexuality and Lesbian Existence" first published in 1980 became a key text, which aimed to "bridge over the gap between *lesbian* and *feminist*" (1993, 227 emphasis in original). Rich pointed out that many feminist thinkers failed entirely to address the question of sexuality, and operated with the presumption that heterosexuality was *the* natural preference for women. Rich's essay also proposes an extension of definitions of lesbianism, to include not simply sexual desire in a narrowly defined sense, but rather, a continuum of "woman-identified experience" involving various forms of intimacy and ways of organising social relations. For Rich, to simply identify as a lesbian is not enough; rather, one must take up a consciously lesbian feminist position.

Queer theory in practice: Compulsory heterosexuality

Rich originally wrote about compulsory heterosexuality to address the implicit bias towards/assumption of heterosexuality in feminist writing. Rich suggests that resistance to compulsory heterosexuality can be a central feminist tactic against the domination of men over women. She writes, "Heterosexuality has been both forcibly and subliminally imposed on women. Yet everywhere women have resisted it, often at the cost of physical torture, imprisonment, psychosurgery, social ostracism, and extreme poverty" (1993, 241). In her original writing, Rich was largely sceptical of the possibilities for queer coalition and was predominantly focused on compulsory heterosexuality as it related to *women's* experience.

However, extending from Rich, queer theory encourages us to think about the ways that compulsory heterosexuality is imposed upon people of *all* genders in very subtle ways in daily life. Here are just a few examples:

- It is considered "normal" for children to talk about having or wanting boyfriends/girlfriends but only if heterosexual. Same-sex relationships in childhood are always understood in terms of friendship.
- Homosexuality and other queer sexualities require disclosure and "coming out", yet no one is expected to declare that they are heterosexual.
- Sex education in schools is often focused on reproduction and presumes a man–woman pairing.
- Many organisations presume that people are in opposite-sex relationships unless otherwise disclosed. For example, if you are a woman making a booking for you and your "partner" the other person is likely to respond, "what is his name?"

In the same year, French feminist Monique Wittig published an equally influential essay, "The Straight Mind" (1980). Similarly to Rich, Wittig discusses the compulsory nature of heterosexuality, and argues that this is unconsciously absorbed and reproduced by individuals. Yet, unlike Rich, Wittig specifically points to the binary gender system as the foundation of heterosexuality. She suggests that sexual difference is a political construct, and writes: "If we, as lesbians and gay men, continue to speak of ourselves and to conceive of ourselves as women and as men, we are instrumental in maintaining heterosexuality" (1980, 108). She argues that the language of gender must be challenged, as the symbolic basis of the heterosexual imaginary that pervades society. It is on this basis that Wittig claims "Lesbians are not women" (1980, 110). Both Rich and Wittig's ideas were highly influential on later queer theorisations of gender, particularly Butler's *Gender Trouble* as discussed in Chapter 5. As Jagose suggests, lesbian feminism was central to later queer theories given its focus on gender, sexuality and compulsory heterosexuality (1996, 57).

The politics of difference

Simultaneously to questions about the place of sexuality in the women's movement, other questions about identity were being raised. This move towards challenging the monolithic "woman" subject as it was constructed in some feminist thought would also be taken up by later queer theorists who focused on *deconstruction* of identity categories as central to the queer political project.

In particular many women of colour began to raise critiques around the whiteness of the women's movement, and the racism inherent within some feminist organising. In the late 1970s a group of Black lesbian feminists called the Combahee River Collective emerged in Boston in the USA, offering a critique of mainstream feminism. As Barbara Smith notes in an interview in 2017, the Combahee River Collective emerged in response to the failure of the feminist movement to deal with issues of race, the racism of the anti-war movement and the sexism of the Black liberation movement. The group also formed as a radical alternative to the National Black Feminist Organization (NBFO), which they saw as "politically insufficient" (Taylor 2017, 4). The Combahee River Collective aligned, at times, with some parts of the Gay Liberation movement, who they saw as "understanding that the '-isms' connected with each other" (Taylor 2017, 45) and with groups of

Queer theory in practice: Psychoanalysis

As discussed in Chapter 2, psychoanalytic engagements with questions of sexuality had an important impact in thinking around sexuality into the twentieth century. Jacques Lacan's re-reading of Freud's psychoanalytic theory in the 1960s was particularly influential on much feminist thought that would in turn influence queer theory.

Elizabeth Grosz (1989, 25) sums up the contributions of Lacan for feminist thought as such:

- An idea of the subject as constructed.
- Emphasis on sexuality as central to identity.
- A philosophical (not simply clinical) approach to psychoanalysis.
- A linguistic approach to psychoanalysis.
- Identification of the patriarchal dictates of language and the symbolic.

Grosz suggests that it was through Lacan's interventions that Freud became a source of interest in academic feminism at the time. For example, in "The Straight Mind" Wittig critiques Lacan's assumptions about sexuality and "the Unconscious", arguing that the discourse of heterosexuality in society prevents disclosure of anything other than misery about sexuality to the analyst (1980, 104–105).

Though many feminists challenged aspects of Lacan's work, his linguistic emphasis and focus on the construction of the sexual subject had an impact not only on feminist thought, but on queer theorists such as Butler, which we discuss in further detail in Chapter 5.

socialist feminists who had focused their attention to race and class critique. As Smith recalls,

It's not like it was all smooth sailing, because we were organizing across identities. We were doing that intersectional organizing. But of all the feminists ... socialist feminists were best aligned with the work of Combahee. Because they had a race and class analysis that was actually a solid race and class analysis as opposed to, "Oh, I really don't care if people are different." (Taylor 2017, 50)

In 1977 the Combahee River Collective released a statement of their views as a group of black lesbian women, suggesting that their struggle was both *with* and *against* black men. In particular, they argued that the separatist elements emerging within the women's movement failed to address how considerations of race trouble clear notions of solidarity. As Taylor notes, the group understood that "Black men and women may experience racism differently in the world, but they had common interests in overcoming it – interests that could not be realized in struggles separated along the lines of gender" (2017, 7). With this in mind, the Combahee River Collective coined the term "identity politics" to refer to the understanding that identity was key to the experience of oppression, and thus identity had a significant role in shaping the political outlook and revolutionary politics of oppressed people. While the Combahee River Collective were not the first to understand that Black women experienced multiple or compounded oppressions, they argued that oppression was "interlocking" – an important precursor to later theories of intersectionality. Explaining this, the Combahee River Collective explicitly addressed questions of sexuality, stating:

> The most general statement of our politics at the present time would be that we are actively committed to struggling against racial, sexual, heterosexual, and class oppression, and see as our particular task the development of integrated analysis and practice based upon the fact that the major systems of oppression are interlocking. (1977)

For the Combahee River Collective, understanding these "interlocking" oppressions was the key to the possibility of radical and revolutionary politics. As Smith recalls, one of the most important aspects of the Combahee River Collective's Black feminism was that it understood class oppression as being central to the experiences of Black women. Smith notes how this shaped the group's critique: "One would expect Black feminism to be antiracist and opposed to sexism. Anticapitalism is what gives it the sharpness, the edge, the thoroughness, the revolutionary potential" (Taylor 2017, 69).

Though some prominent white feminists attempted to address the question of race, many failed to offer a sustained engagement, merely drawing parallels between the civil rights movement and women's struggles rather than meaningfully acknowledging those residing in the intersections of these battles. For instance, feminists such as Firestone addressed race, but collapsed it under the theory of patriarchy. As she suggests,

> Like sexism in the individual psyche, we can fully understand racism only in terms of the power hierarchies of the family ... as in the development of

sexual classes, the physiological distinction of race became important culturally only due to the unequal distribution of power. Thus, *racism is sexism
extended*. (Firestone 1970, 108)

Accounts such as this flattened the experience of racism, even as they
attempted to address them. Other feminist accounts failed to consider the
question of race altogether. As we discuss at length in Chapter 7, some queer
theorists have also failed to address race, placing it to one side in favour of a
focus on sexuality.

Queer theory in practice: Wages for Housework

Wages for Housework was a radical feminist movement that began in
Italy in 1972 and grew momentum on a global scale through the 1970s.
Taking a Marxist feminist approach to advocate for women's rights
and critique gendered divisions of labor, the Wages for Housework
movement sought to subvert capitalist systems of power that saw
many women exploited via unwaged labor in domestic and reproductive spheres. Rather than simply seeking to reward household workers
with a wage, the movement sought to destroy the household as a unit
of social reproduction within the capitalist system. On this note, one
of the founders of the movement, Silvia Federici, also argued that "heterosexuality is a form of socially necessary labor inclusive of sex, care
work, and emotional management" (Capper and Austin 2018, 445),
and viewed lesbian identity as "a historically specific strategy of work
refusal" (Capper and Austin 2018, 445). In her 1975 speech "Capitalism
and the Struggle against Sexual Work", Federici argued, "coming out is
like going on strike" (2017, 144).

Beth Capper and Arlen Austin highlight that in the mid-1970s, two
key groups emerged from the Wages for Housework movement seeking to address Black and lesbian struggles over reproduction. The Black
Women for Wages for Housework (BWfWfH) and Wages Due Lesbians
(WDL) were groups that "centered those reproductive workers often
rendered disposable or superfluous to white heteronormative reproductive imaginaries" (Capper and Austin 2018, 449). Both groups saw:

> heteronormativity, as a modality of a work-discipline, especially
> targeted women of color (and) lesbians who were refused by, or who

refused, the regulatory ideals of (white) femininity associated with the housewife, and who faced criminalization, sexual violence, forced sterilization, welfare austerity, and the loss of child custody for their transgressions. (Capper and Austin 2018, 448)

As such, Capper and Austin suggest that their politics resonate with the contemporary queer(s) of colour critique. These groups also represent an important touchpoint in feminist, Black, gay and lesbian, and queer political genealogies.

As bell hooks also suggests, many feminists in the mainstream women's movement of the USA did not attend to questions of race. hooks suggests that Friedan's *Feminine Mystique*, for example, did not consider the racial dynamics of domesticity, or work: "[Friedan] did not discuss who would be called in to take care of the children and maintain the home if more women like herself were freed from their house labour and given equal access with white men to the professions" (1984, 2). While hooks felt emboldened through her involvement with women's liberation, by way of consciousness raising she also came to feel her marginalisation in the movement. Similarly, in her experience with civil rights groups, she felt that she was being asked to place her concern for women's liberation to one side (hooks 2015, x).

Others reflected similar sentiments, often rallying under the banner of "Third World Women", for example as Cherríe Moraga contends, one of the key questions was "what are the particular conditions of oppression suffered by women of colour?" (1983, 2). Similarly, Gloria E. Anzaldúa's *Borderlands/La Frontera* reflected on Chicana lesbian identity, and the idea of a border identity and consciousness that emerges between places and sites, that expresses itself at the level of the body and experience (1987). For Anzaldúa the "mestiza" who exists in the borderlands occupies not only a place of betweenness, but that very locationality offers a bridge: "She has the choice to be a bridge, a drawbridge, a sandbar, or an island in terms of how she relates to and defines herself in the world" (Anzaldúa 2013).

These critiques of white feminism reveal the plurality of feminist perspectives of the "second wave" that did not simply operate around a singular "gender" framework. This illustrates Butler's argument that the distinction made in the 1990s between queer theory and feminist theory relied on the false premise that feminism up to that point had *only* been concerned with questions of gender. Importantly the critiques offered by many women of colour were made *within* various feminisms – so (e.g.) even though many prominent lesbian feminist figures were white, women of colour were also an integral part of these movements (Garber 2006, 83).

INTERSECTIONAL FEMINISM

Building upon foundations laid by Black feminism, in 1989 legal feminist scholar Kimberlé Crenshaw introduced the term "intersectionality" as a means of exposing the specifics of the marginalisation of Black women in the USA in legal terms (see Table 3.2 for a comparison with earlier Black feminism). Though Crenshaw was writing from a legal perspective, her theory provided a term for an issue many previous feminists had identified, and was subsequently taken up far beyond the legal sphere. In her original paper introducing the term, Crenshaw examines a specific discrimination case, where Black women could not appeal to either sex discrimination law (because some white women were not discriminated against) nor race discrimination law (because some Black men were not discriminated against).

Crenshaw described anti-discrimination law, feminist theory and anti-racist policy discourse as "single-axis frameworks" that tended to highlight only the experiences of relatively privileged members of a particular grouping. She argued that the discrimination faced by Black women at the specific intersection of sex and race was not adequately captured under the law. Crenshaw describes intersectionality as a way to account for multiple oppressions:

> Discrimination, like traffic through an intersection, may flow in one direction, and it may flow in another. If an accident happens in an intersection, it can be caused by cars travelling from any number of directions, and sometimes, from all of them. Similarly, if a Black women is harmed because she is in the intersection, her injury could result from sex discrimination or race discrimination. (1989, 149)

In this sense, Crenshaw's analysis was not intended to provide a sense of oppression as merely layered via a single axis, but rather, to see this as multiplicative and occurring at the intersections of multiple axes of oppression. Crenshaw located this marginalisation in anti-discrimination law but she also saw it reflected in feminist theory and anti-racist politics, arguing that both had "the tendency to treat race and gender as mutually exclusive categories of experience and analysis" (1989, 139).

Table 3.2 Earlier Black feminist and intersectional approaches to sexual oppression/freedom

	Earlier Black feminism	*Intersectional feminism*
MULTIPLE-AXIS-CENTRED	Women's sexual oppression is one facet of a larger system of interlocking oppressions. Occupying certain sexual *and* racial identity positions entails unique struggles ("racial-sexual oppression"). An economic revolution that is also feminist and anti-racist is required.	Women's sexual oppression occurs at the intersections of domains of oppression. Occupying certain sexual *and* racial identity positions entails unique issues of discrimination and injustice. The law can be adapted to better address the intersections.

Though Crenshaw's 1989 essay focuses on race and gender, it exposes how viewing subjectivity through a single axis may erase and distort the experience of those who encounter marginalisation through any relation of race, gender, sexuality, ethnicity, nationality, age, ability or other facets of identity. What Crenshaw's early work highlights is that this "single-axis framework" is reflected not only in the hegemonic power structures, but also in the discourses that critique those structures, which undermines their capacity for resistance. Explaining this in relation to feminist theory she writes:

Because ideological and descriptive definitions of patriarchy are usually premised upon white female experiences, feminists and others informed by feminist literature may make the mistake of assuming that since the role of Black women in the family and in other Black institutions does not always resemble the familiar manifestations of patriarchy in the white community, Black women are somehow exempt from patriarchal norms. (1989, 156)

Rather than simply incorporating marginalised groups into established analytical structures, Crenshaw called upon both feminist theory and anti-racist policy discourse to rethink their critical frameworks with intersectionality in mind. With specific focus on the experiences of Black women, she argues:

[T]he intersectional experience is greater than the sum of racism and sexism, [so] any analysis that does not take intersectionality into account cannot sufficiently address the particular manner in which Black women are subordinated. (1989, 140)

This argument is echoed in the common contemporary feminist axiom, "If your feminism isn't intersectional, then who's it even for?" Intersectionality has gained popularity in recent years, having recently become something of a buzzword in feminist spaces. However, before entering mainstream feminist discourse, it was taken up in queer critiques (see Moraga 1996; Ng 1997). We trace the specific ways that intersectionality has been taken up within queer theory in more detail in Chapter 7.

Key debate: Anti-foundationalism vs. intersectionality

In *Are the Lips a Grave? A Queer Feminist Ethics of* Sex (2013), Lynne Huffer looks back at feminist history to highlight the shared genealogies of queer and feminist theory. Huffer focuses on the work of theorists Luce Irigaray, Leo Bersani and Foucault, all of whom contribute in important ways to the development of queer and/or feminist theory, and all of whom share a philosophical commitment to anti-foundationalism, which is focused on questioning and undoing sexual subjectivity. Huffer suggests that anti-foundationalism was central to feminist theorising in the 1970s but was supplanted by the concept of intersectionality, which cemented a paradigm shift. This shift saw the feminist focus on theorizing "difference" move from the question of sexual difference to a more sociological meaning, grounded in a knowable subject. Intersectionality, for Huffer, made "an empirically grounded theoretical claim about legible positions on a social grid that made identities more complex than previously conceived" (2013, 14).

According to Huffer, how we see queer theory in relation to feminism is dependent on how we see queer theory in relation to the rift between intersectionality and anti-foundationalism. On the one hand, if we understand the emergence of queer theory as part of the paradigm shift towards intersectionality we would understand queer sexuality as attached to a subject with an identity. However, if we were to see queer theory through anti-foundationalism, we would find "neither selves not intersections, just an abyssal ungrounding that not only troubles identity but also undoes subjectivity itself" (Huffer 2013, 16). What Huffer means by this is, if we see queer theory as primarily anti-foundationalist, then it shares very little with feminism. To combat this she suggests we could revisit feminist genealogies in order to locate particular lines of thinking that unite queer and feminist theory.

ANTI-PORNOGRAPHY FEMINISM

While feminisms shifted in various directions during the 1970s, the politics and representation of sexuality in the public sphere had also been changing. As discussed in Chapter 2, revolutionary gay and lesbian politics was unfolding. Simultaneously to this, as Brain McNair argues, the "sexual revolution" of the time was embraced by many on the left, and seen as intimately bound up with the countercultural forces emerging in the 1960s (1996, 12). However, many feminists began to grow sceptical of the promises that could be delivered to women in the context of sexual liberation, which they saw as largely dominated by men's sexual interests. Radical feminists came to argue that sexual liberation under patriarchy was far from liberating for women. Feminists such as Susan Brownmiller (1975) turned their attention to questions of men's sexual domination of women through rape, with her book *Against Our Will* arguing that men hold a fundamental ability to rape women which in turn influences gender power dynamics. Furthermore, with the intensification of sex in the public sphere occurring with the "golden age" of pornography in the 1970s, pornography became a key target of radical feminist concern. In 1976 the group Women Against Violence in Pornography formed in San Francisco, and similar groups emerged across the West in subsequent years.

Radical feminist sentiment against pornography grew through the 1970s. Morgan most famously suggested, "Pornography is the theory, and rape is the practice. And what a practice. The violation of an individual woman is the metaphor for man's forcing himself on whole nations, on nonhuman creatures, and on the planet itself" (Morgan 1978). Following from Morgan into the 1980s, Andrea Dworkin and Catharine MacKinnon emerged as key anti-pornography advocates in the USA. Dworkin was a prominent activist and speaker, citing Firestone, Millett and Morgan as key influences on the development of her feminist thought (Dworkin 1997). MacKinnon was a law graduate from Yale, and, like the radical feminists, much of her early work focuses on using Marxist class theory as an analogy for the domination of women (MacKinnon 1982). MacKinnon was also anti-abortion, as she suggested that the need for abortion was a symptom of the male culture of sexual liberation that oppressed women. As she writes, "The availability of abortion removed the one remaining legitimized reason women have had for refusing sex besides the headache", citing *Playboy* founder Hugh Hefner's support of abortion as reason enough for scepticism (1987, 99).

Dworkin and MacKinnon met in the 1970s, and in 1983 taught a course together critiquing pornography. Following this, the Minneapolis council

Key concept: The erotic

As Audre Lorde argued in her 1978 essay "The Uses of the Erotic: The Erotic as Power", being critical of pornography did not have to mean dismissing sex and intimacy altogether. Rather, "the erotic" could be distinguished from the pornographic, and indeed could be harnessed as a creative force.

According to Lorde, while the pornographic is a male model of sexuality all about surface and sensation and the alienation of sex under patriarchal capitalism, the erotic is a source of power involving connection, joy, bodies and feeling. As she writes,

> When I speak of the erotic ... I speak of it as an assertion of the lifeforce of women; of that creative energy empowered, the knowledge and use of which we are now reclaiming in our language, our history, our dancing, our loving, our work, our lives. (1993, 341)

Lorde's essay was intended as an intervention into feminist debates about pornography at the time which often did not consider the possibility of the erotic. Lorde identified as a Black lesbian feminist, and claimed the erotic has potential to challenge "a racist, patriarchal, and anti-erotic society" (343). Given Lorde's focus on *desire* rather than sexual *identity* per se, her essay on the erotic became a key text for queer theorists in the 1990s.

asked them to draft an ordinance in relation to pornography. Together they drew up *The Antipornography Civil Rights Ordinance*. They designed the legislation such that pornography was seen as a special case of sex discrimination, where individuals could sue the makers, sellers, distributors or exhibitors of pornography if they felt that they were harmed by pornographic imagery (Dworkin 1997). As Dworkin describes:

> It holds pornographers accountable for what they do: they traffic in women (contravening the United Nations Universal Declaration of Human Rights and the Convention on the Elimination of All Forms of Discrimination Against Women); they sexualize inequality in a way that materially

promotes rape, battery, maiming, and bondage; they make a product that they know dehumanizes, degrades, and exploits women; they hurt women to make the pornography and then consumers use the pornography in assaults both verbal and physical. (1997, 71)

Dworkin and MacKinnon's targeting of pornography cannot be understated as key to the debates about sex, sexuality and pornography that are still unfolding today – and, most importantly, the version of feminism that many queer theorists rejected/sought to distinguish themselves from in the 1990s (to today).

Dworkin and MacKinnon frequently called attention to the "realness" of pornography, strongly dismissing the defence that it is just "fantasy". For Dworkin and MacKinnon pornography is not merely a representation of harm that might inspire men to harm women; pornographic materials are inherently harmful – Dworkin suggests that when we watch a woman being tied up, she is *really* being tied up. MacKinnon similarly writes, "Pornography is masturbation material. It is used as sex. It therefore is sex", and further "With pornography, men masturbate to women being exposed, humiliated, violated, degraded, mutilated, dismembered, bound, gagged, tortured, and killed. In the visual materials, they experience this *being done* by watching it *being done*" (1993, 17 emphasis in original).

Dworkin's partner John Stoltenberg also wrote against pornography. In his seminal text *Refusing to Be Man: Essays on Sex and Justice*, he argues that pornography fundamentally reflects male domination. Stoltenberg suggests, "Pornography tells lies about women. But pornography tells the truth about men" (1990, 121). Both Stoltenberg and Dworkin also wrote about gay male sexual cultures. Fred Fejes suggests that they saw gay male identity as "a variation in an overall phallic based heterosexual masculine identity" (2002, 96). For Stoltenberg and Dworkin, gay male pornography, S/M practices and leather subcultures were exaggerated hypermasculine expressions of violence and domination. Dworkin saw the sexual act of penetration as an articulation of power, writing that "Fucking requires that the male act on one who has less power and this valuation is so deep, so completely implicit in the act, that the one who is fucked is stigmatized as feminine during the act even when not anatomically male" (1981, 23). More broadly, Stoltenberg also argued that masculinity is socially constructed (neither a "role" nor a "sex"), and that "manhood" needs to be actively rejected (1990, 185). Stoltenberg's work also tracks the demise of the ordinance which came to a head in the Supreme Court in 1986.

Key debate: Is all sex rape?

Dworkin's analysis extended beyond pornography to critiquing the dynamics of heterosexual sex more generally. In her book *Intercourse*, originally published in 1987, she suggests,

> [M]en possess women when men fuck women because both experience the man being male. This is the stunning logic of male supremacy. In this view, which is the predominant one, maleness is aggressive and violent; and so fucking, in which both the man and the woman experience maleness, essentially demands the disappearance of the woman as an individual; thus, in being fucked, she is possessed: ceases to exist as a discrete individual: is taken over. (2007, 80)

For Dworkin, women are possessed in sex because the act of penetration involves an assertion of men possessing women. Men cannot be possessed in the same way – despite their literal envelopment during penetration. The only cultural space where men can be understood as possessed by women in sex is via the trope of the "evil" woman.

In other words, the ability for women to have sexual power remains in the space of mythology only. This popular discourse supports the idea that it is a man's right to possess a woman through intercourse; for the woman in control is to be feared. The idea of the dangers of women too uncontrollable in their display of sexuality publicly is also used to justify the way in which sex must remain private. That is to say, Dworkin argued that sex is largely about social control.

Because of Dworkin's radical extension of her anti-pornography sentiment to heterosexual sex practices generally, she has frequently been read as conflating all sex with rape. Dworkin herself rejected these claims, suggesting that her critique was merely of the dominant view of sex and women as subordinate/possessed.

Anti-pornography feminists and the new right

Though the ordinance was ultimately unsuccessful, many feminists have since argued that the contentions of Dworkin and MacKinnon had other far-reaching effects. The approach of the anti-pornography feminists impacted debates about how feminism should define itself relative to sex and sexuality, and in turn has impacted queer theorists' sometimes reluctant identification with feminism. An important issue for queer theorists has been how Dworkin and MacKinnon's legislation sat comfortably with the socially conservative right, with this unlikely coalition making it more difficult for sexual minorities.

To contextualise, when this collation emerged, from the late 1970s to the 1980s, there was a conservative backlash to the new era of sexual liberation that expressed itself particularly in the political sphere – known as the "New Right". As the pornography industry grew, during the 1970s laws started to appear around child pornography, and, as Rubin suggests, a child pornography "panic" swept the USA (1984, 272). In 1977 a political coalition called "Save Our Children" formed in Florida, which connected homosexuality to child abuse. They sought to overturn the law in Dade County that made it illegal to discriminate on basis of sexual orientation (Fetner 2001). Their success heralded a wave of Christian right-wing family-values and anti-gay activism across the USA. Former pageant queen and pop star Anita Bryant was at the centre of much of this conservative campaign, and was outspoken against homosexuality, pornography, abortion and sex education.

Rubin suggests that we understand the rise of this New Right also in terms of the wider political context of the Cold War. She writes, "[I]t is precisely at times such as these, when we live with the possibility of unthinkable destruction, that people are likely to become dangerously crazy about sexuality" (1984, 267). The late 1970s saw a move to social conservatism and a new version of economic liberalism across the West, involving the roll-out of neoliberal and socially conservative policies. Given this context, a confluence between anti-pornography aims and the directives of the New Right emerged.

How did feminist tensions around questions of sexuality play out during the so-called sex wars

The "sex wars"

As Lisa Duggan, Nan Hunter and Carole Vance argue, the view of many of the anti-pornography feminists elided the possibilities for pleasure, female agency or the ability to consent. They argue,

> Pornography carries many messages other than woman-hating; it advocates sexual adventure, sex outside marriage, sex for no reason other than pleasure, casual sex, anonymous sex, group sex, voyeuristic sex, illegal sex, public sex. Some of these ideas appeal to women reading or seeing pornography, who may interpret some images as legitimating their own sense of sexual urgency or desire to be sexually aggressive. Women's experience of pornography is not as universally victimizing as the ordinance would have it. (1995, 56–57)

Key debate: *Deep Throat*

One example of the shared approach of the right and anti-pornography feminists was around the pornographic film that had wide cinema release in 1972, *Deep Throat*. As Nicola Simpson describes, "Deep Throat made money and ushered in the era of 'porn chic', when suddenly it was fashionable to stand in line at X-rated theatres ... and compare reviews of hard core films at dinner parties" (2004, 664). The new political right that was also emerging at the time decided to target *Deep Throat* given its popularity – arguing against the film's distribution, confiscating reels from cinemas and attempting to prevent screenings.

The debate around *Deep Throat* became one of censorship, and leading female star Linda Lovelace was at first vocal in defending the film. However, in 1980 Lovelace released an autobiography called *Ordeal*, detailing her exploitation at the hands of her partner during filming. She became involved in the anti-pornography feminist movement, who were vocal supporters of Lovelace. MacKinnon (1982) frequently cites Lovelace in order to demonstrate how pornography operates to make women into objects. Dworkin (1985) similarly uses Lovelace's story and *Deep Throat* as an example of the abuse inherent to pornography.

These competing views around pornography would come to be the key locus of the emerging (so-called) "sex wars". As Lyn Comella explains, the "sex wars" generally refers to a period during the 1980s that involved "an ideological turf war over who would define feminism's relationship to sexuality" (2008, 205). The "sex wars" revealed important differences between feminists on questions of power in terms of theorising domination and agency. While anti-pornography feminists saw sexual culture in terms of its fraught relation to masculine patriarchal domination, the pro-sex feminists that emerged in response saw personal expressions of sexuality as a key site of empowerment and catharsis. In many ways, the pro-sex feminists aligned with earlier discourses of Gay Liberation (discussed in Chapter 2) in terms of understanding that freedom of sexual expression was integral to liberation.

Key concept: Pro-sex/sex radical feminism

In response to the anti-pornography feminists, a new group of feminists formed who called themselves the "pro-sex" feminists or "sex radical feminists". The antics of the anti-pornography feminists led to a greater mobilisation of feminists around the issue of S/M. Khan writes, "One consequence of this discursive proliferation was the growth of a resistance discourse, one that appropriated much of the language of the anti-sadomasochists but reversed its normative agenda" (2014, 92).

One key proponent of S/M feminism was Patrick Califia. While Califia agreed with the anti-pornography feminists that there exists an "erotic tyranny", he argued that sadomasochism must be untangled from this. Originally published in 1981, Califia suggests,

> S/M eroticism focuses on whatever feelings or actions are forbidden, and searches for a way to obtain pleasure from the forbidden. It is the quintessence of non-reproductive sex. Those feminists who accuse sadomasochists of mocking the oppressed by playing with dominance and submission forget that *we* are oppressed. We suffer police harassment, violence in the street, discrimination in housing and in employment. We are not treated the way our system treats its collaborators and supporters. (1996, 234 emphasis in original)

Califia's argument doesn't shy away from the feminist contention that the personal is political, but rather suggests that the personal is a site through which to work through the oppression of the political – it is a cathartic space, and a site from which to take back power. Califia argued that the anti-pornography feminists were encouraging vilification of minorities. Califia went on to be an important voice within transgender studies, as noted in Chapter 6.

The key peak of the sex wars, and the anti-pornography sentiments that were circulating, occurred in 1982 at the conference *Towards a Politics of Sexuality* held at Barnard College in New York City. The year prior, in 1981, the organising committee of the conference created a pamphlet, "Diary of a Conference on Sexuality", which outlined some of the things they wished to explore through the conference. Not taking a straightforwardly anti-pornography radical feminist line, questions canvassed in the pamphlet included (but were not limited to):

1. How do women get sexual pleasure in patriarchy given that if women venture out of the restrictive limits of the patriarchy they are punished?
2. What is the relationship between the political, economic, and social structures of one's sexuality?
3. Does the identity of "femininity" cut across one's choice of object, sexual preference, and specific behaviour? (Alderfer et al. 1981)

Days before the conference was due to begin, pressure from feminist anti-pornography groups, who felt they had been left out of the event, pressured the Barnard administration to confiscate 1,500 copies of the diary that had been published for the event. At the conference itself, anti-pornography feminist protestors handed out leaflets, as Comella reflects,

> "Represented at this conference," the leaflet read, "are organizations that support and produce pornography, support sex roles and sadomasochism, and have joined the straight and gay pedophile organizations in lobbying for an end to laws that protect children from sexual abuse by adults". (2008, 204)

The anti-pornography feminists, sporting t-shirts that read "for a feminist sexuality" and "Against S/M", also targeted groups in their materials that organised around issues of lesbian sadomasochism (S/M) and bondage, abortion rights and butch/femme lesbian identity. Echoing earlier feminist arguments around the problems of role-playing, their central contention was that S/M promotes problematic power dynamics, and that butch/femme lesbianism recreates power dynamics of heterosexuality, mimicking heterosexual gender relations. As Ummni Khan reflects, the lesbians who defended sadomasochism were seen by the anti-pornography feminists as "injecting patriarchal ideas behind feminist lines" (2014, 91).

THE SEXUALITY/FEMINISM SPLIT

Following these events, in 1984 Rubin articulated the key schisms between feminism and sexuality in her essay "Thinking Sex". "Thinking Sex" expresses deep concern about the sex wars and the potential outcomes for "sexual deviants". As Rubin writes, "Most people mistake their sexual prefer-ences for a universal system that will or should work for everyone" (1984, 283). Despite suggesting that the lines around sexual moralism ought to shift, Rubin was nonetheless – like many feminists – very concerned with issues around pleasure and consent. Rubin's argument therefore ought not to be understood as "anything goes", but rather be seen as founded around con-cern for the marginalisation of sexual minorities. Rubin's highly influential essay suggests that engagements with questions of sexuality ought to break from feminist perspectives, even as she wrote the piece with a feminist audi-ence in mind.

Rubin had herself been a feminist activist during the 1960s. However, an encounter with a lesbian from the Gay Liberation Front in 1971 introduced her to new ideas around sexuality. She reflects, "The language enabled me to reinterpret my own experience and emotional history" (2011, 15). From this point Rubin found herself focusing on lesbian archives. However, over time she became increasingly concerned with "moral panics" around sexuality, following work by Jeffrey Weeks in 1981 (see Weeks 1989), with feminist campaigns colluding with the right. "Thinking Sex" describes in detail the convergence between some feminists in the 1980s and right-wing evangelical Christians in the USA around the issue of pornography, and in this way evi-dences a sticking point between feminism's focus on gender sometimes to the detriment of questions of sexuality.

As part of this discussion, Rubin argues that in society particular sexual arrangements and acts operate within a "sex hierarchy", where some are val-ued ("the charmed inner circle") and others remain abject ("the outer limits") (1984, 281) (see Table 3.3). For example, Rubin includes "married", "hetero-sexual", "monogamous" and "no pornography" in the inner circles, and con-trasts these with "in sin", "homosexual", "promiscuous" and "pornography" in the outer circle.

Though some of the arrangements on Rubin's chart may have shifted today, the general point remains that some acts and practices are seen as more acceptable, while others remain (at best) questionable within the mainstream. Rubin suggests that this operates as a "system of erotic stigma", and highlights how particular feminist critiques of sex have inad-vertently perpetuated this hierarchy (1984, 280). Here, Rubin lays the groundwork for attending to questions of sexuality outside of anti-pornog-raphy feminism, and, in turn, a theoretical jumping-off point for later queer theorists such as Butler. As Jagose notes (disagreeing with the contention): "the controversial analytic separation of gender and sexuality ... has been

Table 3.3   Rubin's sex hierarchy outlined in "Thinking Sex"

Culturally acceptable/valued sex practices ("the charmed inner circle")	Culturally unacceptable/abject sex practices ("the outer limits")
Heterosexual	Homosexual
Married	In sin
Monogamous	Promiscuous
Procreative	Non-procreative
Free	For money
Coupled	Alone or in groups
In a relationship	Casual
Same generation	Cross-generational
At home	In the park
No pornography	Pornography
Bodies only	With manufactured objects
Vanilla	S/M

prominently theorized as key to distinguishing between feminist and queer theoretical projects" (2009, 164).

Rubin also argues that feminist critiques of S/M at the time echoed puritanical responses to sexuality that has seen homosexuality vilified over a long period of history. Rubin suggests that this feminist reaction was in part a response to sexual liberation of the 1960s and 1970s, and that simultaneously a group of "sexual radicals" was beginning to band together away from feminist critique. Rubin writes,

> In one sense, what is now occurring is the emergence of a new sexual movement, aware of new issues and seeking a new theoretical base. The sex wars out on the streets have been partly responsible for provoking a new intellectual focus on sexuality. (1984, 310)

In other words, the feminist anti-pornography reaction also helped provoke a new form of scholarship on questions of sex, which in turn would influence queer theorising.

THE IMPACT OF THE "SEX WARS" ON QUEER THEORY

It was not until the "sex wars" of the 1980s that the tension between feminists and sexual politics came to a head, where theorists such as Rubin argued that feminist rubrics for understanding sexuality needed to be placed to one side. For Rubin, while the anti-pornography feminists and New Right alike were worried about the state of the world driving people to perversion, she argues that what happened during the 1970s and early 1980s was a tightening of norms such that people were forced to be normal – where sexual minorities were created and pushed to the limits of society. Along these lines, Hunter (2006) suggests that the difficult debates around sexuality involved in the "sex wars" meant that feminists were somewhat absent from important movements around sexuality into the 1980s and 1990s. She writes,

> [T]here was virtually no feminist commentary, for example, on the characterization of AIDS as a divine punishment for sex. Nor did feminists draw the obvious analogy between the early birth control movement and safe-sex campaigns ... the bitterness of the internal conflict about pornography disabled most feminists from intervening forcefully in these debates. (2006, 16)

From this perspective, the "sex wars" debate drove a wedge between feminists on the question of sexuality, where those in the anti-pornography camp were unwilling to engage with gay rights campaigns, and those on the sex radical side largely found themselves turning to engage in discussions around sexuality studies, and, eventually, queer theory.

Elisa Glick suggests that one key questions of the "sex wars" debate ("Is S/M feminist?") would even later be reframed through queer theory to ask, "Is S/M subversive or genderfuck?" (2000, 21). While these two questions differ in terms of their mode of address (collective vs. individual) and stake (politics of feminism vs. resistance to heteronorms), both questions seek to understand "what kind of sex *counts* as progressive" (Glick 2000, 21). Tracing key points in debates such as these it is important to keep in mind, as Walters suggests, "Like sex itself, feminism is messy. And perhaps one lesson of those debates is that we would do well to revel in that messiness rather than to divide ourselves into neat and tidy categories of pro-sex and anti-sex feminists" (2016, 2).

Queer theory in practice: Feminist comics

Paying attention to more ephemeral pieces of women's writing such as comics and zines can help us to see further points of connection between queer and feminist genealogies. Margaret A. Galvan (2016) suggests that we can look at image-text media produced by writers in the 1970s and 1980s to see how some feminist comics artists "urge[d] their affiliated social movements to be more inclusive through their visual representations of queer bodies" (Galvan 2016, 2).

Writing about comics and the "sex wars", Galvan argues that "female comics artists foregrounded sexuality alongside the activist concerns of both feminism and gay rights in the late 1970s, forecasting further engagement with this topic in the 1980s" (Galvan 2016, 24). Comics such as *Tits & Clits* and *Wimmen's Comix*, both of which began in 1972 and ran into the late 1980s and early 1990s, represented an array of marginalised identities, considered feminism and sexuality to be intimately linked and were significant "shapers of rhetoric and ideas" (Galvan 2016, 26).

Feminist writers would later take up issues that were first engaged with in these comics such as S/M, pornography, and lesbian identity. In this way, the comics were "forerunners of theory" as they functioned to generate and sustain feminist discourse, and in many cases went beyond mainstream feminist thinking by presenting a "capacious vision for feminism that need not result in complete separatism and that can embrace and support other disenfranchised identities" (Galvan 2016, 79).

QUEERING THE "THIRD WAVE"

As the terminology of queer theory emerged, postmodern and poststructural theories had also taken hold in the academy, and many feminists and queer theorists alike were turning to methods of subversion and deconstruction in their writing about gender. Along with Butler and Sedgwick, feminist thinkers such as Diana Fuss (1995), Denise Riley (1988; 2000) and Elspeth Probyn (1993; 1996) offered complex engagements with questions of subjectivity, desire and identification. Simultaneously the so-called third wave of feminism was born. This period involved a greater turn away from the liberation politics of feminism past, to a greater focus on cultural representation.

The new emphasis on representation saw the rise of the feminist music scene (such as the riot grrrl movement in punk music), zine culture and feminist interventions in the art world (such as Guerrilla Girls). As Pilcher and Whelehan suggest, feminists of the third wave believed "that popular culture can be the site of activism, and that media such as music can be used to communicate political messages" (2017, 168). Furthermore, third-wavers explicitly identified as such and sought to respond to the perceived limitations of the "second wave". As Clare Snyder suggests, the third wave can be understood as:

- responding to critiques of the "woman" category and taking on intersectional feminist perspectives;
- adopting postmodern techniques and understanding "truth" as multiple;
- rejecting grand narratives of feminism, particularly those ideas around sex and sexuality that emerged during the sex wars. (2008, 175)

All of these aspects of so-called third wave feminism can be understood to overlap with the interests of queer theorists, as outlined throughout this book. For many third-wavers queer identifications and affiliations were seen as central to their feminist activism (Gillis and Munford 2004, 169).

Queer theory in practice: The sexual politics of SlutWalk

The transnational "SlutWalk" phenomenon can be understood as adopting a feminist pro-sex position while simultaneously offering a critique of women's sexual oppression, engaging with questions of sex and sexiness that neither fully reject nor wholly endorse mainstream models of sexuality. Whether SlutWalk represents "third wave" politics is debated.

SlutWalk has its origins in Toronto, Canada, when in 2011 a police officer suggested that women should prevent assault by not "dressing like sluts" (Friedman et al. 2015, 2). In response, protests occurred all over the world, attempting to reclaim the word "slut" and combat the notion that women should have to change the way they dress or express their sexuality in order to prevent assault. The movement has faced some feminist critique, particularly around what is used to signify "slut" and the different experiences of raunch for different women across intersections of race and gender (Friedman et al. 2015, 5).

There have been many significant developments in feminist theorising relevant to queer theory since the 1990s, much of which is discussed throughout the remainder of this book. However, specifically during the "third wave" period, two key developments with important synergies for queer theory are transnational feminist and transfeminist approaches. Both of these developments are directly related to the rise of postmodern thinking around critiques of the "subject" in Western thought.

Transnational feminism is specifically concerned with challenging the Western-centrism of feminist activism and theory, a concern that has also influenced queer theory approaches to sexuality. As Inderpal Grewal and Caren Kaplan explain, many women outside of a US context have rejected the terminology of "feminism" as a distinctly Western construct, and instead have placed other modes of collectivism around issues of ethnicity, religion and so on at the forefront of their struggle (1994, 17). However, as Garber also points out, when considering the intersection of gender and sexuality in a transnational context, some queer women's histories have been overlooked or erased in favour of focusing on men (2006, 89).

Different from transnational feminism, but sometimes adopting a transnational approach, is transfeminism, a branch of feminist thought that centres the experiences of trans people in feminist theory and activism. As Emi Koyama defines, "[Transfeminism] is not merely about merging trans politics with feminism, but it is a critique of the second wave feminism from third wave perspectives" (2003, 244). While some "second wave" feminists argued for the abolishment of the gender system, some also laid claim to a biologically based sex as co-dependent with gender (Hines 2014, 84). Transfeminism arose in the 1990s as a way to respond to these critiques, often drawing on queer theory ideas from theorists such as Butler who offered a challenge to the "naturalness" of "sex" underlying the "sex/gender distinction". In Chapter 6 we discuss the history of transgender studies and its connections with queer theory in more detail.

CONCLUSION: QUEER FEMINISM TODAY

Despite new feminisms emerging, debate continues about the state of feminism, who is included or excluded, and what the relationship between feminist and queer theories is. Perhaps the relationship is best encapsulated by Elizabeth Weed's description that feminism and queer theory are part of "the same family tree of knowledge and politics" (Weed 1997, vii).

Yet, while much feminism today considers questions of sexuality and queer *identity*, these approaches do not necessarily draw on queer *theory*. Theorists such as Sara Ahmed and Jack Halberstam demonstrate ways to explicitly use feminist and queer theories together, under the rubric of what we might call "queer feminism". For example, while Ahmed discusses the idea of being a "feminist killjoy" at length, she defines the killjoy in terms of being affectively out of step with dominant paradigms – in other words, the feminist killjoy is a figure who "queers" the rules about how one ought to feel (Ahmed 2010). Similarly, Halberstam considers how to develop a queer form of feminism, taking Lady Gaga as his starting point. He suggests possibilities for "feminism to go gaga" or, in other words, ways we might "queer" feminism through challenging compulsory heterosexuality and the gender binary (2012a, xiv).

The history of feminism sketched out in this chapter helps us to understand some foundational ideas of gender and sexuality underpinning queer theory. In thinking about what a queer feminist approach might look like today, like Ahmed and Halberstam we might think about ways to make our feminism queerer and our queer theory more feminist.

Further reading

Elizabeth Weed, and Naomi Schor (eds.). (1997). *Feminism Meets Queer Theory*. Bloomington: Indiana University Press.

This collection includes important essays on feminism "meeting" queer theory, including pieces from Butler, Braidotti and Rubin.

Annamarie Jagose. (2009). "Feminism's Queer Theory." *Feminism & Psychology,* 19(2): 157–174.

This paper unpacks the key connections and tensions between feminism and queer theory.

Diane Richardson, Janice McLaughlin, and Mark E. Casey (eds.). (2006). *Intersections Between Feminist and Queer Theory*. New York: Palgrave.

This collection offers a range of important reflections on the nexus of feminist and queer theories, including pieces from Garber, Jackson and Halberstam.

Keeanga-Yamahtta Taylor (ed.). (2017). *How We Get Free: Black Feminism and The Combahee River Collective*. Chicago: Haymarket Books.

The 40th-anniversary reprint of the Combahee River Collective statement contains interviews with collective members with key observations about queerness, intersectionality and feminist theory.

QUESTIONS TO CONSIDER

- How do you think the earlier feminist movement helped shape ideas around sexuality today?
- How did feminist tensions around questions of sexuality play out during the so-called "sex wars"?
- Does sexuality need to be theorised independently from feminism?

Recommended films

Born in Flames (**Lizzie Borden 1983**) is a fictional documentary-style film exploring issues of sexism, sexuality, race and revolution. *Born in Flames* centres women of colour in an imagined post-social revolution future. It illustrates possible approaches to a revolutionary context that has failed to address intersecting oppressions.

Inside Deep Throat (**Fenton Bailey and Randy Barbato 2005**). This documentary looks at the controversy surrounding the 1972 pornographic film *Deep Throat*. The documentary includes footage and interviews with various key persons including many feminists involved in the debate around the film and the tensions around the influence of sexual liberation in culture more broadly.

Itty Bitty Titty Committee (**Jamie Babbit 2007**) is an independent comedy focused on the activism of a "third wave" lesbian feminist group. The film dramatises some "third wave" feminist concerns and the connections between queer and feminist identities.

---

4 AIDS and Acting Up

KEY TERMS AND CONCEPTS	HIV and AIDS, necropolitics, anti-essentialism, ACT UP, Silence = Death, Queer Nation, the Queer International, Transgender Nation, gay shame

AIDS AND QUEER THINKING

What role did AIDS (Acquired Immune Deficiency Syndrome) activism in the 1980s and 1990s play in shaping ideas in queer theory? How did some of the fraught politics of the time impact on ideas that would become central to queer perspectives? Why and how did the term "queer" emerge with AIDS activists in the first place? While our first two chapters considered the role of early social movements around sexuality and gender in laying the foundations for queer theory, this chapter looks to a more specific event that continues to shape queer theory discussions. Here, the history of the AIDS crisis can be understood as playing a seminal role in shaping queer theorising, both in terms of the activism that emerged around the issue and the way that AIDS and its impact crystallised conceptualisations of life, death, reproduction and futurity for the LGBTIQ community and discussions of sexuality and gender in the academy.

This chapter explores the mechanisms by which AIDS came to influence and act as an "impetus" for queer theory discussions (Mykhalovskiy and Rosengarten 2009, 187). Many queer theorists have noted the impact of AIDS on shifting notions of identity, power and knowledge (e.g., see Jagose 1996, 93–96; Barker and Scheele 2016, 53), and here we seek to expand upon the role of AIDS discourse in shaping queer theory. The advent of AIDS shaped queer thinking and community formations in ways that are still having ramifications, even as we appear to discuss and recognise this time in LGBTIQ history less and less. The extreme homophobia of early AIDS policy, particularly the lack of government response in the USA, is oft forgotten (Gould 2009b, 229). As historian Graham Willett argues, HIV and AIDS cannot be understood merely as a health-related issue, but rather, have historically been

---

Key terms: HIV and AIDS

In this chapter, we predominantly refer to "AIDS", rather than "HIV and AIDS". The latter is used to distinguish between AIDS from Human Immunodeficiency Virus (HIV), a distinction used frequently in public health discourse today. Today it is understood that HIV *can* lead to AIDS, and specifying this is particularly important given that we are now in a treatment era in which the diagnosis of HIV rarely leads to AIDS *if* there is sufficient access to medication. However, as this chapter explores, the discursive construction of the "AIDS epidemic" in social imagination influenced activism – and most importantly, queer theory. As such, we refer to "AIDS" here as the cultural object that has taken on a life of its own under this all-encompassing signifier.

---

intimately bound up with the political – in terms of mainstream political (policy) responses – and social activism (2000, 166).

Furthermore, the politics of AIDS have been intimately bound up with sexuality and identity. The peak period of AIDS activism in the 1980s saw the emergence of a renewed sexual politics, and a general focus on sex and sexuality not least because AIDS was perniciously seen as a homosexual disease. As early theoretical reflections on AIDS argued, "AIDS does not exist apart from the practices that conceptualize it, represent it, and respond to it" (Crimp 1987, 3). In this sense, though AIDS is *not* specific to the gay community, its early association with gay men, and the ensuing discourse conflating AIDS with male homosexuality, constructed it as a disease that was a special issue for the gay community to grapple with. As Paula Treichler has argued, "The AIDS epidemic is cultural and linguistic as well as biological and biomedical" (1999, 1).

Indeed, when AIDS was first beginning to be recognised by public health scientists in the early 1980s, it was colloquially dubbed "Wrath of God Syndrome" (WOGS) and officially "Gay-Related Immune Disorder" (GRID) (Fela 2018, 87). It was only later that AIDS would be defined and understood as something other than a "gay plague". Willett describes how in an Australian context, even after only one death, the press called for various measures such as banning gay people from travelling between the USA and Australia, from being teachers, being on public transport and more (2000, 169). While the 1960s and 1970s had enjoyed the increasing visibility of gay people in the public sphere, the politics around AIDS were deeply homophobic, with discourse around AIDS effectively calling for the radical erasure of gay people from public life. As Joshua Gamson argued at the time, "AIDS activists find themselves simultaneously attempting to dispel the notion that AIDS is a gay disease (which it is not) while, through their activity and leadership, treating AIDS as a gay problem (which, among other things, it is)" (1989, 356). However, in turn, as homophobia spread in mainstream discourse and policy response to AIDS, this period became a time of re-invigorated activism around sexuality (Jagose 1996, 94).

Looking at how the crisis unfolded and what impact it had on the LGBTIQ community worldwide is difficult, not least because different policy responses emerged in different contexts. For example, Australia had a relatively well coordinated response to AIDS, where the gay community was highly active on the issue early on, and the Federal government had reasonably responsive policy (notwithstanding its homophobic discourse). In contrast, in the USA, then President Ronald Reagan failed to even refer to the term "AIDS" until several years into the crisis, with thousands of lives already lost. Reagan's assistant at the time, Gary Bauer, argued that the lack of action on the issue was due to the fact that AIDS was not yet a mainstream disease – that is, it had not yet crossed over to a general population beyond gay men and intravenous drug users (Grover 1987, 23).

Despite different policies in various contexts, many activist responses to AIDS were a shared endeavour, with strategies and conceptualisations around activist resistance circulating beyond the boundaries of individual countries. These shared ideas and experiences are directly relevant to our understanding of queer theory. As has been noted previously, there is an explicit connection between the specific terminology of "queer" as an umbrella term for LGBTIQ sexuality and the AIDS crisis, given the use of the term by many AIDS activists, including Queer Nation (Sullivan 2003, 37), discussed in further detail in this chapter. More broadly, it has been noted that defining sexual identity in terms of "queer" emerged within a context of poststructuralist theory which was focused on the deconstruction of linguistic identifiers (Jagose 1996, 93). In this context, "queer" offered a conceptual identification that was anti-essentialist and politically efficacious for responding to a virus (HIV) that spread based on *bodily practices* rather than identity (as the mainstream media at the time would have one believe).

In this sense the emergence of the language of "queer" simultaneously to the AIDS crisis, *and* the utility of this term for AIDS organising, ought not be understood as merely coincidental. Rather, the newly developing period of poststructural thought, the term "queer" and the unfolding event of AIDS emerged in confluence (Jagose 1996, 94). AIDS necessitated sex to be talked about explicitly, and articulated to a mainstream audience to overcome any negative and stigmatising discourse that may have fatal consequences (Berlant and Warner 1995, 345). Yet as Leo Bersani also crucially points out, AIDS also shifted public feelings around homosexuality from "fear" to "compelling terror" (1996, 19). As we explore at the end of this chapter, though there was mass LGBTIQ community mobilisation and powerful resistance to state homophobia, this period contributed significantly to the sense of "gay shame" experienced within the community, an affect arising from "the stigma of gay sexual difference" (Gould 2009b, 223). The sexual acts associated with male homosexuality came to be imagined as marked by death in profound ways that would impact upon queer theory discussions for decades to come.

THE UNFOLDING CRISIS

Though the crisis extended across the world in different ways, it is generally the USA that takes centre place in discussions of AIDS. It is important to note that AIDS was first identified in the USA in 1981, and therefore the USA was the medical and discursive origin of AIDS from which it came to be socially constituted. At the time, doctors across the USA noted that gay men were presenting with similar and unusual symptoms, such as pneumonia and Kaposi's sarcoma, indicating compromised immune systems (Grover 1987, 18). Hundreds of gay men were suddenly becoming ill, with the virus seemingly affecting gay men in particular, fuelling beliefs about the immorality of gay male sex (Gould 2009b, 231). From this the term GRID was first used, followed by AIDS in the following year, classifying the problem as a syndrome, caused by HIV. Though women were also identified as having the syndrome, AIDS nevertheless continued to be imagined as a particularly gay male issue (Treichler 1999, 42), was understood only in terms of affecting white men despite prevalence in Black and Latino communities (Hammonds 1987, 34), and indeed early on was presumed to be simply an unpleasant effect of a gay "life-style" (Crimp 1988, 238). This particular framing of AIDS as an effect of homosexuality was undoubtedly primed by the existing historical association of homosexuality as a "contagion" and threat to the heterosexual way of life (Edelman 1994, 307).

Despite hundreds of reported cases in the USA by 1982, there was little media attention on the issue outside of the gay press, despite early activism and fundraising on the issue within the LGBTIQ community. Notably, gay press materials from the USA were banned from circulation in the UK until 1986, severely limiting communication on the issue between affected

Queer theory in practice: Trans experiences of the AIDS crisis

Though the AIDS crisis was imagined predominantly as an issue for gay men, many others within the LGBTIQ community were affected but could not easily access treatment. As Stryker describes, many transgender people were affected who survived on sex work, shared hormone needles or were involved in gay male spaces, yet already experienced barriers in accessing healthcare due to poverty and stigma (2008, 113). In the USA into the 1990s AIDS organisations came to recognise transgender people as a vulnerable group, and specific funding and initiatives were directed to trans communities (Stryker 2008, 132).

communities (Watney 1987b, 13). In April 1983, *The New York Times* picked up the issue, following outcry over a large AIDS benefit in Madison Square Garden that they failed to cover (Nelkin 1991, 297). Simultaneously, in the UK at this time, a "moral panic" emerged among the general population, though there was little government action (Weeks 1989, 301). Although AIDS was officially classified as a syndrome, the popular discussion of it as a "disease" perpetuated the false fear that it was easily communicable (Grover 1987, 20). As greater attention to AIDS emerged, talk turned to the possible susceptibility of heterosexuals, with a focus on bisexual men and contact with sex workers as possible risk factors. This expansion of imagining the risk of AIDS for a broader community increased both fear and interest in the syndrome (Nelkin 1991, 297). As Bersani contends, "Nothing has made gay men more visible than AIDS. If we are looked at more than we have ever been looked at before – for the most part proudly by ourselves, sympathetically or malevolently by straight America – it is because AIDS has made us *fascinating*" (1996, 19 emphasis in original).

Despite growing awareness, the danger of AIDS to women remained largely undiscussed, as medical experts argued that transmission from women to men was less likely than from men to women or other men. In other words, because women were not understood as dangerous carriers, there was little focus on the risk to women who themselves might be affected (Treichler 1999, 45). Yet, in New York City in 1987, AIDS-related illnesses were the leading cause of death among women aged 25–29, many of whom were Black and Latino (Worth and Rodriguez 1987, 63). Where safe sex campaigns were targeted at women, focus was on women taking responsibility for ensuring that male partners

Queer theory in practice: AIDS and the politics of disgust

Ramzi Fawaz's work, "Political Disgust and the Digestive Life of AIDS" (2015), focuses on the political significance of disgust in the AIDS crisis, using Tony Kushner's play *Angels in America* as a point of exploration. Drawing on affect theory (discussed in more detail in Chapter 7), Fawaz describes:

> I treat the visceral as a potent cultural site where the literal and the figurative aspects of embodiment are so tightly wound as to become coterminous, so that linguistic representations of the body figuratively invoke, and materially elicit, affective responses. (2015, 123)

Here Fawaz focuses on vomiting as a key point of interest. Nausea might be a response to the shock of a HIV diagnosis and indeed the symptoms of AIDS, but nausea might also be provoked by disgust at the lack of political and institutional responses to AIDS. Fawaz suggests that we should seek to understand how the negative affects (feelings, bodily sensations) of AIDS were able to be mobilised politically and creatively, to signify AIDS in a way that didn't do away with the abject, but rather, found a way to rework it for political ends.

As Fawaz acknowledges, engagement with disgust in the context of the AIDS crisis can be traced to Douglas Crimp's (1987) work and Bersani's key 1987 essay *Is The Rectum a Grave?* (discussed in Chapter 8), among others. These theorists argued for the materialities of AIDS to be better represented, particularly given that such embodied aspects were utilised for political ends to promote stigma and association between homosexuality and disgust, disease and death.

used protection (Patton 1987, 72). Furthermore, within the gay male community there was some sense that not only were lesbians not at risk of AIDS, but that they were not interested in activism around the crisis. As Douglas Crimp argues, such views among (some) gay men were simply a result of demoralised politics, and that divisions within the community on the issue were not inevitable given the coalitional politics of the earlier gay and women's liberation political movements (1988, 251). Indeed, with the emergence of some later

AIDS activists groups, lesbians and other women ended up playing a central and visible role in organising (Cvetkovich 2003, 174).

Prior to the emergence of AIDS, as Crimp points out, earlier social movements around gender and sexuality had made particular self-identifications possible/claimable with pride. However, following the decline of the social movements of the 1960s, differences within the gay and lesbian movement had also forced a bunkering down into notions of essential identities as well as an orientation towards more liberal rights-based discourse. Within this context of a downturn in activism, AIDS arose, causing a crisis that Crimp claims, "brought us face-to-face with the consequences of both our separatism and our liberalism" (1993, 314). In other words, following the peak of Gay Liberation and second wave feminism, coalition building had become more difficult. The model of identity politics that had emerged became an obstacle with the emergence of AIDS, requiring a response that moved beyond the assumption that the syndrome was simply an issue for white gay men.

Queer theory in practice: AIDS and bisexual stigma

Though AIDS was initially imagined as a gay men's disease, as understanding of the multiple populations affected grew, so too did panic increase around "who" might spread HIV between groups. To this end, many media reports promoted a particular form of stigma around bisexuality and the risk of contracting AIDS, particularly bisexual men. As Marshall Miller outlines, even when not discussing AIDS specifically, media representations of bisexuality in the 1990s promoted a skewed notion of HIV transmission by promoting the stereotypes that (2001, 98):

1. Bisexuals are non-monogamous and have multiple sexual partners at once.
2. Bisexuality is a trend and a dangerous "decision" in the face of the AIDS crisis.

Miller describes, "Bisexual men were seen as the logical link and became an easy target for blame" (2001, 99). Miller suggests that far from enhancing HIV prevention strategies, this framing linking AIDS and bisexuality merely promoted biphobia.

Regardless of these internal debates what was entirely clear was that the minority communities most affected by AIDS were seen as *the problem*, rather than in need of assistance (Cole 1996, 280); the mainstream response to AIDS was focused on keeping straight white men safe. In the USA, this focus on preserving white male health, occurred within the larger context of the emergence of the New Right, with a focus on family values and "healthy" muscular/strong masculinity (Cole 1996, 287). Though Reagan finally addressed the issue of AIDS in 1985, it was not until 1987 that his administration set up a commission on AIDS (Nelkin 1991, 304). Much discussion focused on the possibilities of compulsory testing and quarantine, a move which many saw as reinforcing homophobia rather than effectively responding to the issue, as Bersani reflects: "To put this schematically: having the information necessary to lock up homosexuals in quarantine camps may be a higher priority in the family-oriented Reagan Administration than saving the heterosexual members of American families from AIDS" (1987, 201). Similarly, in the UK, it was not until 1986 that the government, led by Margaret Thatcher, decided to act on AIDS, with a large amount of funding dedicated to an education campaign focused on monogamy, only suggesting use of protection outside of monogamous relationships (Weeks 1981, 303). Such responses marked casual sexual relationships as both deviant and dangerous (Sontag 1989, 73). The political response (or lack thereof) to the AIDS crisis and the shaming around sexuality that emerged would later shape the activism to come, and in turn, the insights into heteronormativity that queer theory would begin to pose in the 1990s.

Queer theory in practice: AIDS and the New Queer Cinema movement

New Queer Cinema is a queer independent film movement of the 1990s. The term was coined by film theorist B. Ruby Rich to refer to a wave of queer films that were met with acclaim at the Sundance Film Festival in 1991 and 1992. These films included Jennie Livingston's *Paris is Burning* (1990), Todd Haynes' *Poison* (1991) and Tom Kalin's *Swoon* (1992). Films grouped under the banner New Queer Cinema reject so-called "positive" LGBTIQ representation and evoke queer as an aesthetic strategy by defying cinematic conventions. As Monica B. Pearl suggests, "this defiance can take the form of being fragmented, non-narrative, and ahistorical" (Pearl 2004, 23). Many films within the movement focus on the experience of marginalised groups within the lesbian and gay community such as Black gay men, sex workers and transgender people of colour.

There are strong connections between the AIDS crisis and New Queer Cinema. Many theorists argue that the AIDS crisis actually gave rise to the aesthetics and politics of the movement. As Monica B. Pearl suggests, "New Queer Cinema *is* AIDS cinema" (Pearl 2004, 23), not only because it emerged from a particular historical context, but because the narratives and "formal discontinuities and disruptions [of the films], are AIDS-related" (Pearl 2004, 23).

While not all films within New Queer Cinema deal with the subject of AIDS, the movement is built on a disruptive form of expression that is reflective of the cataclysm of the AIDS crisis, which not only had far-reaching impacts on individuals and communities but also on the understanding of identity itself. As the HIV virus "becomes part of the body that it infects", the AIDS crisis represented a major disruption of identity, undermining any understanding of self or subjectivity as "whole, sacrosanct, inviolable, and definable" (Pearl 2004, 24).

Writing about this in 1993, José Arroyo argues that as gay men, "[w]e know different things about ourselves and we know ourselves differently (and part of that change is questioning who is 'we' and what is the self)" (1993, 92). From this sparked New Queer Cinema's "Homo Pomo" (Rich 2004, 16) approach to identity and the desire to "utilize irony and pastiche, represent fragmented subjectivities, [and] depict a compression of time with sometimes dehistoric [and dystopic] results" (Arroyo 1993, 92).

AIDS ACTIVISM AND THE EMERGENCE OF "QUEER"

As discussed so far, with AIDS came a homophobic offensive against the LGBTIQ community, but in turn the community responded with re-invigorated activism (Seidman 1996, 10). As Bersani argues, "it is as if AIDS, the devastating depletory of the body's energies, had energized the survivors" (1996, 20). However, before the use of the term "queer" in this space, prior to an orientation towards a more coalitional-based politics, early emphasis on *pride* was key. Pride was seen as essential in order to overcome the shame and stigma of AIDS that was being promoted within medical and policy discourse, particularly to avoid individuals dis-identifying with AIDS, which had the potential for fatal consequences (Gould 2009b, 233). In response to the shaming of gay men – with the mainstream idea circulating that those suffering had brought on the illness themselves – initially a discourse of gay responsibility emerged. As Deborah Gould notes: "This gay pride ... pointed toward gay similarities with dominant society – gays as responsible, mature caretakers" (2009b, 236). This orientation reinforced ideas of what ought to be shamed (namely "promiscuity"), while simultaneously emphasising the need for gay pride.

Key concept: Necropolitics

Central to the social constitution of AIDS during this time was medical discourse that provided particular framings which then fed into homophobic state responses. AIDS revealed the problematic ways that medical expertise could be deployed to manage populations and occlude lived experience (Berlant and Warner 1995, 345).

Though *History of Sexuality: Volume 1* preceded AIDS, Foucault's insights from this text are useful for making sense of the response of the medical establishment to the crisis. As Foucault explains, a historical shift had occurred, from sovereign arrangements of power of letting live, to bio-political arrangements of managing life and letting certain people die. Foucault writes,

> A power whose task is to take charge of life needs continuous regulatory and corrective mechanisms. It is no longer a matter of bringing death into play in the field of sovereignty, but of distributing living in the domain of value and utility. (1976, 144)

The response to AIDS is perhaps the most obvious example of this turn towards the management of life, particularly in the USA where certain populations were left to die.

As theorists such as Che Gossett have pointed out, this wasn't just "gay" populations. "HIV Criminalization" and the "war on drugs" were also part of this, affecting an array of people, communities "of colour, queer, transgender, gender non-conforming, poor and disabled" (2014, 31). Here, Gossett reminds us that the politics of life are also the politics of death, drawing on the notion of "necropolitics", that is, the normative politics that determine who should die (or, as Gossett also discusses, be incarcerated), while others live.

The delayed policy response largely came only after public pressure around protecting "life" more broadly, particularly the lives of children. However, those children who became the focus of AIDS' moral panic were tainted by the association with homosexuality. For example, Dorothy Nelkin notes that the haemophiliac boy Ryan White who had famously contracted AIDS from a blood transfusion, was accidentally referred to by one media source as a "homophiliac" (1991, 305). As Cindy Patton remarks,

> AIDS has provided a sophisticated screen for constituting and reconstituting identities, and a deadly opportunity to link specific institutional practices with both gay assertions of self-knowledge and new-right assertions that homosexuality is an object of scientific knowledge. Importantly, if race had once served as a quasi-genetic metaphor for visualizing and policing difference, HIV, as a form of genetic interference, now provides the vessel for essentializing differences. (1993, 153)

However, while medical discourse referred to AIDS "victims", and attempted to individualise the issue by emphasising the need for individuals to manage their sexual activities to avoid the "dangers" of promiscuity, a new term emerged to counter this language: Persons with AIDS (PWAs) (Treichler 1987, 48). Such responses were part of AIDS activists not only re-framing the terms of the discussion, but also countering medical knowledge as the only valuable perspective from which to understand and engage with AIDS. As Max Navarre reflects, "I am a person with a condition. I am not that condition" (1988, 143). While there remained some in the LGBTIQ community who attempted to engage with medical arguments about "innate" sexuality in order to mobilise the community (harking back to positions taken up during the homophile movement), others began to turn to a more diffuse notion of sexual identity reflected by "queer" identity (Seidman 1996, 11).

Part of this shift had its basis in the practicalities of LGBTIQ communities responding to AIDS. This was in spite of the prevailing discourse at the time focusing on white gay men: as Allan Bérubé explores, gay men have stereotypically been imagined as white, and whiteness has functioned as an unmarked norm in gay communities (2010). However, AIDS itself *did not* discriminate so easily. As Bersani notes, AIDS acted as a "boon to the cause" of homophobia because "it never stops killing" (1996, 29). As such LGBTIQ community responses had to turn towards a focus on safe sex *practices* rather than sexual *identities*, meaning that the new activism emerging out of the AIDS crisis began to challenge prior conceptions of clear lines of identity (Jagose 1996, 94). To this end, HIV-prevention strategies turned to a focus on categories based on sexual activities such as "men who have sex with men" (MSM) to identify risk groups (Hames-García 2011a, 75). From within this context of de-emphasising identity, along with the need for a coalition-based politics to address the crisis, use of the term "queer" emerged. In relation to the emergence of coalition work, Patton also suggests, "regardless of how you contracted the virus, you become nominally queer" (1993, 154). According to Patton, a "queer paradigm" had emerged wherein sexually non-normative communities were seen as vulnerable to AIDS, but once you contracted HIV your sexuality was irrelevant: non-normative status was then attached to you via the virus. As Crimp also suggests, AIDS confronted activists with the limits of earlier identity politics: "It is within this new political conjuncture that the word 'queer' has been reclaimed to designate new political identities" (1993, 214).

Notably this linguistic shift also occurred within a broader context of postmodern/poststructuralist thought which involved a turn towards deconstruction of categories. Treichler goes as far as to suggest that the anti-essentialising aspects of postmodern theory at this time was "a godsend in the struggle against AIDS" (1999, 272). The activist efforts to address the AIDS crisis necessarily led to a shift in conceptualising identity that had profound effects on queer theory to come. As Berlant and Warner note: "The labor of bringing sexual practices and desires to articulacy has tended to go along with a labor of ambiguating categories of identity. Just as AIDS activists were defined more by a concern for practice and for risk than by identity, so queer commentary has refused to draw boundaries around its constituency" (1995, 345). While the initial AIDS activist response involved a turn towards affirming homosexuality, the designation "queer" was seen to challenge the fixity of sexual identity offered by those promoting pride (the activists) and shame (mainstream discourse) alike. As Seidman suggests, the approach to un-unified sexual identity as signified by "queer", that is central to queer theory more broadly (1996, 11).

Unleashing power: ACT UP

Central in the shift towards coalitional AIDS activism was the emergence of a group in New York in 1987, which called itself ACT UP, which stood for "AIDS Coalition to Unleash Power". The aim of the group was to increase pressure on governments and other agencies to invest in targeting AIDS, or more succinctly, to "get drugs into bodies" (Halcli 1999, 142). Between 1987 and 1991, ACT UP chapters emerged across the USA, as well as in Europe, Canada and Australia (Christiansen and Hanson 1996, 167), from Adelaide to Windy City (Halcli 1999, 141).

Key term: ACT UP

ACT UP described themselves as "a nonpartisan group of diverse individuals united in anger and committed to direct action to end the AIDS crisis" (Crimp 1987, 7). Many women were involved in ACT UP chapters, looking to AIDS activism in order to leave behind "the vehemence and bitterness of the feminist sex wars of the early 1980s" (Cvetkovich 2003, 175).

ACT UP have been described as heralding in a new "*queer* sensibility" that differed from existing "establishment-oriented gay leadership and institutions" (Gould 2009a, 256). As Crimp describes, the activists involved were "mostly a bunch of queers". However, he also points out that in this context queer didn't just mean taking part in certain sexual practices (such as men having sex with men), but rather, queer reflected one's place in society, one's vulnerability to contracting the disease, which was not as simple as sexual identity (1993, 317–318). Many of the activists involved had HIV themselves, or friends or family members who were affected (Halcli 1999, 142).

The first years of ACT UP involved shifting discourse on the "punitive moralism" of AIDS, and exerting pressure on governments and drug companies to undertake research and develop new accessible treatments (Crimp 1993, 303). ACT UP protests were often theatrical, artistic and confrontational in style. Various artists became central to ACT UP, with autonomous art groups such as Gran Fury affiliating with ACT UP to create political art installations and hundreds of graphic posters (Crimp and Rolston 1990, 16). ACT UP's signature direct action activity was to stage "die-ins" in public places, where protestors would lie down and have others draw chalk outlines around them, to highlight the brutal reality of the crisis (Christiansen and Hanson 1996, 157). Other theatrical stunts involved highlighting issues around sexuality specifically, with actions such as the "kiss-ins" held during the "Nine Days of Protest" coordinated by the AIDS Coalition to Network, Organize, and Win (ACT NOW) across the USA in 1988 (Crimp and Rolston 1990, 53). Kiss-ins were seen as a way to enact sexual resistance against homophobia, as the leaflet that featured at the kiss-ins, "WHY WE KISS", explained:

> We kiss in an aggressive demonstration of affection.
> We kiss to protest the cruel and painful bigotry that affects the lives of lesbians and gay men.

We kiss so that all who see us will be forced to confront their own homophobia.
We kiss to challenge repressive conventions that prohibit displays of love between persons of the same sex.
We kiss as an affirmation of our feelings, our desires, ourselves. (Crimp and Rolston 1990, 55)

Another example of one of ACT UP's many militant theatrics occurred in 1990, when ACT UP Chicago protested against the lack of an AIDS ward in Cook County Hospital. Activists from several caucuses within the Chicago chapter, including the Women's and People of Color groups, blocked traffic with mattresses covered in slogans about AIDS. Though over 100 people were arrested, the protest was successful in getting a ward opened (Stockdill 1997, 9).

During their direct action stunts and other activities, ACT UP made the symbol of the pink triangle prominent, alluding to the Nazi practice of forcing homosexuals incarcerated in concentration camps to wear pink triangles as identification (Edelman 1994, 302). Just as "queer" was given new meaning at this time, so too was the pink triangle reclaimed as a signifier of resistance in the face of PWAs being seen as deviants marked for death. Indeed, ACT UP's main slogan was "Silence = Death", originally created by a group of six gay men that identified at the "Silence = Death Project" who then became part of ACT UP (Crimp and Rolston 1990, 15). As Edelman reflects:

Silence = Death can be read as a post-AIDS revision of a motto popular among gay militants not long ago – "Out of the closets and into the streets" – and as such it similarly implies that language, discourse, public manifestations are necessary weapons of defense in a contemporary strategy of gay survival. (1994, 302)

Here we also see the symbiosis between the ideas of the time – the focus on the linguistic and representational in poststructuralist thought – and the actions and slogans being taken up by activists. Activist groups such as ACT UP (as well as Queer Nation that followed) are frequently associated with postmodernism because of pastiche tactics employed during protest, such as creating billboards and other posters imitating advertisements (Patton 1993, 147). Furthermore, artistic pursuits around ACT UP, such as the posters and artworks created by Gran Fury, were action-oriented, taking art out of institutions and into the streets (Crimp and Rolston 1990, 19). Despite the new ideological shift towards questions of cultural representation, away from earlier movements centred around redistribution and the restructuring of society, many activists who had been involved in the earlier Gay Liberation and feminist movements were also part of ACT UP. As such, ACT UP reflected a new period of protest that differed from earlier social movements, but that was also inflected with the spirit of an earlier time (Willett 2000, 191).

ACT UP groups in the USA had a major influence on activists in many other countries, and similar ACT UP groups formed across the world albeit in different political contexts. For example, ACT UP groups began forming

---

Queer theory in practice: The politics of life and death

In one canonical ACT UP speech, Vito Russo – who had also been a key figure during the 1970s – talks about the difficulty of "living" with AIDS, given that people tend to think of PWAs as either in a state of "dying", or not suffering at all. He reflects:

> So, if I'm dying from anything, I'm dying from homophobia. If I'm dying from anything, I'm dying from racism. If I'm dying from anything, it's from indifference and red tape, because these are the things that are preventing an end to this crisis. If I'm dying from any-thing, I'm dying from Jesse Helms. If I'm dying from anything, I'm dying from the President of the United States. And, especially, if I'm dying from anything, I'm dying from the sensationalism of newspa-pers and magazines and television shows, which are interested in me, as a human interest story – only as long as I'm willing to be a helpless victim, but not if I'm fighting for my life. (1988)

Helms, who Russo refers to here, was one of the many US politicians who argued for the quarantining of homosexual people who tested positive for HIV (Crimp 1987, 8). We see in Russo's speech that he isn't railing against death from AIDS per se, but rather the slow death of a homophobic society.

However, while ACT UP activists such as Russo advocate for life (here we see he is "fighting" for it), as we discuss in Chapter 8, queer theo-rists influenced by the AIDS crisis such as Bersani and Edelman would respond to the same issue from another angle, that is, they would come to embrace "death" as the rejection of normativity.

in Australia in 1990, but while in the US context ACT UP was a necessary response to a conservative government slow to act on the issue, the story in Australia was rather different given a much swifter response to the issue generally. Nonetheless, ACT UP in Australia employed similar direct action, performance-based, disruptive antics to their US counterparts. For example, in 1991, the Australian National Council on AIDS was encouraging the Federal government to introduce new experimental drug treatments that had been trialled in the USA and UK, though they had not been tested in Australia. When the health minister refused this recommendation, ACT UP activists staged protests, such as digging up a famous floral clock in Melbourne and replacing it with a graveyard, and abseiling onto the floor of Federal Parliament House during question time (Willett 2000, 190). The effect of these actions, and lobbying from other groups, was an expansion of clinical trials in Australia and a change of regulations that made it easier to access new drugs.

Queer theory in practice: ACT UP and needle exchange

Though the actions and activities of various ACT UP groups were wide and varied, of particular note is ACT UP New York's involvement in a needle exchange programme in the early 1990s, as it demonstrates the group's aims to tackle AIDS as it affected a diversity of populations.

Though the New York chapter was dominated by white middle-class gay men, as Christina Hanhardt discusses, "needle exchange presented both an opportunity and a challenge for ACT UP to expand its identity across race and class lines" (2018, 427). The New York chapter disseminated information across ACT UP in order to educate other members about needle exchange and complex issues around race and class, and illegally distributed needles in at-risk neighbourhoods. However, these activities also provoked some tensions with some leaders of Black communities, who claimed that the exchange programme facilitated access to drugs.

Hanhardt (2018) suggests that because of the conflicts and complications of this activity, the ACT UP involvement in needle exchange has rarely been included in historical reflections on the period.

Bashing back: Queer Nation

While at first ACT UP mostly involved coalitional organising around sexuality, a split emerged in the group between those who thought that a more offensive approach to tackling homophobia specifically was needed. On this basis, it was from an ACT UP New York meeting that the group "Queer Nation" then emerged in 1990 (Berlant and Freeman 1993, 198). Crimp reflects:

> As queers became more and more visible, more and more of us were getting bashed. Overburdened by the battles AIDS required us to take on, ACT UP couldn't fight the homophobia anymore. That, too, was a full-time struggle, a struggle taken on by the newly formed Queer Nation. I don't want to oversimplify this capsule history. Queer Nation didn't take either the queers or the queerness out of ACT UP. But it made possible, at least symbolically, a shift of our attention to the nonqueer, or the more-than-queer, problems of AIDS. (1993, 316)

According to Crimp, ACT UP had suffered from a proliferation of antagonism within the group, rather than broadening of alliances (1993, 317). ACT UP groups began to decline, and by 1998 there were only a handful of chapters remaining.

Unfortunately, some historical reflections on the period merely list ACT UP and Queer Nation alongside each other as examples of AIDS activism, rather than drawing out the unique aspects of the two groups. Unlike ACT UP, the politics of Queer Nation centred on "outing" and "bashing back", and enhancing militancy, which was perceived to have been lacking (Crimp 1993, 302). Like ACT UP, Queer Nation held kiss-ins, in an attempt to confront the public with sexuality and erotics (Berlant and Freeman 1993, 208), but the rage and anger expressed in Queer Nation materials acted to create further distance from the victim status that had been placed on the community with the AIDS crisis. As E. Rand writes, Queer Nation's approach meant that, "Being queer, in this sense, is no longer associated with passivity or victimization but with anger, strength, and the ability to defend oneself" (2004, 295). The Pink Panthers group also emerged from Queer Nation (eventually organising separately), acting as a street "foot patrol" dressed in "black T-shirts with pink triangles enclosing a black paw print" with the slogan "Bash Back" (Berlant and Freeman 1993, 206). Furthermore, Queer Nation marked a distinct turn towards constructing "queer" as an identity, as R. Anthony Slagle explains: "While Queer Nation uses many of the strategies that characterize identity politics, the collective identity of the queer

---

Key concept: From Queer Nation to queer theory

Academics working on questions of gender and sexuality turned to Queer Nation to unpack the possibilities of employing a more strategic and deconstructed notion of identity in social movement politics. Simultaneously, the notion of "queer theory" began to be articulated, and early academic imaginings of the possibilities of "queer" are discussed in the following chapter.

Queer Nation provided a key source of inspiration and an exemplar of queer politics for queer theory discussion in the years following its emergence. As several early queer theory discussions identified, the challenge for academics working in this space was to maintain the political (and not just "theoretical") angle of queer. This tension, and the paradoxes and contradictions of working with deconstructed identification as the basis for identity work, would come to be a persistent issue for queer theorists.

As Duggan suggested at the time, "The continuing work of queer politics and theory is to open up possibilities for coalition across barriers of class, race, and gender, and to somehow satisfy the paradoxical necessity of recognising differences, while producing (provisional) unity" (1992, 16).

---

movements is based not on a unitary identity but rather emphasizes that members are similar because they are different" (1995, 88). In other words, Queer Nation helped to cement "queer" as a category distinguished by its aim to deconstruct sexual identity.

Perhaps because of the stigmatisation of the LGBTIQ community that had occurred throughout the AIDS crisis, Queer Nation sought to actively *shame* heterosexuality. As Gould suggests, "nonrecognition may become reciprocal" (2009b, 224) – in other words, "gay shame" can transform into heterosexuals becoming alien, unrecognisable, to queers themselves. In 1990, Queer Nation handed out thousands of leaflets at New York and Chicago pride parades titled on one side "Queers Read This", which among the opening pages read:

I want there to be a moratorium on straight marriage, on babies, on public displays of affection among the opposite sex and media images that promote heterosexuality. Until I can enjoy the same freedom of movement and

Queer theory in practice: Queer Nation in Taiwan

Tracking the appearance of queer theory discourse in Taiwan in the 1990s, Fran Martin describes how the language of "Queer Nation" was adopted by a lesbian publication, *Ai Bao*, in 1994. Martin suggests that rather than simply repeating the Western idea of Queer Nation and remaining US-centric, reference to Queer Nation in *Ai Bao* is distinctly local. She writes:

> The unevenly globalized "nation" in this redeployment of Queer Nation becomes an ambivalent sign, indexing the weakening of the ties of the nation-state on culture while simultaneously pointing to their continuing hold. (2003, 2–3)

The language of Queer Nation appeared at this time in resistance to specific nation-state homophobia. Furthermore, Martin points out that Queer Nation as referred to in this context of Taiwan Mandarin language reflects multiple possibilities beyond Western concepts of "queer" and "nation". This leads Martin to claim that, "appropriation is not the same as replication and that translation is also rewriting" (2003, 4).

Martin challenges the US-centrism that sees concepts as "travelling" globally without understanding the specificity of the take-up of ideas in context. In other words, though Martin's research shows that the idea of Queer Nation was adopted in Taiwanese gay and lesbian culture, this iteration is specific to the context and cannot be understood as a "replica" of the US group (2003, 5).

sexuality, as straights, their privilege must stop and it must be given over to me and my queer sisters and brothers. Straight people will not do this voluntarily and so they must be forced into it. Straights must be frightened into it. Terrorized into it. Fear is the most powerful motivation. No one will give us what we deserve. Rights are not given they are taken, by force if necessary. It is easier to fight when you know who your enemy is. Straight people are your enemy. (Anonymous 1990)

Here we can see Queer Nation as a more distinct break from the Gay Liberation and feminist movements of the 1970s, involving a turn away from structural accounts of oppression and towards a clearer focus on individuals as the source of suffering, in this case, "straights". Yet, perhaps paradoxically, Queer Nation's view of identity was nonetheless "situational and strategic", not essential (Rand 2004, 297). The other side of the same leaflet was titled "I Hate Straights", presenting an anti-assimilationist manifesto that painted straightness as a dangerous social affliction (Berlant and Freeman 1993, 200). The idea of this propaganda was to point out the danger that *heteronormativity* posed to LGBTIQ persons. Activists had also begun to notice the rampant nationalism of the USA at the time, apparent also within LGBTIQ communities. Many within the LGBTIQ community continued to adhere to an "ethnic model" of sexual identity based on notions of biology and desire (Duggan 1992, 12). Along these lines, according to Berlant and Freeman, Queer Nation acted as a kind of postmodern parody to this nationalist complex, emphasising fluidity over fixity. They suggest, "Its tactics are to cross borders, to occupy spaces, and to mime the privileges of normality – in short, to simulate 'the national' with a camp inflection" (1993, 196).

Key concept: The queer international

In her work *Israel/Palestine and the Queer International* (2012), Sarah Schulman describes how Queer Nation influenced her idea of the "queer international". As she describes, the "nationalism" inflected by Queer Nation was satirical, given the effective exile from public citizenship that those living with AIDS experienced.

Schulman draws on this historical idea of a non-nationalistic "queer nation", and puts this into conversation with the issue of Israel and Palestine, resulting in a concept of the queer international. Schulman describes this as:

> [A] worldwide movement that brings queer liberation and feminism to the principles of international autonomy from occupation, coloni-alism, and globalized capital. (2012, 66)

Schulman suggests that a transgressive global queer solidarity is possible. We discuss the issue of sexual citizenship in further detail in Chapter 5.

Racism, whiteness and AIDS

While the historical event of the AIDS crisis and the activist response shaped queer theory, it is also important to note that the general myopia of the movement around questions of race also arguably influenced a lack of attention to race and intersectionality within some segments of queer theory. In the decade between 1981 and 1991, Black men in the USA made up a disproportionate number of AIDs cases, yet this was a cause for little public concern given the assumption that it was normal for Black men to die young (Harper 1993, 239). Furthermore, following medical discourse claiming AIDS emerged from Africa, the political "New Right" had begun to rhetorically connect homosexuality and Africa, marking both homosexuality and Blackness as unnatural/diseased (Patton 1993, 157). This endemic racism impacted on the response of Black communities in the USA to AIDS, with Black leaders and commentators largely remaining silent on the issue. The general lack of organisation against AIDS in Black communities cannot be understood in terms of resistance to the *health issue* as much as the *social baggage* of AIDS, as H.L. Dalton reflects, "[O]ur leaders, however defined, seem to run away from the issue of AIDS. They talk about it as little as possible and even more rarely involve themselves in efforts to develop constructive solution" (1989, 209). The emphasis on "Africa" as the origin of AIDS enrolled African Americans as responsible by association, adding to the reluctance of many to address and thereby further associate themselves with the issue (Dalton 1989, 211).

Where AIDs was spoken about there was distancing from the issue of homosexuality – with Black leaders wanting to maintain what cultural capital they had in the face of racism (Cohen 1996, 379). Similar dynamics were noted in Latino communities in the USA, with a general silence around the issue prevailing among marginalised groups (Alonso and Koreck 1993). This is not to claim that AIDS activists were predominantly white, rather, that racism impacted upon how AIDS was constructed as an issue, which in turn led to a general failure to centre racial politics in response to the crisis. In many cases, communities formed in marginalised groups in order to respond to the health crisis. As Lionel Cantú argues, for example, "HIV/AIDS has had a tremendous influence over queer Latino social space", insofar as responding to the crisis necessitated the imagining and formation of a Latino "community" (2009, 151). However, it is to say that the mainstream awareness and activist response to the impact of AIDS on marginal groups remained sidelined. Indeed, in many academic commentaries produced during the period, race was rarely focused on despite the clear racism of AIDS discourse in the public arena, and activists of colour were often made invisible (Cohen 1996, 369). Further, where more liberal responses to AIDS were on the front foot against the "New Right", there was still an emphasis on "colour blindness" that meant race was infrequently attended to. As Evelynn Hammonds argues, such blindness "buries racism along with race" (1987, 29). Though Hammonds was one of the earliest commentators on the question of race and AIDS, few took up the concerns she raised around the continuing racism of AIDS discourse.

As Cohen argues, the emergence of "queer" politics promised a new anti-assimilationist vision to interrupt normativity (1997). Indeed, as Ana Maria Alonso and Maria Teresa Koreck called for, on the issue of silence on AIDS in Latino communities, there was a need to build "new coalitions based on a post-modernist consciousness of 'affinity' rather than an essentialist construction of 'identity' and establishing political alliances with those who are

---

Key debate: The whiteness of queer theory

Understanding the racial dynamics of this context, and the failure of some activists and thinkers writing about AIDS to more distinctly centre questions of race, is important to keep in mind when examining the queer theory that was influenced by the epidemic. This historical failure cannot simply be rectified by re-writing the queer theory canon, but rather, necessitates more deeply understanding the racial dynamics influencing what has emerged as theory.

As Michael Hames-García contends, "to *add* race and colonialism to queer theory is to overlook the formation of queer theory as thoroughly grounded in the Eurocentric narratives of the coloniality of power" (2011b, 42 emphasis in original). However, while Hames-García emphasises Eurocentric ideas as the problematic white origin of queer theory, as we also pose in this book, ideas are not merely influenced by earlier ideas, but also shaped by material conditions.

Looking to the whiteness of thinking around AIDS helps us to understand that the inattention to race – as seen in some seminal queer theory texts that emerged in the 1990s – was also because of the racial and racist dynamics of AIDS politics that queer theorists were influenced by.

also 'other' and 'different'" (1993, 122). Yet, as Cohen contends, queer did little to disrupt the racialised normativity widespread in much gay and lesbian political organisational structures:

> [Q]ueer politics has served to reinforce simple dichotomies between heterosexual and everything "queer". An understanding of the ways in which power informs and constitutes privileged and marginalized subjects on both sides of this dichotomy has been left unexamined. (1997, 438)

For Cohen, much queer politics has involved an over-emphasis on sexuality, to the detriment of other dimensions of oppression (1997, 440), an issue which we explore further in Chapter 7. Cohen argues that materials such as "I Hate Straights" produced by Queer Nation illustrate a narrow focus on a heterosexual/queer divide, rather than attending to additional concerns over race, gender and class oppression (1997, 448). Furthermore, some have noted that the actions carried out by Queer Nation hinged on particular racial and class dynamics, as Mary L. Gray suggests, "[Queer Nation's] class and race privilege also gave them knowledge of what would be most disruptive, yet tolerated – namely, displays of an urban stylized queer sexuality with purchase power" (2009, 225). Where there was desire to attend to and centre questions around gender, race and class within some Queer Nation groups, there was also resistance from those who wished to focus only on sexuality (Gray 2009, 228). Importantly, LGBTIQ press also often characterised Queer Nation merely as a new wave of militant gay and lesbian activism, rather than highlighting the more complex vision of "queer" identity that some aspired towards – and in turn, where there was attention to more intersectional issues, this was sometimes occluded (Gray 2009, 229).

The racialised aspects of AIDS history, and the racialised ways that activist history is remembered, reported and recorded, is essential to keep in mind in the following sections as we explore some of the key queer theory ideas that emerged in the wake of ACT UP and Queer Nation. Further, we might wonder how queer perspectives, influenced by the postmodern focus on deconstruction, can adequately account for structures of oppression. While we continue to explore key texts in queer theory throughout this book, Cohen's contention that queer activism can easily slip into an over-simplified binary of the queer versus not queer, that ignores questions of race and racism, is worth keeping in mind throughout.

Queer theory in practice: Transgender Nation

Shortly after Queer Nation emerged, a subgroup called Transgender Nation formed in San Francisco in 1992. As Stryker describes, this group began in part in response to concern around how trans issues were being sidelined or erased by some members in Queer Nation (2008, 135).

Though Queer Nation declined, the presence of Transgender Nation signalled a new queer appreciation of trans issues, a departure from the vitriol experienced within some strands of feminist organising (discussed in Chapter 3). Stryker suggests that the formation of this group played some part in the addition of "T" to LGB organising (2008, 137), a change that we consider in much more detail in Chapter 6.

CONCLUSION: QUEER THINKING AFTER AIDS

Though this chapter has focused on the influence of the AIDS crisis on ideas of queer identity and theory, we might also note the changing landscape of AIDS politics since the 1980s that has perhaps turned in a more conservative direction. As Anne Cvetkovich argues, as well as being connected to the emergence of radical ideas, AIDS activism can also be understood as the foundation of "mainstream gay politics and consumer visibility", as she laments "something got lost along the way" (2003, 156). Or, as Cantú contends, "the institutionalization of HIV/AIDS prevention" among other social changes had provided both space for community formation while simultaneously constructing limitations on imagining identity within Latino groups (2009, 146). More broadly, there has been a turn away in LGBTIQ activism from the shame and stigmatisation associated with the mainstream discourse of the AIDS crisis, towards an attempt to embrace pride and forget a darker past associated with death. As Heather Love argues, homonormativity (discussed extensively in Chapter 6) has emerged where the murky side of queer life has been replaced by "lighter and airier versions of gay life" (2008, 52). She continues:

> Emotional conformism, romantic fulfilment, and gay cheerfulness constitute the dominant image of gay life in the contemporary moment. Not only are gays being represented as shiny, happy people in major media outlets, but traces of the history of gay unhappiness are being expunged as well. (2008, 55)

While groups like Queer Nation argued against assimilation, much LGBTIQ politics in the past decade has focused on issues such as marriage equality, ostensibly campaigning on the basis of *similarity* rather than *difference*. In other words, many political demands from the LGBTIQ community today are about aspirations towards normality, a fantasy of "being normal" (Love 2008, 53).

Yet, these shifts in LGBTIQ activism have not occurred without debate and friction between those advocating for "equality" versus those arguing against "assimilation". For example, in 1998 in New York, a new group calling themselves "Gay Shame" emerged in order to interrupt the mainstreaming and corporatisation of LGBTIQ communities (Sycamore 2008, 269). The debate over "gay shame" generated a great deal of discourse that is still playing out in queer theory discussions today, and highlights the ongoing tensions between the academy and activists, queer theory versus queer activism, and what is "queer" versus what is "mainstream".

There is disagreement about whether the concept of gay shame is a useful rallying point on the basis of shared oppression (being shamed), whether it relates to something more fundamental (how shame structures queer identity), or whether it is a specific queer activist strategy (we should "shame" mainstream LGBTIQ advocacy). As Gould argues, the concept of gay shame can

---

Key concept: Gay shame

Various gay shame groups have emerged across the world, sharing tactics including interrupting various pride marches, holding speak-outs, and staging "Gay Shame Awards" to disgrace various LGBTIQ individuals and groups involved in mainstreaming activities (Sycamore 2008, 272).

In 2003, academics who had been engaging with this emerging issue in LGBTIQ activism decided to hold a "Gay Shame Conference" at the University of Michigan, which was met with scrutiny from Gay Shame activists who challenged the level of "critical thinking" involved in the organisation of the conference (Sycamore 2008, 286).

As Halberstam also argues, the Gay Shame Conference was marked by racial dynamics that saw white men dominating panels and discussion. As Halberstam suggests, "If queer studies is to survive gay shame, and it will, we all need to move far beyond the limited scope of white gay male concerns and interests" (2005, 231).

be productive for forming collectives based on the shared experience of *being shamed*, while still recognising differences between individuals (2009b, 223). Further, both Didier Eribon (2004) and Sally R. Munt (2008) argue that shame is fundamental to the constitution of gay identity in the West. Munt argues that in Western culture it is through the Judeo-Christian shame narrative of Adam and Eve that the idea of sexual difference comes from. Munt contends: "shame produces shamed subjectivities, however it is an aspect of the dynamism of shame that it also can produce a reactive, new self to form that has a liberatory energy" (2008, 80). Munt concludes that shame can be a driving force for transformation. In contrast to these academic approaches, some queer activists have rallied the idea of gay shame in terms of *shaming* certain LGBTIQ mainstreaming efforts. For example, prominent Gay Shame activist Mattilda Berstein Sycamore describes handing out fliers in San Francisco that read: "Are you choking on the vomit of consumerist 'gay pride?' – DARLING spit that shit out – GAY SHAME is the answer" (2008, 271).

The mainstreaming and corporatisation of the pride marches around the world and the turn away from the militant politics seen during the AIDS crisis continues to be a source of trouble and contention for activists, organisers and academics. As Love suggests, "If there were ever a time that we needed our cynicism, it is now – when the future that is being marketed to us is so insanely bright" (2008, 63). It is our hope that our account of AIDS, and the activism around it that helped to shape early queer theory thinking, might go some way to attending to the history of "queer unhappiness" that Love suggests we turn to (2008, 63).

Further reading

Douglas Crimp, and Adam Rolston. (1990). AIDS Demo Graphics. Seattle: Bay Press.

This work gives a great sense of the kinds of actions undertaken by ACT UP, detailing protests held by ACT UP New York in the 1980s. The work includes many images and posters from protests and actions which give an excellent sense of the representational and discursive strategies employed by the group.

Michael Warner (ed.). (1993). *Fear of a Queer Planet: Queer Politics and Social Theory*. Minneapolis; London: University of Minnesota Press.

A collection of seminal texts on queer theory and activism, including numerous key pieces reflecting on the AIDS crisis.

Cathy J. Cohen. (1997). "Punks, Bulldaggers, and Welfare Queens: The Radical Potential of Queer Politics?" *GLQ: A Journal of Lesbian and Gay Studies,* 3: 437–465.

This important article from Cohen explores the limitations of the "queer" politics promised by AIDS activists, in terms of engaging with questions of gender, race and class.

QUESTIONS TO CONSIDER

- What were the similarities and differences between the politics of ACT UP and the earlier period of Gay Liberation and second wave feminism?
- Why was reclaiming the term "queer" useful for AIDS activism, and what were its limitations?
- What did the racial politics of the AIDS crisis reveal about the limits of some queer activism?
- Is "gay shame" a useful idea? How does "gay shame" jar with the idea of "gay pride"?

Recommended films

Chocolate Babies (**Stephen Winter 1997**). This film looks at issues of race and class in the context of the AIDS crisis, and the failure of mainstream AIDS activism to attend to the queer Black people being affected.

The Gift (**Louise Hogarth 2003**). This documentary explores the phenomenon of "bugchasing" – that is, of those seeking to become infected with HIV. For more on "viral sex" see Gregory Tomso 2008.

BPM (Beats Per Minute) (**Robin Campillo 2017**). This film offers a fictional account of the real-life activities of ACT UP in Paris during the 1990s. The film explores personal and activist struggles around AIDS at the peak of the crisis.

5 Outing the Closet

KEY TERMS AND CONCEPTS	the heterosexual matrix, gender melancholy, gender performativity, subversion, drag, camp, the closet, queer reading, paranoid reading, reparative reading

QUEER THEORY ARTICULATES ITSELF

When did queer theory come out of the closet? Or, as we might also say, when did queer theory *challenge the notion of a closet altogether*? As discussed in Chapter 1, in an academic context feminist and film theorist de Lauretis coined "queer theory" at a conference that she had organised at the University of California, Santa Cruz, in 1990 and she later published it in her introduction to a special issue of *Differences: A Journal of Feminist Cultural Studies* in 1991. De Lauretis used the term "queer" as a means to "mark a certain critical distance" (1991, v) from the terms "lesbian and gay" which she understood as having become "the standard way of referring to what only a few years ago used to be simply 'gay' ... or just a few years earlier still, 'homosexual'" (1991, iv). In proposing queer theory, de Lauretis sought to challenge these stable identity categories as a strategy of resistance, one that afforded individuals the possibility "not to adhere to any one of the given terms, not to assume their ideological liabilities, but instead to transgress and transcend them – or at the very least problematise them" (1991, v).

In this chapter we take a close look at the theoretical articulations of queer theory that gained traction alongside de Lauretis' work in the 1990s, with a particular focus on the works of Butler and Sedgwick. Both Butler and Sedgwick take a poststructuralist approach to sex, gender and sexuality, seeking to deconstruct the relationships between these categories and problematise normative models of identity. Though de Lauretis coined the term, as William Turner writes in *A Genealogy of Queer*, Butler and Sedgwick, "laid much of the conceptual groundwork for the emerging field in the early 1990s" (2000, 106). However, as we will see, Butler and Sedgwick's work developed separately and along slightly different trajectories.

To begin, this chapter explores the work of Butler, particularly *Gender Trouble* first published in 1990 (and updated with subsequent prefaces; see Butler 1999), with a focus on her critique of the gender binary and her theory of gender performativity. As we explain, this is the idea that gender involves the repetition of acts in a pre-determined social context over time, which makes gender appear natural and innate. We also look at the significance of psychoanalysis, particularly the work of Freud, to Butler's theory, including notions of gender mourning and melancholia, and her re-thinking of the "primary prohibition" against homosexuality. Consideration is also given to Butler's discussion of subversion, including her comments on drag. In the latter half of this chapter, we outline Sedgwick's key theoretical contributions, particularly her work in *Epistemology of the Closet* (1990), starting with her axioms and conception of "the closet". From here we explore Sedgwick's notion of queer reading practice and outline her ideas of paranoid versus reparative reading, which continue to be central to many contemporary queer theorists.

WHAT'S SO QUEER ABOUT JUDITH BUTLER?

Butler's writing reflects her philosophical training in phenomenology, German Idealism (particularly the work of Georg Wilhelm Friedrich Hegel) and The Frankfurt School (with a particular focus on neo-Marxist critique). While her work operates within feminist, psychoanalytic and Marxist frameworks, she is best known for her contributions to queer theory. She is most famous for her book *Gender Trouble: Feminism and the Subversion of Identity*, first published in 1990, but Butler has published many influential books and articles interrogating intersections of power, identity, gender and sexuality.

In her early work, *Subjects of Desire: Hegelian Reflections in Twentieth-Century France* published in 1987, she traces Hegel's notion of the desiring subject through modern French philosophy. The following year, her essay "Performative Acts and Gender Constitution" laid out the first iteration of her theory of gender performativity, which would later be developed in *Gender Trouble* in 1990. Through each of these works, Butler theorises identity formation and subjectivity with notions of the body, sex, sexuality, language and speech. As Sarah Salih notes, Butler's works reveal a lifelong dedication to interrogating "the ways in which identity norms are taken up and subject positions assumed" (2004, 2).

Notable works: Butler

- *Subjects of Desire: Hegelian Reflections in Twentieth-Century France* (1987)
- *Gender Trouble: Feminism and the Subversion of Identity* (1990)
- *Bodies That Matter: On the Discursive Limits of "Sex"* (1993)
- *The Psychic Life of Power: Theories of Subjection* (1997)
- *Excitable Speech: A Politics of the Performative* (1997)
- *Antigone's Claim: Kinship Between Life and Death* (2000)
- *Precarious Life: The Power of Mourning and Violence* (2004)
- *Undoing Gender* (2004)
- *Giving an Account of Oneself* (2005)
- *Frames of War: When Is Life Grievable?* (2009)
- *Parting Ways: Jewishness and the Critique of Zionism* (2012)
- *Dispossession: The Performative in the Political* (co-authored with Athena Athanasiou 2013)
- *Senses of the Subject* (2015)
- *Notes Toward a Performative Theory of Assembly* (2015)

As we explore through this chapter, Butler developed a theory that suggested identity to be "a contingent construction which assumes multiple forms even as it presents itself as singular and stable" (Salih 2004, 2). Butler's theorisation had a profound and far-reaching impact upon the ways that gender, sex and sexuality have been understood within and beyond academia in the post-1990s era. Butler argued that feminism's focus on the "woman" question was deeply flawed because the subject of its analysis – woman – was an exclusionary construct that was stabilised only via a gender binary underpinned by heterosexuality (Butler 1999, 3). As Butler writes in the 1999 preface to *Gender Trouble*:

> I was most concerned to criticise a pervasive heterosexual assumption in feminist literary theory. I sought to counter those views that made presumptions about the limits and propriety of gender and restricted the meaning of gender to received notions of masculinity and femininity. (1999, vii)

Butler suggests that the term "woman" (or "man") does not refer to a singular, coherent or stable identity category. Instead she asserts that all such categories are unstable constructions that depend on regulation and ritual in order to exist. As Salih argues, this line of argument leaves "little room for belief in identity categories as stable, self-evident, or 'natural'" (2004, 6).

Like many poststructuralist writers, Butler has been criticised for the difficulty and density of her work. However, she asserts that her style of writing is part of her critical project, arguing, "neither grammar nor style are politically neutral" (1999, xviii). Hence, when we discuss Butler's work, we need to acknowledge her prose as an aspect of her methodology; it functions to deconstruct the grammatical norms that naturalise identity formation. In offering subsequent commentary in preface form to *Gender Trouble*, Butler reveals a little more about her thinking behind this. She writes:

> The dogged effort to "denaturalize" gender in this text emerges, I think, from a strong desire both to counter the normative violence implied by ideal morphologies of sex and to uproot the pervasive assumptions about natural or presumptive heterosexuality that are informed by ordinary and academic discourses on sexuality. The writing of this denaturalization was not done simply out of a desire to play with language or prescribe theatrical antics in the place of "real" politics, as some critics have conjectured (as if theatre and politics are always distinct). It was done from a desire to live, to make life possible, and to rethink the possible as such. (1999, xx)

With this in mind, we move on to exploring Butler's key contributions to the field of queer theory as it developed through the 1990s.

Butler's approach to sex and gender

What is the relationship between sex, gender and sexuality? Does sex determine gender? Does gender determine sexuality? These questions are at the centre of Butler's project. Butler's discussion in *Gender Trouble* opens with an interrogation of what she describes as "the compulsory order of sex/gender/desire" (1999, 9). By this, she means the fantasy that a person's sex is naturally aligned with their gender and their sexual identity. In other words, this is the assumption that a person assigned female at birth (sex) will ideally grow up to be a feminine woman (gender) and her desire will be directed towards a man (e.g., a person of the opposite sex/gender). Butler calls this set of expectations the "heterosexual matrix" (2008, 7) that underpins the gender binary (see Figure 5.1).

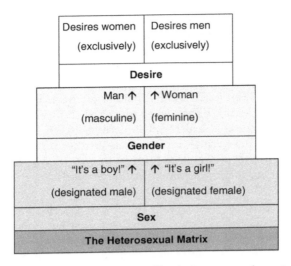

Figure 5.1   The gender binary as determined by the heterosexual matrix, adapted from William Leonard's wedding cake model

For Butler, the concept of the "heterosexual matrix" is a "grid of cultural intelligibility" where sexes, genders and desires are maintained and natural-ised under a binary heterosexual logic (1999, 194). Another way of think-ing about this is via Leonard's wedding cake model, which represents these binary logics as a three-tiered cake (2005, 94). The bottom tier of the cake represents sex; it is split into two sides correspondingly labelled as male and female. The second tier represents gender; it too is split according to a binary of masculine and feminine which aligns with the binary of sex. The top tier represents sexuality; it presents heterosexuality as the natural result of the lower tiers and the pinnacle of the model. In this model, sex (seen as "natu-ral") underpins gender, which in turn is the foundation of desire. According to Butler, the "coherence" and "continuity" of sex, gender and desire are "socially instituted and maintained norms of intelligibility" that stabilise what we understand as identity (1999, 23). When we see this pattern repeated over and over across a sustained period of time, we come to see it as natural and normal.

While earlier feminist discourse sought to distinguish between sex and gender, as Butler highlights, by making this distinction feminist scholars had asserted that sex had been reinforced as a "natural" basis upon which gender was built. To critique the assumed naturalness of this sex/gender relationship,

Butler draws attention to some possible discontinuities between "sexed bodies and culturally constructed genders" (1999, 10). For Butler, understanding gender via binary oppositions reifies the assumed causal relationship between sex and gender, because it assumes that gender difference mimics sexual difference. Even if we assume there is a binary sex (an idea which Butler later challenges) and if we assert that there is no causal relationship between this binary sex and gender, then it would be possible for the construction of "man" or masculinity to relate to either male or female bodies, and the same for "woman" and femininity. Hence, as Butler suggests:

> If gender is the cultural meanings that the sexed body assumes, then a gender cannot be said to follow from a sex in any one way. Taken to its logical limit, the sex/gender distinction suggests a radical discontinuity between sexed bodies and culturally constructed genders. Assuming for the moment the stability of binary sex, it does not follow that the construction of "men" will accrue exclusively to the bodies of males or that "women" will interpret only female bodies. (1999, 10)

Taking this even further, Butler argues that if we think of gender as more flexible and fluid than sex (which we often do), then there is "no reason to assume that genders ought also to remain as two" simply because we think of sex as a binary (1999, 10).

Importantly, Butler does not ask us to consider gender as cultural versus sex as biological/natural. Butler argues that perhaps this thing we call "sex", which we may have always thought to be natural and never thoroughly interrogated, is just "as culturally constructed as gender" and she suggests, "perhaps it was always already gender" (1999, 10–11). Throughout *Gender Trouble*, Butler outlines a queer proposition: that it is not enough to re-think our assumptions about what gender is and how it works, we must also do the same for sex. However, if we were to think of sex as a constructed category that was always already inflected by gender, then our existing definitions of gender also need revising.

What is gender anyway?

In *Gender Trouble*, Butler prompts us to reflect further on the question of gender. As we have noted, a long-held view within feminist discourse was that gender functioned as the cultural interpretation of a person or subject's sex. However, Butler's work suggests that sex does not operate as an

Queer theory in practice: Butler outside the West

Butler's approach to sex and gender relies on Western conceptions of sex and gender, and thus her work may not be applicable in the same way outside of a Western context. As Marie-Paule Ha suggests, we can "trouble" Butler's work through thinking it through in a Chinese context, which historically involves a different theorisation of the body than offered in Western medicine. She writes:

> Within the Chinese cosmological framework, the gender markers of the Chinese body ... differ radically from those of its European biomedical counterpart ... within the Chinese body schema, the categories of "male" and "female" were explained in terms not of biological differences but of relative predominance of yin and yang. (Ha 2010, 140–141)

Ha's conclusion is that even though Western medical frameworks have been adopted in China, at a social level "many Chinese in fact function within a plurality of body schemas" (2010, 142). Ha suggests that students should think through localised examples outside of the West such as this that might trouble Butler's work in its application.

"interior 'truth'" (1999, 44) or essence to gender identity. For Butler, gender is the apparatus that makes us believe in this myth of a natural inner truth. As we have noted, Butler's work suggests that gender is the discursive and cultural means by which sex is produced. Gender is thus a set of power relations; it is the reason that we think of a sex as binary, natural, "as 'prediscursive,' prior to culture, a political neutral surface *on which* culture acts" (Butler 1999, 11, emphasis in original). Querying (and indeed queering) the hegemonic discourse of gender requires a lot of conceptual work, in particular "a radical rethinking of the categories" and formations of identity (Butler 1999, 16). Deconstructing the concept of gender, she asks whether there is "'a' gender which persons are said to *have*" or whether gender is "an essential attribute that a person is said to *be*" before putting forward her argument that gender is neither of these things (1999, 11, emphasis in original). Butler's most cited contribution to queer theory is her argument that gender is a *doing*, not a *being*.

Butler suggests that gender does not refer to a singular, coherent or stable identity category. Instead she asserts that the appearance of a "gendered self" is "produced" via "the regulation of attributes along culturally established lines of coherence" (Butler 1999, 32–33). As Butler highlights, genders are unstable productions, dependent upon socio-cultural regulation to exist. By this she means that those gendered behaviours and attributes that we commonly associate with femininity or masculinity are in effect imposed upon us by normative sexuality (within the heterosexual matrix). However, as she notes, forms of sexual practice do not *produce* certain genders, rather, that heterosexuality is maintained by policing a strict gender binary.

Taking this a step further, Butler asserts that the production of gender is performative. Though it might be tempting to think of gender as a sort of act that is performed by a subject who exists in some form of pre-gendered state, Butler argues that there is no *doer* behind this process. This is because, for Butler, the production of gender *constitutes* identity. She borrows a line from Friedrich Nietzsche to make this argument. In his 1887 *On the Genealogy of Morals*, Nietzsche argues that "there is no 'being' behind doing, effecting, becoming; 'the doer' is merely a fiction added to the deed – the deed is everything" (Nietzsche 2010, 45). Extending from this, Butler argues that identity is an effect rather than a cause, writing: "There is no gender identity behind expressions of gender; that identity is performatively constituted by the very 'expressions' that are said to be its results" (1999, 33). Here Butler destabilises norms of identity formation by suggesting that there is no identity behind the expression of gender. For Butler, identity is retroactively constructed and comes to be *through* these expressions.

Gender melancholy

Foundational to her theory of gender formation, Butler draws on psychoanalysis to put forward a theory of gender as melancholic. Through this she aligns heterosexuality with the lost possibility for same-sex desire. In Freud's "Mourning and Melancholia" and *The Ego and the Id*, both mourning and melancholia are theorised as reactions to loss (1962, 2001). Freud views mourning as a healthy reaction to loss (a reaction that is ultimately resolved), but melancholy as a pathological response wherein the subject cannot let go of the lost object. In Freud's account of melancholia, this loss is refused and subsequently internalised into the self (or ego) through imitation. In simple terms, Freud argues that this loss is incorporated into identity, essentially suggesting that the melancholic becomes what they cannot love.

Butler takes up these ideas in her discussion of gender formation, arguing that we could use them to re-think gender and sexuality. Butler suggests that masculinity and femininity are "rooted in unresolved homosexual cathexes" (1999, 69) and she makes a complex argument to explain this, asserting that:

> The melancholy refusal/domination of homosexuality culminates in the incorporation of the same-sexed object of desire and reemerges in the construction of discrete sexual "natures" that require and institute their opposites through exclusion. (1999, 69)

In other words, there is a taboo around homosexuality which cannot be mourned, which means that we become what we cannot love, in gendered terms. In relating this notion of melancholia to the formation of subjectivity, Freud refers to the incest taboo (otherwise known as the Oedipus complex) to explain the ways that the child identifies with and against their parents along gendered lines. Butler alters this argument suggesting that there is a taboo against same-sex desire that comes before the incest taboo. For Butler, gender formation is the result of this prohibition becoming internalised and incorporated into identity. According to this argument, we mimic the gender that we are not allowed to have an attraction to. As Butler's work suggests, the taboo initiates a loss of a love-object, which is then recuperated into identity through the internalisation of the taboo. In other words, this theory suggests that heterosexuality is based on a social repudiation of homosexuality. Taking a Foucauldian approach, she considers how these prohibitions against homosexuality function as a generative force, producing the very possibilities that they are thought to prohibit. Butler also suggests there is a melancholic refusal of heterosexuality involved in the formation of homosexuality. However, this is complicated by the layers of prohibition that inflect same-sex desire.

Gender performativity

In her first theorisation of gender performativity, Butler suggests that gender is not an attribute or essence, but "an identity instituted through *a stylised repetition of acts*" (1988, 519). Butler's argument rests on the idea that gender comes to exist through "the stylization of the body" (1988, 519). However, she does not mean to suggest theatrical bodies, instead focusing on how this formation of gender functions within the everyday. She refers to "the mundane way in which bodily gestures, movements, and enactments of various kinds constitute the illusion of an abiding gendered self" (1988, 519). In *Gender*

Trouble, she revises her argument to highlight the role of regulation and temporality in this process, writing that:

> [G]ender is the repeated stylization of the body, a set of repeated acts within a highly rigid regulatory frame that congeal over time to produce the appearance of substance, of a natural sort of being. (Butler 1999, 44)

Hence, Butler suggests that gender involves the performative repetition of acts in a pre-determined social context over time in such a way that it appears to be natural and innate. It is important to note the difference between *performance* and *performative*, because Butler does not view the expression of gender as a performance per se. As we have noted, Butler views gender as the process that constitutes subjectivity rather than as an active choice and performance on the part of the subject.

The idea of the "performative" comes from the philosopher John Langshaw Austin, who theorised performative as speech acts that perform actions. For Butler, an example of this is the proclamations "It's a boy!" or "It's a girl!" that call embodied subjects into a world of gender, whereby their bodies are thus rendered understandable/legible ("intelligible" as Butler would suggest). Butler's notion of performativity also borrows from the work of Jacques Derrida, who theorised the notion of *"différance"* which refers to the deferral of meaning and the deconstruction of the notion of origin. For Butler this means challenging the very notion of an original "sex" underlying gender. Following Austin and Derrida, Butler's gender performativity can be explained as "an expectation that ends up producing the very phenomenon that it anticipates" (Butler 1999, xiv). In her preface to the tenth anniversary edition of *Gender Trouble*, Butler further clarifies her use of the term "performativity", arguing that in her work:

> [P]erformativity is not a single act, but a repetition and a ritual, which achieves its effects through its naturalization in the context of a body, understood, in part, as a culturally sustained temporal duration. (1999, xv)

Butler's contribution to queer theory is her insistence that "what we take to be an internal essence of gender is manufactured through a sustained set of acts, posited through the gendered stylization of the body" (1999, xv). Her work seeks to deconstruct the foundations of identity by demonstrating how gender, which we have traditionally thought to be an interior feature, is produced through the repetition of bodily acts.

Queer theory in practice: Performativity as bodily practices

What does gender performativity look like in practice if there is no "doer" behind the deed? Fundamentally, Butler is concerned with how a gender binary is produced and reproduced in society in a way that occludes the socio-cultural aspects of this, and masquerades as "natural".

An example of this might be to think about the assumptions we have about differences between men's versus women's bodies. It is assumed that men are always naturally bigger and stronger than women, and that women are always naturally smaller and weaker. In reality, men and women come in all shapes and body sizes, but even taking this diversity into account some may claim there is a "natural" difference.

However, if we look at the bodily practices that men versus women are expected to adopt, we can understand how bodily acts solidify into seemingly "natural" differences. For example, typically:

- boys are expected to be active, go outside, and use their bodies, whereas girls are expected to be relatively less active;
- girl's/women's clothing and shoes often allow less mobility than boy's/men's;
- in gyms, many women exclusively use the cardio area while men use the weights area;
- women are expected to diet and eat salads/light food, whereas men are expected to eat protein and red meats/heavy food;
- men are expected to take up physical space ("manspreading") whereas women are expected to take up very little space;
- men are expected not to express themselves in ways that might be read as "feminine", including walking and sitting in particular ways.

While many people do not conform to these expectations, on a societal level (including the ways that "normal" men and women are represented) they play out in ways that shape a "natural" sense of men as bigger and stronger, and women as smaller and weaker. These acts of eating, sitting, walking, working out and so on, repeated over time on a societal level, is gender performativity: "gender" emerges from the stylised repetition of acts shaped by gender norms. These may slowly shift and change over time and context.

In her later work, Butler uses the same logic to think about sex and sexuality. For instance, in her later essay "Imitation and Gender Insubordination", she deconstructs the hierarchical relationship between heterosexuality and homosexuality, through which homosexuality is considered a "bad" copy or version of an original heterosexuality. In this work she argues that both homosexuality and heterosexuality are produced, and that heterosexuality only maintains stability via repetition (Butler 2004a, 119–137).

Subversion and drag

A core tenet of Butler's work is the suggestion that if identity categories are not innate, if they are always in the process of formation, then they can be refused, resisted and subverted. We can see this idea operating in Butler's discussions of subversion, which she locates as a deconstructive strategy to undermine the power of existing gender norms.

Butler suggests that certain enactments of gender, such as drag performances and butch/femme relationships, can be subversive because they question the foundations of gender norms; such enactments can "suddenly and significantly upset" the assumptions that we make about sexed bodies (1999, 140). For Butler, the norms of gender can be split, exaggerated and parodied. Such subversive actions highlight "the strange, the incoherent, [and] that which falls 'outside'" (Butler 1999, 140), revealing the constructed nature of what is often considered to be "natural" and "normal". As she writes: "Only from a self-consciously denaturalized position can we see how the appearance of naturalness is itself constituted" (1999, 140).

Underlying Butler's argument is the perspective that "power can be neither withdrawn nor refused, but only redeployed" (1999, 158). Hence, she posits certain subversive bodily acts as deconstructive strategies, writing:

> [T]he more insidious and effective strategy it seems is a thoroughgoing appropriation and redeployment of the categories of identity themselves, not merely to contest "sex," but to articulate the convergence of multiple sexual discourses at the site of "identity" in order to render that category, in whatever form, permanently problematic. (1999, 163)

Thinking about this in relation to lesbian cultures, Butler suggests that butch and femme identities both recall and displace heterosexual exchange, meaning that they are "internally dissonant and complex in their resignification of ... hegemonic categories" (1999, 157). The implication of this is that both identities put "the very notion of an original or natural identity into question" (Butler 1999, 157).

From this discussion, Butler also outlines some initial thoughts on drag as a subversive bodily act, though as we will see her views on drag are tempered through her later writing. In *Gender Trouble*, Butler elaborates on her theory of gender performativity to emphasise the role of "corporeal signification" in the production of gender (1999, 173). By this she means that certain "acts, gestures, and desire" create the illusion of an inner truth to gender but that this is produced *"on the surface of the body"* (Butler 1999, 173, emphasis in original). What Butler does here is suggest that there is an interior and exterior element to gender. This idea becomes essential to her thoughts on drag.

Feminist theory had earlier viewed drag as an imitation of an original gender identity. Drag was viewed as a problematic style of performance because it was thought to mock and degrade women. Complicating this critique, according to Butler, are the slippery relations between the "imitation" and the "original", and the internal and external realms of gender. Drag performances are commonly thought to play upon a distinction between a performer's sex and the gender of performance. For instance, we know self-proclaimed drag superstar RuPaul Charles to be a male-identified person who performs as a woman on stage and screen. Some would suggest that the pleasure of RuPaul's performance lies in this awareness. Butler complicates this neat sex/gender distinction by highlighting that when we watch a drag performance, we actually witness three contingent dimensions of gender: anatomical sex, gender identity and gender performance. Hence, Butler argues:

> If the anatomy of the performer is already distinct from the gender of the performer, and both of those are distinct from the gender of the performance, then the performance suggests a dissonance not only between sex and performance, but sex and gender, and gender and performance. (1999, 175)

So for Butler, drag is a subversive tool because it teases out the distinctness of these three aspects of gendered experience, which are naturalised as a unified picture through the heterosexual matrix. Butler also views drag as an imitation of gender that implicitly reveals how all genders are produced through imitation.

Butler's comments on drag build upon Esther Newton's *Mother Camp: Female Impersonators in America*, published in 1972, which suggests that drag can reveal the mechanisms through which gender is socially constructed. From this, Butler suggests that drag exposes mechanisms of gender production, in particular the interior and exterior qualities of gender, and "fully subverts the distinction between inner and outer psychic space" (1999, 174). She also considers drag as a subversive tool to parody "the notion of a true gender identity" (Butler 1999, 174). This is an important point, as Butler does not consider drag as a parodic imitation of an original gender. Instead, she makes a bolder claim, arguing that what drag parodies is "the very notion of an original" (1999, 175). According to this view, drag is not a parody of any so-called "real" women; it is instead a parody of the assumption that a natural gender exists.

Responses, critiques and lasting influence

As Tim Dean notes, in the early 1990s, Butler's writing and Livingston's film *Paris is Burning* helped to canonise each other. On the one hand, this disseminated the emerging discipline known as queer theory beyond the academy, while at the same time "intensifying academic attention to issues of

---

Key concept: Camp

In 1964 New York writer Susan Sontag published her infamous essay, "Notes on 'Camp'". In the essay Sontag describes camp as a "sensibility" that involves "love of the unnatural: of artifice and exaggeration" (1982). For Sontag camp described an aesthetic mode that was not necessarily tied to homosexual subcultures, yet her description of camp in terms of "the love of the exaggerated, the 'off', of things-being-what-they-are-not" has distinctly *queer* overtones. In the 1970s Esther Newton took up the term in application to a study of drag queens in the USA, emphasising the aspects of both humour and glam involved (1972).

As Nikki Sullivan writes, camp "foregrounds the performative character of gender, sexuality, race, class, and so on" (2003, 193). Reading Butler with Sontag, we might see how camp style reveals the imitative, performative aspects of gender. Importantly, though often associated with gay men, camp is not exclusive – as Katrin Horn points out, camp can be a queer subversive style for anyone. As she suggests, pop singer Lady Gaga is exemplary of someone who adopts camp style, to reveal their own artifice (2010).

Queer theory in practice: *Paris is Burning*

In the years following *Gender Trouble*, Butler qualified her views on drag, re-focusing her argument in relation to the documentary film *Paris is Burning* (Jennie Livingston 1990). Filmed throughout the 1980s, *Paris is Burning* documents New York City's underground drag ball culture wherein participants contest a range of categories in which they perform social norms. The film combines footage of drag balls with interviews of contestants, providing insight into LGBTIQ culture with a specific focus on people of colour within the LGBTIQ community and the significance of groups known as "houses" (a term borrowed from fashion-house) which functioned as chosen families for the contestants. *Paris is Burning* was a key text in the emergent New Queer Cinema, a film movement that developed alongside queer theory in the early 1990s. Film critic B. Ruby Rich argued that *Paris is Burning* was among a group of films that broke with humanist approaches to the politics of gender and sexuality on screen, radically deconstructing the very foundations of identity (Rich 1992, 30–35).

In *Paris is Burning*, Butler saw the powerful evocation of subversive models of kinship. These were enacted in defiant and affirmative ways through the various "houses" and alternative family models presented by the film. However, in addition to this, she saw a simultaneous reiteration of norms that led her to question her initial comments on the subversive potential of drag. Butler argued that the film prompted her to question whether parody is an effective means of displacing dominant norms. Qualifying her initial views on drag, Butler argues in *Bodies That Matter*, first published in 1993:

> Although many readers understood my book *Gender Trouble* to be arguing for the proliferation of drag performances as a way of subverting dominant gender norms, I want to underscore that there is no necessary relation between drag and subversion and that drag may well be used in the service of both the denaturalisation and the reidealisation of hyperbolic heterosexual gender norms. At best, it seems, drag is a site of certain ambivalence. (Butler 2014, 85)

In an important qualification to her earlier comments on drag, Butler stresses the influence of heterosexual privilege, which leads her to argue that there are some forms of drag produced by and for heterosexual culture. As evidence of this, she cites examples such as Jack Lemmon in *Some Like it Hot* as "high het entertainment", Hollywood moments wherein heterosexuality "concede[s] its lack of naturalness and originality but still hold onto its power" (Butler 2014, 85).

With a particular focus on evocations of race, class and gender within the film, Butler ultimately concludes that *Paris is Burning* offers a deconstructed vision of identity because it suggests, "the order of sexual difference is not prior to that of race or class in the constitution of the subject" (2014, 89). What *Paris is Burning* highlights for Butler are the intersecting norms of class, race and sex that constitute subjectivity – it is important to note that she doesn't view any of these as coming before the others. Ultimately, Butler concludes that drag is only subversive "to the extent that it reflects on the imitative structure by which hegemonic gender is itself produced and disputes heterosexuality's claim on naturalness and originality" (2014, 85).

transsexualism, cross-dressing and non-white identity" (Dean 2000, 68). Since then, many have responded to and developed Butler's work (including Butler herself), continuing the project of deconstructing sex, gender and sexuality. Butler's ideas have had profound influence in the development of queer theory, and have been taken up by activists and academics alike. For instance, Butler's approach to gender has been adopted in legal studies, literary studies, media and cultural studies, sociology and political theory. Her notion of performativity has also been taken in many directions in film, video visual art and the performing arts. However, this project has not been without critique.

In *Second Skins: The Body Narratives of Transsexuality*, published in 1998, Jay Prosser discusses the impact of *Gender Trouble*, noting key misreadings of Butler's work, which have had profound impact on the understanding of transgender subjectivity. In the first instance, Prosser points out the assumption that gender performativity involves a subject who gets to perform gender at their will (1998, 28). Secondly, and perhaps more importantly, Prosser identifies that transgender subjectivity has been taken as inherently queer and subversive (1998, 29) (this issue is discussed in more detail in Chapter 6). As Prosser argues, "transgendered subjectivity is not inevitably queer" (1998, 31). Prosser argues that trans people do not necessarily "trouble", unfix or *queer* gender in the way that Butler suggests, and he argues that many people may desire to simply "be" rather than be enrolled in "doing". Finally, Prosser argues that Butler's work lacks relevance to trans lives because it cannot account for identity to be desired. Explaining this, he writes:

> One is not born a woman, but *nevertheless* may become one – given substantial medical intervention, personal tenacity, economic security, social support, and so on: becoming woman, in spite of not being born one, may be seen as a crucial goal. (1998, 33)

This notion of Butler's theory being incompatible with lived experience is taken up in many critiques of her work. In John Champagne's *The Ethics of Marginality: A New Approach to Gay Studies*, Butler's work is critiqued as insufficiently responsive to lived experience. Champagne's perspective is that Butler's early theorising was as part of a larger problem with poststructuralist theory conflating sexual politics with style (Champagne 1995). A similar argument is posed by Martha Nussbaum, who claims that Butler's theoretical approach "makes only the flimsiest of connections with the real situation of real women" (Nussbaum 1999). For Nussbaum, Butler's work is limited because it suggests that parody and subversion are the only possible modes of resistance, and that these must work within the pre-established boundaries of power.

Butler's later book, *Undoing Gender*, published in 2004, attempts to ground her work in dialogue with politics and lived experience as part of her shift towards an ethical theoretical framework. As she writes in her introduction to this book:

> [M]y own thinking has been influenced by the "New Gender Politics" that has emerged in recent years, a combination of movements concerned with transgender, transsexuality, intersex and their complex relations to feminist and queer theory. (2004b, 4)

In *Undoing Gender*, Butler asks what it means to "undo restrictively normative conceptions of sexual and gendered life" (2004b, 1) and she devotes time to critically reflect on the experiences of those marginalised groups, pushing at the edges of what is culturally recognised as human. In relation to trans people she questions "why violence against transgender subjects is not recognised as violence, and why this violence is sometimes inflicted by the very states that should be offering such subjects protection from such violence" (2004b, 30).

Trans theorist and activist Viviane Namaste puts forward an argument against Butler's approach in *Undoing Gender*. Namaste asserts that theorists, following Butler's lead, have long looked at trans bodies to ask questions about the formation of gender without thinking about the lived experience of trans people. In her essay "Undoing Theory: The 'transgender question' and the epistemic violence of Anglo-American feminist theory" Namaste questions "the extent to which transsexual women themselves have been served by such an academic feminist project" (2009, 12). In Butler's work, Namaste sees the exclusion of trans people, which she links to a broader history of marginalised people being excluded from academia and the production of knowledge.

Namaste also finds Butler's tight focus on issues of gender to be problematic because it excludes other frames of analysis. Namaste argues that Butler fails to consider questions of labour and capital in relation to trans bodies. For instance, while Butler shows how drag performances raise questions about how gender comes into formation, Namaste highlights how "they are also inextricably linked to matters of work" (Namaste 2009, 19). Hence, for Namaste, Butler's contributions to queer theory provide little insight into the lived-experience of trans people, and in fact, may be "complicit with broader social relations of capitalism" (Namaste 2009, 21).

As we have noted, transgender theorists such as Namaste and Prosser have critiqued Butler's work. These are not the only arguments against Butler, but they are evocative of broader tensions between queer theory and trans lived experience, which are taken up further in the following chapter where we consider queer approaches to identity politics.

In 2016, Butler was prompted to reflect upon the legacy of *Gender Trouble* in an interview with Sara Ahmed for the journal *Sexualities*. In this interview, Butler links her earlier writing to her more recent projects focusing on the vulnerability and liveability of LGBTIQ experience. She also muses over the changing nature of the term queer, which over time has been used in contradictory ways: queer has been engaged to reject the politics of identity, as an umbrella term to refer to many identities and as an identity in itself. In this interview, Butler raises questions that suggest her theoretical approach to gender and sexuality has been greatly informed by the responses to her work. For instance, she asks:

> If "queer" means that we are generally people whose gender and sexuality is "unfixed" then what room is there in a queer movement for those who understand themselves as requiring – and wanting – a clear gender category within a binary frame? Or what room is there for people who require a gender designation that is more or less unequivocal in order to function well and to be relieved of certain forms of social ostracism? (quoted in Ahmed 2016, 490)

To answer this, she suggests that we must re-think the questions that we pose within queer theory, shifting the conversation from identity to liveability – one key question Butler poses is "what kind of a life do I want to live with others?" (quoted in Ahmed 2016, 491). As we will see in the final chapters of this book, this shift in Butler's approach transports her from the emergent queer to queer theory's future, relating her project to contemporary debates around intersectionality and queer futurity. However, before we can move to queer theory's new directions, it is necessary to consider the field's other key influencer, Sedgwick.

WHAT'S SO QUEER ABOUT EVE KOSOFSKY SEDGWICK?

Sedgwick (2 May 1950 – 12 April 2009) was a feminist, literary critic, poet, artist and teacher. She grew up in Dayton, Ohio and Bethesda, Maryland and later studied at Cornell University. Like Butler, Sedgwick completed her PhD at Yale. Across her academic career, Sedgwick taught at many universities including Boston University, Amherst College, University of California, Berkeley, Dartmouth College, Duke University and City University of New York. However, it was her time at Duke University where she gained notoriety as a key voice in the emergent field of queer theory.

Sedgwick's writing reflects her training in feminist theory and literary criticism. While she is most famous for her book *Epistemology of the Closet*, first published in 1990, she produced many influential books and essays over the course of her life. As we will see, what Sedgwick brought to queer theory was a methodology for deconstruction that enabled a deep interrogation of sexuality, gender, bodies and pleasure in and across Western culture. As she describes in an interview with *The New York Times* in 1998, "It's about trying to understand different kinds of sexual desire and how the culture defines them" (quoted in Smith 1998).

Sedgwick's first book, *Between Men: English Literature and Male Homosocial Desire*, published in 1985, laid out her initial thoughts on this and her methodology for deconstruction. In her preface to the 1992 edition of this book, she describes herself as a "deconstructive and very writerly close reader" (vii). Reading literary texts including works by Charles Dickens, George Eliot, William Shakespeare, Alfred Tennyson and others, Sedgwick uncovers traces of desire between male characters. She pays particular attention to "erotic triangles" (1992, 20) through which the plot is driven by a volatile relationship between men who both vie for the affection of a woman. Through this, she highlights how desire informs relations between men and how this desire is transmitted through women. The purpose of this is to interrogate the relationship between power and sexuality, carefully teasing out the limits of a cultural system wherein desire between men emerges only under the pretence of heterosexuality.

In *Epistemology of the Closet*, Sedgwick uses this methodology to highlight how "the closet" functions as a structuring metaphor in Western culture. In this work she traces correlations between "the closet" and structures of knowledge, drawing heavily on the works of Herman Melville, Henry James, Friedrich Nietzsche, Marcel Proust and Oscar Wilde. While *Epistemology of the Closet* is credited as a pioneering text in queer theory, Sedgwick did not explicitly engage with the term "queer" until her 1993 book *Tendencies*. In this book, which collected a series of her essays including "Jane Austen and the Masturbating Girl" and "How to Bring Your Kids Up Gay", she famously defined queer as "the open mesh of possibilities, gaps, overlaps, dissonances and resonances, lapses and excesses of meaning when the constituent elements of anyone's gender, of anyone's sexuality aren't made (or can't be made) to signify monolithically" (1993, 8). *Tendencies* was the first volume of the influential Duke University Press *Series Q*, which brought together gender, sexuality and cultural studies to interrogate intersections of sex, gender, sexuality class, race, nationality and culture – the series concluded upon Sedgwick's death in 2009.

Touching Feeling: Affect, Pedagogy, Performativity, published in 2003, was the last of Sedgwick's books to be published in her lifetime. In this work she reflects upon the emergence of queer theory, paying particular attention to the affective conditions of the era. As we will discuss in this chapter, Sedgwick's later work lays out "tools and techniques for nondualistic thought" (2003, 1) through which she seeks to interrogate emotion in many forms. Sedgwick was diagnosed with breast cancer in 1991 and her work from the late 1990s onwards – particularly her poetry, prose and literary criticism – muses on her experiences and feelings stemming from this.

As we explore through the latter parts of this chapter, Sedgwick developed an approach to the study of sexuality, bodies, feeling and power, which has proven useful to many critics, scholars and artists. Across her work, Sedgwick demonstrates that any analysis of the relation between sexual desire and political power must move along two axes. The first "needs to make use of whatever forms of analysis are most potent for describing historically variable power asymmetries" (1992, 7). By this she means gender, race, class or nationality. The second axis is that of representation, as she argues that this is the

Notable works: Sedgwick

- *Between Men: English Literature and Male Homosocial Desire* (1985)
- *Epistemology of the Closet* (1990)
- *Tendencies* (1993)
- *Fat Art, Thin Art* (1995)
- *Performativity and Performance* (1995, coedited with Andrew Parker)
- *Shame & Its Sisters: A Silvan Tomkins Reader* (1995, coedited with Adam Frank)
- *Gary in Your Pocket: Stories and Notebooks of Gary Fisher* (1996, coedited with Gary Fisher)
- *Novel Gazing: Queer Readings in Fiction* (1997, coedited with Jacob Press)
- *A Dialogue on Love* (2000)
- *Touching Feeling: Affect, Pedagogy, Performativity* (2003)
- *The Weather in Proust* (2011)

only way to get insight into the "range of ways in which sexuality functions as a signifier for power relations" (1992, 7). With this in mind, we can move on to exploring Sedgwick's key contributions to queer theory as it developed through the 1990s.

Sedgwick's Axioms

In *Epistemology of the Closet*, Sedgwick lays out seven axioms (see Table 5.1). These are statements that underscore her work and serve as queer starting points for her later arguments, so it is worth exploring them in some detail. The first is simple but far-reaching: "people are different from each other" (2008, 22). Sedgwick argues that critical and political thought is limited by its use of only a small number of axes for distinguishing and understanding people. These are typically gender, race, class, nationality and "sexual orientation". The latter axis is Sedgwick's key site for analysis, and she argues that there is a problem with viewing sexuality as an "orientation" towards people of a particular gender – in the case of heterosexuality, homosexuality and bisexuality. Sedgwick highlights that sexuality extends along many dimensions that cannot be described in this limited way. She notes that certain things could differentiate people who may seem to have identical configurations of class,

Table 5.1   Sedgwick's Axioms and some examples illustrating her claims

Sedgwick's Axiom	Practical example
1. "People are different from each other" (2008, 22)	While many people experience sexual attraction towards others, some people never do and describe themselves as asexual.
2. "The study of sexuality is not coextensive with the study of gender; correspondingly, antihomophobic inquiry is not coextensive with feminist inquiry. But we can't know in advance how they will be different" (2008, 27)	Having sex in public versus in a private setting is primarily about sexual acts, not gender per se. However, in addition to attending to questions of sexual space/desire/acts/etc., we may wish to bring in other lenses around gender, race, class and so on for analysis.
3. "There can't be an a priori decision about how far it will make sense to conceptualize lesbian and gay male identities together. Or separately" (2008, 36)	Homophobic discourse in popular media/politics/culture might implicate both lesbians and gay men (and others), creating a shared interest.
4. "The immemorial, seemingly ritualized debates on nature versus nurture take place against a very unstable background of tacit assumptions and fantasies about both nurture and nature" (2008, 40)	The idea of the "gay gene" ("nature") ignores the regime of compulsory heterosexuality that pervades everyday life. However, understanding sexuality from a purely constructivist ("nurture") lens does not eliminate cultural bias against homosexuality.
5. "The historical search for a Great Paradigm Shift may obscure the present conditions of sexual identity" (2008, 44)	Even though we might have a huge range of words for sexual identifications today, terms and identifiers will continue to change and complexify. We shouldn't presume that we fully "know" sexuality in the present.
6. "The relation of gay studies to debates on the literary canon is, and had best be, torturous" (2008, 48)	We can work under the assumption that minority canons relevant to lesbian and gay studies can be found in any context.
7. "The paths of allo-identification are likely to be strange and recalcitrant. So are the paths of auto-identification" (2008, 59)	While we may presume that homosexuality simply means desire for "same-sex" coupling, it may be bound up with much more complicated schemas of identification "with" and "as".

race, gender and sexual orientations. For instance, she suggests, "Even identical genital acts mean very different things to different people" (2008, 25). According to Sedgwick, we could disrupt dominant ways of thinking about sexuality by taking some of these differences seriously. In doing so, we could also consider many more dimensions of identity *and* reveal different forms of oppression and subordination.

Sedgwick's second axiom builds on this and relates to the conflation of gender and sexuality within critical inquiry. She asserts that we can't study gender and sexuality through the same lens because "in twentieth-century Western culture gender and sexuality represent two [distinct] analytic axes" (2008, 30). While Sedgwick acknowledges that gender is definitionally built into sexuality in that "without a concept of gender there could be … no concept of homo – or heterosexuality" (2008, 31), she highlights that there are many other dimensions of sexuality that have no connection to gender (such as when an individual's sexual desire is *regardless* of gender, or where preference is based on something other than gender). Taking a Foucauldian approach, she notes that the reduction of sexuality to a hetero/homo binary is the result of medical, legal and psychological discourse that emerged in the nineteenth century.

Sedgwick's third and fourth axioms relate to the conceptualisation of lesbian and gay identities. In the former, she argues that we cannot make assumptions

---

Queer theory in practice: *How to Bring Your Kids Up Gay*

In 1991 Sedgwick published an essay, "How to Bring Your Kids Up Gay". In this piece, Sedgwick further disentangles sexuality and gender, highlighting how these categories have been represented in co-dependent binaries in studies of sexuality. She argues that early studies of sexuality development rely on the assumption "that anyone, male or female, who desires a man must by definition be feminine" (1991, 20), and vice versa for those who desire women.

This assumption has had a profound impact on psychological and psychoanalytic debates on youth sexuality, which Sedgwick notes have tended to promote a cultural acceptance of homosexuality only when it is founded upon gender conformity (such as males not being *too effeminate*). This has meant that those who do not conform to traditional gender roles have been typically marginalised and pathologised.

about the relevance or irrelevance of one identity to the other. In the latter, she argues that we need to re-think the commonly recited essentialist versus constructivist debates on sexuality and identity. She argues that these debates "take place against a very unstable background of tacit assumptions and fantasies about nurture and nature" (2008, 40). Sedgwick draws attention to a deadlock between the essentialist and constructivist positions on identity, clouding every conceptual tool we have for analysing it. Furthermore, both accounts of sexuality can be skewed towards arguments for the elimination of homosexuality, which she encourages us to resist. She puts forward an alternative, which she describes as a universalising versus minoritising approach and she explains them in relation to the question of sexuality (see Table 5.2).

In her fifth axiom, Sedgwick critiques what she calls "the historical search for a Great Paradigm Shift" (2008, 44). She argues that those who seek to uncover a "transhistorical" essence of homosexuality or provide a genealogical account of homosexuality's origin, problematically juxtapose notions of "the past" with a unified image of contemporary gay experience. She writes that "in counterposing ... the alterity of the past [against] a relatively unified homosexuality that 'we' do 'know today'" these accounts "underwrite the notion that 'homosexuality as we conceive of it today' itself comprises a coherent definitional field rather than a space of overlapping, contradictory, and conflictual definitional forces" (2008, 45). Hence, for Sedgwick, a more productive, and indeed queerer approach to historical projects, involves a deep analysis of the "relations enabled by the unrationalized coexistence of different models [of sexuality] during the times that they do coexist" (2008, 47).

Table 5.2   Sedgwick's universalising vs. minoritising models

Universalising model	*Minoritising model*
This model views sexuality through a universalising lens. It suggests that sexuality is fluid, and that all people are capable of experiencing a range of sexual desires.	This model views sexuality through a minoritising lens. It suggests that sexuality is reasonably fixed, and that only a minority of people experience non-heterosexual desire.
Sedgwick's question: "In whose lives is homo/heterosexual definition an issue of continuing centrality and difficulty?" (2008, 40)	
Universalising answer: Questions of sexuality are relevant to everyone, across a spectrum of sexualities.	**Minoritising answer:** Questions of sexuality are only relevant to a select few, those in the homosexual minority.

Sedgwick's final two axioms relate to the literary canon and to issues of identification in literary theory, feminist theory and activism. In the first instance, she argues that "the relation of gay studies to debates on the literary canon is, and had best be, torturous" (2008, 48) and she reflects upon the power structures at play in the process of canonisation (and re-canonisation). Through this she suggests that the literary canon is a space of white, heterosexual privilege and that the establishment of mini-canons could create opportunities for greater acceptance of LGBTIQ literature. In the second instance, she notes, "the paths of allo-identification are likely to be strange and recalcitrant. So are the paths of auto-identification" (2008, 59) and she reflects on the difference between *"identifying with"* and *"identifying as"* (2008, 59–63, emphasis in original). These final axioms seek to justify her analyses of particular texts (which is always to the exclusion of others) and her critico-theoretical positioning as a seemingly heterosexual woman – we should note she was married to a man but rejected rigid identity categories in favour of a fluid/queer conception of identity – writing about homosocial and homosexual relations between men.

Sedgwick and "the closet"

In *Epistemology of the Closet*, Sedgwick demonstrates how the metaphor of the closet functions in Western culture. The term epistemology refers to the theory of knowledge, so this means her project interrogates the intersection between knowledge and sexuality. Coming "out of the closet" is never simple and it is never something that LGBTIQ people have to do just once. As Sedgwick notes, "the deadly elasticity of heterosexist presumption" means that new closets constantly appear as LGBTIQ people come out of them (2008, 68). Coming out is something that LGBTIQ people must do with every new person they meet:

> [E]very encounter with a new classfull of students, to say nothing of a new boss, social worker, loan officer, landlord, doctor, erects new closets whose fraught and characteristic laws of optics and physics exact from at least gay people new surveys, new calculations, new draughts and requisitions of secrecy or disclosure. Even an out gay person deals daily with interlocutors about whom she doesn't know whether they know or not. (2008, 68)

As we will discuss, Sedgwick does not see the closet operating only in relation to the lives of LGBTIQ people, but she does acknowledge its central place in LGBTIQ experience. She argues, "the closet is the defining structure for gay oppression in this century" (2008, 71), writing that for many gay people, the closet is:

> [S]till the fundamental feature of social life; and there can be few gay people, however courageous and forthright by habit, however fortunate in the support of their immediate communities, in whose lives the closet is not still a shaping presence. (2008, 68)

Sedgwick argues that the closet (and sexuality more generally) has occupied a privileged relation to "identity, truth, and knowledge" in twentieth-century Western culture (2008, 3). She reads the closet through the notion of performativity, which, as we have noted in our discussion of Butler, refers to acts of speech that perform an action. She argues that the closet is performative in that it is part of a "language of sexuality" that "not only intersects with but transforms the other languages and relations by which we know" (2008, 3). However, Sedgwick notes that the closet also problematises what counts as speech and language. This is because being in the closet involves the specific act of not disclosing or speaking about one's sexuality or gender identity. For Sedgwick, this silence is "rendered as pointed and performative as speech ... [which] highlights more broadly the fact that ignorance is as potent and as multiple a thing ... as knowledge" (2008, 4). As she notes, like knowledge, ignorance can be harnessed, licensed and regulated. Here Sedgwick illuminates not only how sexuality is made visible through the closet, but also how it is implicated in structures of oppression. Hence, she argues that the "centrality of homophobic oppression in the twentieth century ... has resulted from its inextricability from the question of knowledge and the process of knowing in modern Western culture at large" (2008, 33–34).

Taking a universalising approach, Sedgwick argues that "many of the major modes of thought and knowledge in twentieth-century Western culture as a whole are structured – indeed fractured" by these relations (2008, 1). She traces this back to what she describes as "a chronic, now endemic crisis of homo/heterosexual definition ... dating from the end of the nineteenth century" (2008, 1). Drawing on Foucault's *History of Sexuality*, which we discussed in Chapter 2, Sedgwick highlights how this was the point where binary ideas of sexual identity came into use in medical, legal and psychological discourse. From this point, she notes that knowledge and sexuality became "conceptually inseparable from one another" (2008, 73) and the concealment of identity (the closet) began to proliferate in cultural texts.

With this in mind, Sedgwick argues that within Western culture, the binary between heterosexuality and homosexuality has been a "presiding master term of the past century, one that has the same, primary importance for all modern Western identity and social organization (and not merely for homosexual identity and culture)" (2008, 11). She argues that the power dynamics and knowledge structures of the closet are not only relevant to LGBTIQ people, but that this metaphor has come to structure many other binaries beyond those implicated directly by its doors. As examples she notes:

> secrecy/disclosure, knowledge/ignorance, private/public, masculine/feminine, majority/minority, innocence/initiation, natural/artificial, new/old, discipline/terrorism, canonic/noncanonic, wholeness/decadence, urbane/provincial, domestic/foreign, health/illness, same/different, active/passive, in/out, cognition/paranoia, art/kitsch, utopia/apocalypse, sincerity/sentimentality, and voluntarity/addiction. (2008, 11)

What Sedgwick suggests here is that the closet not only marks what we know about sexuality, it has been subsumed into our very structures of thought. Hence, her key intervention in *Epistemology of the Closet* is to deconstruct these binaries by revealing the mechanisms through which they work. Sedgwick demonstrates that many of these categories, which are typically presented as symmetrical binaries, are actually part of an "unsettled and dynamic tacit relation" and she describes this as a process:

> [F]irst, term B is not symmetrical but subordinated to term A; but, second, the ontologically valorised term A actually depends for its meaning on the simultaneous subsumption and exclusion of term B; hence, third, the question of priority between the supposed central and the supposed marginal category of each dyad is irresolvably unstable, an instability caused by the fact that term B is constituted as at once internal and external to term A. (2008, 9–10)

Thinking about this in relation to the heterosexual/homosexual binary is revealing. Following Sedgwick's logic, heterosexuality and homosexuality are presented as a symmetrical binary in and through culture. In this binary, homosexuality (term B) is subordinated to heterosexuality (term A), but heterosexuality only gains meaning in relation to homosexuality – via what Sedgwick terms a "simultaneous subsumption and exclusion" of the latter term (2008, 9–10). This means that heterosexuality can only exist in relation to a previously defined homosexuality. Sedgwick suggests that we cannot assume anything about the cultural centrality and/or marginality of these categories nor anything about the power relations between them, because the binary is "irresolvably unstable" (2008, 9–10).

Queer readings: paranoid and reparative strategies

In *Between Men* and *Epistemology of the Closet*, Sedgwick pioneered the usage of a set of conceptual tools for deconstructing assumptions about sex, gender, sexuality and desire, and thereby demonstrating the pervasive mechanisms of oppression and homophobia. These tools were part of an intellectual tradition of "inveterate, gorgeous generativity", "speculative generosity", "daring", "permeability" and "activism" which Sedgwick describes as queer reading (1992, x).

In the introduction to her third book, *Tendencies*, Sedgwick explains what she means by this. She begins by describing the childhood experience of forming intent attachments to "a few cultural objects" (1993, 3). She notes that these might be from high culture or popular culture or both, but they are significant for us as children because their meaning seems "mysterious, excessive, or oblique in relation to the codes most readily available to us" (1993, 3). As a result, they are important to us because they provide "a prime resource for survival" in the world of adults (1993, 3). Taking this childhood experience into adulthood and explicitly enmeshing it with sexuality, desire and queer politics, she writes:

> I think many adults (and I am among them) are trying, in our work, to keep faith with vividly remembered promises made to ourselves in childhood: promises to make invisible possibilities and desires visible; to make the tacit things explicit; to smuggle queer representation in where it must be smuggled and, with the relative freedom of adulthood, to challenge the queer-eradicating impulses frontally where they are to be so challenged. (1993, 3)

What Sedgwick means by queer reading is this process of challenging the dominance of heterosexual representation by making hidden desires visible, making inferred relations overt, and smuggling queerness into texts that were previously thought to deny it. As we have noted, this is what Sedgwick's earlier works achieved in their analysis of homosocial desire and the closet. Sedgwick describes queer reading in relation to her own writing as:

> [A] kind of formalism, a visceral near-identification with the writing I cared for, at the level of sentence structure, metrical pattern, rhyme, was one way of trying to appropriate what seemed the numinous and resistant power of the chosen objects. (1993, 3)

Ultimately, Sedgwick's approach to queer reading positions the strategy as a means of survival for LGBTIQ people who are confronted with exclusion, marginalisation, homophobia, shame and violence on a regular basis. However, in her later work, Sedgwick argued that her conceptual tools for queer reading were informed by a "paranoia" that sometimes undermined the power of her critique.

In her essay "Paranoid Reading and Reparative Reading or, You're So Paranoid, You Probably Think This Essay is About You", published roughly a decade after *Tendencies*, she revised her methodology and delineated two distinct reading strategies. On one hand Sedgwick describes paranoid readings, which she argues had become the dominant form of analysis within queer theory, feminist analysis and poststructuralism more generally. Paranoid readings come from Paul Ricoeur's concept of the "hermeneutics of suspicion" – a phrase used to describe the position of thinkers such as Marx, Nietzsche, Freud and others who have followed in their intellectual traditions. Sedgwick highlights an intimacy between queer theory and paranoia, tracing the idea to Freud who argued that it was linked to the repression of same-sex desire and, following this, to 1970s French theorist and activist Guy Hocquenghem who suggested paranoia revealed the mechanisms of homophobia and heterosexism. By the mid-1980s, Sedgwick argues that paranoia had found a central place within feminist and anti-homophobic theory, eventually becoming a methodology on its own. By the early 2000s, Sedgwick argues that paranoid analysis had come to be the only form of theory, rather than simply one strategy or form of theoretical practice among others.

Queer theory in practice: Queer methods

Given the slippery nature of queer theory, with its focus on deconstruction and destabilisation, how can we "use" queer theory in our research? We discuss different and diverse applications of queer theory in more detail in Chapter 7. However, briefly, we might define queer methods as anything that involves a deconstructive/destabilising bent. As McCann suggests, "[Q]ueer *methodology* is about troubling the subject, employing a queer reading approach, and drawing from multiple perspectives and traditions, all in order to challenge 'dominant logics'" (2016, 236).

Along these lines, Halberstam (1998) proposes "scavenger methodology" as a queer approach to methods, that involves drawing on a range of fields and cultural paraphernalia, such as popular culture, cultural events and other archives and fragments. This approach connects to the queer archival method discussed in Chapter 8. Halberstam suggests that a queer approach means resisting strict disciplinary coherence.

As Plummer (2011) also outlines, ethnography and performance have become key queer methods, often involving insider accounts and/or work that is deeply situated within queer cultures in specific contexts.

As discussed in this chapter, "queer reading" following Sedgwick is one key way to approach the question of queer "method" in queer theory. This involves using reading strategies to see the (otherwise heteronormative) world differently. Alexander Doty (2000) deploys this approach to re-read film classics such as *The Wizard of Oz* in queer ways, understanding characters in these films in terms of camp (exaggeration, artifice, queerness). Queer reading involves over-emphasising subtext, and over-investing in queer elements of the storyline over and above the dominant reading that might otherwise emerge. However, caution is needed: as Martin Ponce (2018) argues, historically gay and lesbian reading practices have often reinforced a white Western literary canon of homoeroticism, only reading and reinforcing particular texts as part of queer tradition.

For Sedgwick, paranoid readings always anticipate their own outcomes, they are rigid and reject "the possibility of alternative ways of understanding or things to understand" (2003, 131), they place an emphasis on exposure and they are imbued with strong negative affect. Sedgwick locates paranoia in studies such as Butler's *Gender Trouble*, drawing attention to Butler's unwavering insistence that there is no subjectivity prior to gender and her repeated usage of terminology such as "reveal". Sedgwick argues these are markers of a paranoid reading of gender formation.

In theorising paranoid reading, Sedgwick reflects on the work of Melanie Klein who views the paranoid as a *position* that is always "in the oscillatory context of a very different possible one" (2003, 128). For Sedgwick that other possible position is reparative reading. In contrast to paranoid reading, a reparative approach is open to possibility and surprise, to alternate outcomes, ways of understanding and things to understand. Sedgwick writes:

> [T]o read from a reparative position is to surrender the knowing, anxious paranoid determination that no horror, however apparently unthinkable, shall ever come to the reader as new; to a reparatively positioned reader, it can seem realistic and necessary to experience surprise. Because there can be terrible surprises, however, there can also be good ones. Hope, often a fracturing, even a traumatic thing to experience, is among the energies by which the reparatively positioned reader tries to organize the fragments and part-objects she encounters or creates. Because the reader has room to realize that the future may be different from the present, it is also possible for her to entertain such profoundly painful, profoundly relieving, ethically crucial possibilities as that the past, in turn, could have happened differently from the way it actually did. (2003, 146)

It is important to note that the paranoid and the reparative are not conceptualised as ideologies, but rather methodological approaches or as strategies for reading and knowing. As we will discuss in later chapters, Sedgwick's reparative approach has had profound influence on the way that contemporary queer theorists think about temporality and the future (issues discussed in more detail in Chapter 8).

Responses, critiques and lasting influence

As we noted in our discussion of Butler, early queer theory was critiqued for its lack of relevance to LGBTIQ lives. In relation to Sedgwick's early writing, we have noted that she did not respond to the immediate politics of Gay Liberation and activist discourse in the USA. Instead, Sedgwick's early writing takes up traditions of European thought and literature. Though her methodology was explained through her works, some critics found their lack of connection to the lived experience of gay men to be problematic.

Nevertheless, Sedgwick's contributions to queer theory have had immense influence. Following Sedgwick, a number of scholars have taken up the closet as a key site for analysis. Many of these have thought about the closet in relation to coming out and the politics of identity, which is our focus in the following chapter. For instance, in the introduction to the edited collection

Inside/Out: Lesbian Theories, Gay Theories, Fuss argues that the hetero/ homo binary is intimately connected with the in/out binary of the closet. Fuss raises the closet as a space where both of these binaries are contested. For instance, she argues that sometimes "to be out is really to be in – inside the realm of the visible, the speakable, the culturally intelligible" but other times it is to be marked as an outsider (1991, 4). Fuss suggests that placing emphasis on coming out of the closet risks further affirming the structures of heteronormativity, because it implicitly suggests heterosexuality to be the norm.

Butler's essay "Imitation and Gender Insubordination", which was first published in *Inside/Out*, also tackles the idea of the closet in relation to identity politics. She argues that the coming out and claiming an LGBTIQ identity actually creates and maintains the closet. She writes:

> Conventionally, one comes out of the closet (and yet, how often is it the case that we are "outed" when we are young and without resources?); so we are out of the closet, but into what? What new unbounded spatiality? The room, the den, the attic, the basement, the house, the bar, the university, some new enclosure whose door, like Kafka's door, produces the expectation of a fresh air and a light of illumination that never arrives? Curiously, it is the figure of the closet that produces this expectation, and which guarantees its dissatisfaction. For being "out" always depends to some extent on being "in"; it gains its meaning only within that polarity. Hence, being "out" must produce the closet again and again in order to maintain itself as "out". (Butler 2004a, 122–123)

Similarly, in the introduction of *Fear of a Queer Planet*, Michael Warner links the closet, coming out and identity politics when he builds on Sedgwick's ideas to incorporate social politics into queer theory. Beyond her contribution to closet discourse, Sedgwick's discussion of queer reading practice and ideas of paranoid versus reparative reading have been central to many queer theory texts, including the writings of Halberstam whom we discuss in later chapters.

In her later career, Sedgwick turned towards analysis of affect and emotion, prompted by her feelings around her cancer, death, homophobia and the AIDS crisis. Her ideas have since been taken up by queer affect theory and her intellectual lineage runs through works of Lauren Berlant (*Cruel Optimism*), Sara Ahmed (*The Promise of Happiness*), Ann Cvetkovich (*An Archive of Feelings and Depression*) and Heather Love (*Feeling Backwards*). Sedgwick also influenced contemporary queer theory through her teaching. During her time at Duke

University, she fostered many queer theory graduate students including José Esteban Muñoz, a scholar whose work we examine when we encounter queer utopias in Chapter 8.

CONCLUSION: QUEERING CRITICAL INQUIRY

Though their work developed along slightly different trajectories (only intersecting in a few terse essays), Butler and Sedgwick laid the foundation for a queer approach to critical inquiry. Both scholars took queer as a means of destabilising, unsettling, revealing, subverting, opening and questioning established norms around categories of sex, gender, sexuality and identity. They sought to reveal the mechanisms through which these categories are naturalised in Western culture. Butler offered a way to deconstruct the relationship between sex and gender, demonstrating how both are produced as effects of the heterosexual matrix. Sedgwick, on the other hand, focused largely on the relationship between gender and sexuality. Her work demonstrates that sexuality is comprised of many characteristics (not just gender of one's "orientation"), challenging the notion that sexual identity is supposed to organise into a seamless unitary category. Both scholars placed significant attention on interrogating the precarity and contingency of the relationships between these categories.

It is important to re-visit the works of these influential scholars as they offer insight into the early development of queer theory as paradigm that resists normalising forces of discourse, identity and the closet. In her introduction to *Tendencies*, Sedgwick considers the power of queer, writing:

[A] lot of the most exciting recent work around "queer" spins the term outward along dimensions that can't be subsumed under gender and sexuality at all: the ways that race, ethnicity, postcolonial nationality criss-cross with these *and other* identity-constituting, identity fracturing discourses, for example. Intellectuals and artists of color whose sexual self-definition includes "queer" – I think of an Isaac Julien, a Gloria Anzaldúa, a Richard Fung – are using the leverage of "queer" to do a new kind of justice to the fractal intricacies of language, skin, migration, state. Thereby, the gravity (I mean the *gravitas*, the meaning, but also the center of gravity) of the term "queer" itself deepens and shifts. (1993, 8)

Though Sedgwick wrote this in 1993, her description of queer's shifting centre of gravity remains a powerful image. This notion of a queer theory that spins outward, intersecting and challenging other discourses is a vital foundation for understanding how queer theory is being developed in current debates and it is a notion that we take up in the following chapters.

Further reading

Judith Butler. (1999). *Gender Trouble: Feminism and the Subversion of Identity*. London: Routledge.

This important book, first published in 1990, introduces Butler's theories on gender formation including gender melancholia and gender performativity. This edition includes a useful preface written by Butler that may help readers to navigate the text.

Teresa de Lauretis. (1991). "Queer Theory: Lesbian and Gay Sexualities. An Introduction". *Differences: A Journal of Feminist Cultural Studies*, 3(2): iii–xviii.

In this essay Teresa de Lauretis coins the term "queer theory", which makes this a useful text for reflecting on the development of the field through the early 1990s.

Eve Kosofsky Sedgwick. (2008). "Introduction: Axiomatic." *Epistemology of the Closet: Updated with a New Preface*. Berkeley and Los Angeles: University of California Press, 67–90.

Sedgwick's introduction to *Epistemology of the Closet* lays out her views on sexuality via the seven axioms which inform her later work.

QUESTIONS TO CONSIDER

- What is *queer* about Butler and Sedgwick's approaches to sex, gender, sexuality and identity?
- Does Butler's notion of gender performativity have relevance for trans and non-binary experiences?
- What problems does Sedgwick's approach to sexuality raise for contemporary understandings of identity politics and LGBTIQ activism?
- In what ways does the closet continue to hold a central space within LGBTIQ culture? How is it represented culturally and how is it implicated in broader structures of contemporary thought?

Recommended films

Orlando (**Sally Potter 1992**). The instability of gender is played literally in this film in which Tilda Swinton portrays a young nobleman named Orlando who is commanded to stay forever young by Queen Elizabeth. Orlando experiences several centuries as a man before one day waking up a woman.

Paris is Burning (**Jennie Livingston 1990**). Documentary exploring New York City's underground drag ball culture wherein participants contest a range of categories in which they perform social norms. This film has a significant place in Butler's writing on drag.

6 Theory Meets Identity

KEY TERMS AND CONCEPTS	identity politics, neoliberalism, strategic essentialism, cultural capital, homonormativity, homonationalism, sexual citizenship, cisgender, transgender studies, transnormativity, phenomenology, non-binary identity, assemblage

QUEER THEORY VERSUS IDENTITY

This chapter examines the tensions between identity politics and queer theory following shifts in thinking about "queer" in both activist (Chapter 4) and academic (Chapter 5) contexts during the 1990s. Here we consider the relationship between queer *identity* and queer *theory* in more depth. Should the aim of our activist and academic work be the acceptance of LGBTIQ identities in society, or should mainstreaming be seen as an unwelcome form of assimilation? Is acceptance antithetical to a queer theory approach? How does the supposed radical openness of queer theory sit with the lived realities of sexuality and gender?

In this chapter we turn attention towards key debates around "homonormativity", and the neoliberal queer subject, as discussed by many queer theorists. Though this chapter considers the enduring relevance of queer theory critiques of identity politics, it complicates any notion of abandoning identity. Rather, here we examine how we can understand lived experiences of queer identity in different ways. Most significantly, this chapter gives time to considering how and why queer theory does not necessarily centre around sexuality, but rather, is also intimately related to questions around experiences and embodiments of gender.

Many queer theorists describe identity politics – in its broad sense, as politics organised around discrete identity formations – as antithetical to the deconstructive aims of queer theory. Some have argued that the intention of the term "queer" was always to remain radically open, not to describe a specific sexual group or orientation. For example, as Moya Lloyd describes: "as a non-identity politics, 'queer' must not become inscribed as '*the* sexual

Key term: Identity politics

Queer theorists frequently engage with and critique "identity politics", though the term is deployed in multiple ways by different theorists. Broadly speaking, the term refers to political activities that are organised around identities, where identity categories are treated as discrete and definable (Riggs 2010, 345). Ronald L. Jackson and Michael A. Hogg offer the following definition: "Identity politics is the political activity and theories rooted in social justice for marginalized, oppressed, or disadvantaged social groups" (2010, 368).

minority' ... thereby alienating and excluding those sexual minorities that do not fit in" (Lloyd 2005, 160 emphasis in original). As discussed in Chapter 4, the advent of the AIDS crisis highlighted the need to focus less on sexual *identity*, and more on sexual *practices*. This was the impetus for using queer as a term that challenged discrete sexual identity categories such as gay and lesbian. As many suggested during the early 1990s, even talking about "identity" does not necessitate talking about distinct categories. Rather, identity can be understood as fluid and dynamic (Anzaldúa 1991).

This new "non-identity politics" approach that emerged in the 1980s and 1990s sat in stark contrast with the earlier Gay Liberation movement (discussed in Chapter 2). While LGBTIQ people and people affected by HIV/ AIDS were activists, the focus of solidarity was not sexual identity in the same way as it had been during the Gay Liberation movement of the 1960s and 1970s. In contrast, in earlier movements identity was the basis upon which people organised. The social movements of the earlier period are considered by many to be illustrative of "identity-based liberation movements" where identity conferred a special understanding of oppression as the basis for fighting back; for example, women led the charge for women's rights (Alcoff and Mohanty 2006, 1–2).

Others have challenged the idea that *all* forms of these earlier movements should be considered "identity politics". For example, Nancy Fraser argues that identity politics is a specific political formation connected with the neo-liberal political and economic shift towards individualism. Fraser suggests that groups such as the women's liberation movement only shifted towards identity politics after the 1970s, when a new focus "recognition" emerged under neoliberal economic regimes (2005, 296). While the aim of coalitions

---

Key term: Neoliberalism

Neoliberalism is a contested term that is sometimes used as a synonym for individualism without reflecting on the historical, economic roots of the term. Neoliberalism is best defined as a political ideology that took hold in the 1980s that has both economic and social dimensions.

- **Economically**, neoliberalism refers to free market and free trade ideology, is pro-privatisation and pro-corporate, and advocates for small government and big business.
- **Socially**, neoliberalism is associated with individualism, depoliticised advocacy and support for ideals of privacy and individual liberty.

We might say that on a cultural level, neoliberalism represents a move against the feminist slogan of the 1970s "the personal is political", towards "the personal is privatised". In terms of activism, neoliberal ideology has encouraged a turn away from structural accounts of oppression, towards individual and depoliticised accounts. As Duggan describes, neoliberalism severely impacted LGBTIQ organising by entrenching homonormative politics (2002).

---

such as Queer Nation (as discussed in Chapter 4) was to challenge normative constructions of sexual identity, such "anti-identity" formations might nevertheless constitute their own form of identity politics. As outlined in Chapter 4, Cohen argued that the language of "queer" politics at the time merely served to entrench a hetero/homo binary (1997, 438). As Fraser also writes,

> Despite its professed long-term deconstructive goal, queer theory's practical effects may be more ambiguous. Like gay-identity politics, it too seems likely to promote group solidarity in the here and now, even as it sets its sights on the promised land of deconstruction ... The queer-theory recognition strategy thus contains an internal tension: in order eventually to destabilize the homo–hetero dichotomy, it must first mobilize "queers". (1995, 83)

Whether we agree with Fraser here or not, what is common to definitions of "identity politics" is the suggestion that: (a) it is organised around identity; and (b) involves striving for some form of justice in relation to that identity.

Key term: Strategic essentialism

Strategic essentialism is a concept proposed by postcolonial theorist Gayatri Chakravorty Spivak in the 1980s, in the context of "Subaltern Studies". Here the subaltern refers to the marginalised/non-elite, specifically within the context of colonialism. Spivak argued that strategic essentialism around discrete (subaltern) identity terms might sometimes be necessary to collectivise for political ends. She described this as "*strategic* use of positivist essentialism in a scrupulously visible political interest" (1996, 214, emphasis in original). Yet she also argued that strategic essentialism should always be adopted with the deconstruction of categories at the forefront of analysis.

Spivak became critical of how her concept was sometimes deployed by activists, as strategic essentialism became a go-to concept for ignoring heterogeneity in the face of demands for homogeneity/single-axis prioritising (Danius, Jonsson and Spivak 1993, 35). As Raksha Pande argues,

> In its wide-ranging adoption, strategic essentialism has lost its deconstructive strain and at its best has become a reference for coming to terms with the inevitability of essentialism in feminist and postcolonial discourses. (2017, 5)

Strategic essentialism is often misread as permitting calls for "unity" (without deconstruction), in order to achieve political goals, which was not Spivak's original aim.

However, as Spivak (1996) argues, "strategic essentialism" around identity might sometimes be necessary in order to make political claims. Sherry Wolf also points out that the danger of queer theory critiques of identity politics is they can veer towards seeing *all* forms of group solidarity as problematic. Instead, we might look to understand what holds particular groups of people together, such as shared experiences of oppression. She writes:

> While identity politics tends to strengthen the divisions between oppressed groups, queer theory unwittingly lends itself to disavowing the validity of oppression entirely by denying the common points of identity between members of subjugated groups. (2009, 195)

Following Wolf, this suggests that we should approach queer theory critiques of identity politics with caution if we are to remain doing justice to questions of oppression. As some such as Seidman have argued, the aim of queer theory is not to eliminate claims to identification altogether but to open the Pandora's box that is the question of sexuality in the first instance: "[T]he aim is not to abandon identity as a category of knowledge and politics but to render it permanently open and contestable as to its meaning and political role" (1996, 12). As we will continue to explore, the difficult question of negotiating identity within queer theory is an ongoing area of discussion and debate.

THE NEW HOMONORMATIVITY

The 1990s ushered in a new era in LGBTIQ politics in the West. As Seidman argues, "In the early 1990s, gays became a visible, seemingly permanent part of the American mainstream" (2002, 125). During this time the idea of the "normal gay" emerged (Seidman 2002, 161). While the AIDS crisis led to some "anti-identity formations" such as Queer Nation (Chapter 4), simultaneously the intensification of neoliberal ideology during the period brought with it a new form of mainstreaming in LGBTIQ politics.

As Duggan describes, in the late 1990s, a strand of advocacy emerged that argued for "full inclusion" and "equality" for gays and lesbians, but against "progressive" visions that clashed with the prevailing social and economic order (2002, 175). Duggan's critique centres on a conservative US-based website that emerged, called the Independent Gay Forum (IGF), which promoted social and economic principles consistent with neoliberal ideology. Duggan termed this politics "the new homonormativity" given its refusal to engage with critiques of heteronormative structures and institutions such as the family (2002, 179). As Duggan defines:

> [Homonormativity] is a politics that does not contest dominant heteronormative assumptions and institutions but upholds and sustains them while promising the possibility of a demobilized gay constituency and a privatized, depoliticized gay culture anchored in domesticity and consumption. (2002, 179)

While queer activists during this period aimed to deconstruct the assumptions underlying heteronormativity (such as discrete sexuality categories and the gender binary), new homonormative advocacy aimed to maintain these foundations and aim for "equality" within an existing system. Importantly, homonormativity is not just about maintaining current "norms", but specifically is about enshrining neoliberal ideas about what should remain in the private sphere. In other words, homonormative politics aims to protect the private rights of LGBTIQ individuals and aims for "equality" in the private sphere, rather than in the public sphere (Nagle 2018, 79). Homonormative politics are concerned with individual domestic liberties such as marriage equality, rather than the collective public issues of Gay Liberation past, such as around housing, employment and education. As Seidman explains, alongside greater "gay normalisation" in the 1990s, there was simultaneously a tightening of other moral codes around sexuality; "a fear that other sexual outsiders will demand inclusion, further fueling anxieties of impending disorder" (2002, 160–161). Homonormative politics of inclusion necessarily advantage upper-middle-class, white and otherwise "normative" LGBTIQ persons who already have a great deal of cultural capital and mobility.

Key concept: Cultural capital

Sociologist Pierre Bourdieu coined the term "cultural capital" to account for the capital that is accumulated and reproduced within certain classes that is not just "economic" (though the economic and cultural forms are intimately linked). According to Bourdieu, cultural capital helps to maintain class distinctions.

Cultural capital has three forms:

1. **Embodied:** cultural capital is embodied, insofar as "external wealth [is] converted into an integral part of the person" (1986, 244–245). An example of this might be one's accent, which may identify to others which region and class one is from.
2. **Objectified:** cultural capital is objectified when one "owns" certain cultural objects, and where the owner also possesses the ability to engage with this on an appropriate symbolic level (such as owning, interpreting and understanding the value of artworks) (1986, 246).
3. **Institutionalised:** cultural capital is institutionalised insofar as it is formally recognised, for example, through an academic certification (1986, 247).

Homonormativity is now a widely used term in queer theory. Some have extended the term; for example, Magdalena Mikulak has proposed the idea of "godly homonormativity", that refers to advocacy for LGBT acceptance within the institution of Christianity (2017, 19). Mikulak's work on LGBT politics in Poland suggests that within the context of a neoliberal state and a mainstream LGBT movement that rejects recognition of religious beliefs, a strand of LGBT activism has developed that supports inclusion within the country's dominant Roman Catholic Church in conservative and homonormative ways.

However, homonormativity is also sometimes employed as a synonym for "normative"-seeming LGBTIQ persons, rather than persons who express the kind of "non-political" sentiments that Duggan described. For example, as Andrew Gorman-Murray (2017) discusses, gay and lesbian "domesticity" (or home life) has frequently been regarded as emblematic of "homonormativity". Yet, attending to the lived experiences of gay and lesbian persons in domestic settings reveals a more complex picture than simple accounts of mainstreaming would suggest. Gorman-Murray suggests that Duggan's critique is firmly based within a US-context, and as such misses the nuances of the private sphere operating in other locations. Gorman-Murray writes: "Quite simply, some lesbians and gay men desire privacy and domestic 'comfort', not to be 'normal' but just to be 'content' ... many remain outside the normative bounds of neoliberalism, being non-professional, undereducated and reliant on social welfare" (2017, 155).

Queer theory in practice: *Queer Eye* for the normative guy

The popular US reality television series show *Queer Eye* (known in its earlier form as *Queer Eye for the Straight Guy*) offers a space to explore issues around homonormativity. In both its older and new versions, *Queer Eye* is essentially a "makeover" show, where five gay men transform the looks and lives of (in most cases) straight men. As critics of the earlier series have suggested, while the show enhances gay visibility in popular culture, it also promotes neoliberal ideas around personal improvement and consumption (Sender 2006). Columnist Laurie Penny describes the new version as the "pornography of emotional labor" and adds that "Money is the silent sixth member of the rescue squad" (Penny 2018). Though a beloved show of many, the question remains as to what is "queer" about *Queer Eye*.

Queer theory in practice: Homonormativity in Lebanon

While some have critiqued the US-centric basis of Duggan's theory of homonormativity, others have deployed the concept to understand the dynamics of LGBTIQ politics in other locations. For example, John Nagle (2018) describes the fraught issues of LGBT organising in Lebanon, where a government power-sharing arrangement organised along sectarian lines means that there are strong incentives to form distinct identity-based groups to enable rights-based claims. The issue here is that this system also often accommodates the views of groups who advocate against sexual minorities. Nagle describes two different political responses to this problem:

> As rights can only be awarded to distinct communities, some activists endeavour to construct "groupness", a unified public identity. Those opposing the homophobia of power-sharing do so by rejecting its core logics: groups must form homogenous and distinct communities. Activists deny this by developing a "non-identarian" politics that emphasises intersectionality and communal unbecoming. (2018, 86)

Nagle suggests that while the power-sharing system encourages both homophobia and homonormativity, there are activists who actively reject these limits through the strategy of "non-groupness" (2018, 86).

One of the most contentious issues involving questions of domesticity and homonormativity is marriage equality – the legal right of LGBTIQ persons to marry. This is also often referred to as "same-sex marriage" or "gay marriage". As Michael Warner writes in his 1999 piece "Beyond Gay Marriage", the issue of marriage equality poses questions for the LGBTIQ community around sex, state interference, normality, mainstreaming and inclusion. As Warner suggests, marriage was never historically the focus of Gay Liberation, yet with increasing liberties and legislative changes in the West the question of marriage equality came to the fore. As historian Graham Willett notes, in Western countries like Australia, marriage came to be seen as a final legislative battleground for LGBTIQ advocates (2010, 195). Yet, debate has been split: some argue that marriage equality leads to further LGBTIQ integration (and support it on this basis) while others argue this is a profoundly homonormative assimilatory shift in LGBTIQ life (and oppose it on this basis) (Yep et al. 2003).

For example, Butler warns that investing in the narrow parameters of "marriage" forecloses other more radical possibilities for sexual life and imagining kinship, negating the non-biological ties that bind many in the queer community (Butler 2002). Butler further suggests:

> Variations on kinship that depart from normative, dyadic hetero-sexually based family forms secured through the marriage vow are figured not only as dangerous for the child, but perilous to the putative natural and cultural laws said to sustain human intelligibility. (2002, 16)

In other words, Butler argues that the heteronormative foundation of marriage cements the idea that any family formations that *do not* fit this logic are dangerous – and thus, that marriage equality further reinforces this logic. Amy Brandzel extends this critique, suggesting that the norms institutionalised by marriage are also connected to racialised and classed notions of who belongs to the nation-state, revealing "the state's interest in promoting the reproduction of certain kinds of citizens" (2005, 195–196).

From homonormativity to homonationalism

Related to the debate around marriage equality, questions of citizenship have come to the fore in queer theory in recent years, with many raising questions about LGBTIQ mainstreaming and the construction of "ideal" (homonormative) queer citizens. The foundation of this is the concept of the citizen as the male head of a family household, who is both masculine and heteronormative (Johnson 2003). Historically, feminist activists have campaigned against this ideal of the (male) citizen, and have argued for full inclusion, with demands around issues such as property and voting rights. Similarly, civil rights activists, LGBTIQ activists, disability advocates and many other groups, have fought for rights within nation-states that have been limited under narrow models of citizenship. As Leti Volpp defines:

> Citizenship differentiates the citizen from the alien and this refers not only to civil, political, and social rights; it also concerns membership within the community of the nation-state. (2017, 155)

The concept of homonormativity underpins the more recent concept of "homonationalism", which is designed to address this question of the normative sexual citizen. In mainstreaming of queer culture under late capitalism,

---

Key concept: Sexual citizenship

The idea of "sexual citizenship" specifically refers to issues around sexuality and reproduction and citizenship, as well as questions around the citizenship/belonging of various sexual subjects (Volpp 2017, 164–165). With the emergence of homonormativity and the attendant emphasis on domesticity, some theorists suggest that there has been a reinvigoration of the "private" over the "public" in debates around sexual citizenship.

For example, Berlant argues that the political has become the personal, not in the way that feminists originally imagined ("the personal is political"), but rather, where all politics is directed towards individual and personal concerns, rather than politics concerning the collective public (Berlant 1997). As McCann further argues, the original feminist sentiment has been distorted into "the personal is the political" where politics is seen to be done at the level of the body (through style, behaviour and so forth) rather than at the level of the collective (2018, 27). Thus, sexual citizenship in neoliberal times refers to a model of normative belonging that is enacted at the individual level, the consequence of which is moving away from politics of collective struggle.

---

heteronormativity collides with homonormativity to produce homonationalism. Coined by Jasbir Puar, homonationalism refers to how LGBTIQ rights are utilised and promoted by some nation-states for the purpose of evidencing progress and exceptionalism, to assist in maintaining border regimes against certain outside populations. Puar suggests that

> [H]omonationalism is fundamentally a critique of how lesbian and gay liberal rights discourses produce narratives of progress and modernity that continue to accord some populations access to cultural and legal forms of citizenship at the expense of the partial and full expulsion from those rights of other populations. (2013, 25)

Puar's theory of homonationalism relates sexuality to projects of imperialism and xenophobia, explaining how "collusions" between "homosexuality and US nationalism" produce violence (Puar 2007, 46). Puar argues that homonationalism describes how particular notions of "us" versus "them" are constructed through the state's invocation of a respectability-based LGBTIQ

Queer theory in practice: Colonial legacies of homophobia

On 6 September 2018, the Supreme Court of India ruled that homosexual acts between adults would no longer be criminalised under Section 377 of the Indian Penal Code (IPC). As Jyoti Puri describes, Section 377 was first introduced in 1860 via British Colonial rule in India (2016, 4). The change came following decades of grassroots activism in India around the rights of sexual and gender diverse minorities.

While laws such as Section 377 have frequently been used in homonationalist rhetoric as evidence of the relative sexual freedoms of the West, Section 377 and laws like it are a colonial legacy. Section 377 remains in place across former British colonised countries, including Singapore, Pakistan and Jamaica.

---

rights discourse, and used against migrant and other populations who are cast as "perverse" in orientalist terms (2013, 25). According to Puar, US culture in particular valorises a particular kind of "acceptable" (but not really "queer") queer culture, presenting itself as tolerant and diverse. Puar's theorising of homonationalism is part of queer theory's geopolitical turn, discussed in more detail in Chapter 7.

Homonationalism, which constructs ideas of ideal citizens, is similar though different to "pinkwashing", which refers to actions taken by states to actively cover up discrimination against LGBTIQ persons through promoting *some* gay rights (Puar 2013, 32). In other words, pinkwashing is a propaganda strategy deployed to distract from LGBTIQ human rights issues through appealing to some limited gay rights.

WOUNDED ATTACHMENTS

As a new "homonormative" identity politics emerged in the 1990s, so too did theorists turn to critiques around this new emphasis on individual identity-based politics. Of particular note is Wendy Brown's work on what she calls "wounded attachments" (1993, 1995). Brown argues that a kind of difference-based "alterity" politics had arisen: those positioned as marginal paradoxically adopted categorisations of otherness (such as "queer") in a political move that repeats the rhetoric of difference (Brown 1993, 53). According to Brown, this categorisation of otherness contributes to the formation of an excluded and injured sense of self, which sits in contrast to a (fantasy) notion of a social ideal. She writes, "without recourse to the white masculine middle-class ideal, politicized identities would forfeit a good deal of their claims to injury and exclusion, their claims to the political significance of their difference" (Brown 1995, 61). In other words, identities require a continual ideal reference point, to maintain coherent (relative) identification. As Stefan Dolgert explains, "For Brown, the danger is that the wounds scored into us by bourgeois discipline have become the only thing that liberal selves can cling to" (2016, 359). Ultimately this obscures the economic operations of class under capitalism, with minority claim-making based on identities that effectively bolster capitalism (insofar as they seek equality *within* the system) rather than critique it. Brown questions the transformative possibilities of such claim-making under capitalism, leading her to ask, "what does politicised identity want?" (1995, 62). Here, Brown turns to Friedrich Nietzsche's concept of "ressentiment", which refers to a politics that is founded on ideas of and attachments to injured subjectivity. The problem with ressentiment, according to Brown, is that it leads to placing demands on the state to resolve "deep political stress in a culture", turning to institutions such as the law to resolve this crisis (1995, 27). Brown suggests that not only are such strategies impotent for naming the economic dynamics that create this stress, they reinforce the power of the state rather than challenge it, and only serve to normalise injured subjects.

Brown has been critiqued for dismissing what is identified as "ressentiment" politics, as necessarily bad. As Dolgert suggests, ressentiment can be utilised: "Maybe what we should be doing is helping to show people where to direct their smashing, against whom their rage should be unleashed, rather than telling them that their rage is uncivilized, barbaric, reactionary, uncouth" (2016, 365). Similarly, as Debra Thompson argues, accusations of "ressentiment" are often used against historically dispossessed groups, and that in fact the emotions mistaken for "ressentiment" (such as anger, rage, resentment) can be politically productive (Thompson 2017, 473).

Brown might also be critiqued for ignoring not only the experience of identity, but the possibilities of solidarity resulting from injury (i.e., from what she would call "ressentiment"). For example, Love points out that queer theory was always intended to create solidarity from the injured: "At its most expansive, queer studies imagined a federation of the shamed, the alienated, the destitute, the illegitimate, and the hated" (2011, 183). As Love also writes of her identification as a lesbian, "This investment in identity is, I realize, a wounded attachment. But if an attachment isn't wounded, what's the point in having it?" (2011, 187).

Queer theory in practice: Trigger warnings

Trigger warnings – the verbal or visual warnings given before an audience is exposed to content that may provoke negative response – have become a hot topic in debates around the politics of injury. As Clare Forstie (2016) describes, trigger warnings came into use in the 1990s, with the formation of online feminist and similar spaces.

Some queer theorists such as Halberstam (2014) have critiqued trigger warnings for reinforcing queer vulnerability and adhering to neoliberal individualistic politics. He suggests:

> [A]s LGBT communities make "safety" into a top priority (and that during an era of militaristic investment in security regimes) and ground their quest for safety in competitive narratives about trauma, the fight against aggressive new forms of exploitation, global capitalism and corrupt political systems falls by the wayside. (2014)

Forstie, however, suggests that trigger warnings ought not be so easily dismissed. She writes:

> The queer classroom is fundamentally affective, political, and imbued with power, and whether trigger warnings enable inclusive and productive individual and social change depends on how we frame and manage the structural and political contexts that run through our classrooms. (2016, 430)

Forstie suggests that the use of trigger warnings be determined based on the specific affects, power dynamics and political discourse at play in one's classroom. Rather than rejecting trigger warnings altogether, Forstie encourages us to think about what function such warnings play in specific contexts.

CONNECTIVITY AND TRANSGENDER IDENTITY

While theorists such as Duggan and Brown were concerned with neoliberal forces, another historic shift was taking place that contributed to new formations around identity: the rise of the Internet. As Steven Whittle argues,

> The growth of home computer use in the 1990s ... was crucial to the development of a new, geographically dispersed, diverse trans community in the 1990s ... Online, this newly formed community was able to discuss its experiences of fear, shame, and discrimination, and, as a result, many community members developed newly politicized personal identities. (2006, xii)

While trans identities of course pre-dated the Internet, the Internet provided a space and platform for sharing experiences. This new form of connectivity meant that previously isolated individuals could find networks of like-minded individuals across the globe. From this, new articulations of identity were made possible, as people began to cohere around similar life experiences, desires and understandings. It was during this time that the term "transgender" came to be commonly used as an umbrella term for a range of gender diverse identities (Williams 2014, 232).

The precise origins of the term transgender are uncertain, but it is known to have been used as early as the 1960s as a broad way to describe a range of gender diverse embodiments and experiences (Williams 2014, 233). Some accounts distinguish between transgender identity as "somebody who permanently change[s] social gender through the public presentation of self, without recourse to genital transformation" and transsexual identity as "somebody who permanently change[s] genitals in order to claim membership in a gender other than the one assigned at birth" (Stryker 2006, 4). Others argue that transgender – often shortened to trans – can be used as an umbrella term for a wide range of gender diverse identifications, gendered bodily modifications and expressions (Williams 2014). Today, some theorists and activists suggest using the term trans* to represent an infinite number of possible gender embodiments. As Halberstam writes, "This terminology, trans*, stands at odds with the history of gender variance, which has been collapsed into concise definitions, sure medical pronouncements, and fierce exclusions" (2018, 5).

Leslie Feinberg's 1992 self-published pamphlet "Trans Liberation: A Movement Whose Time Has Come" is widely cited as influential in early discussions of transgender activism. Feinberg argued that trans is not simply a descriptor but might be a site for collective mobilisation sexuality. On this issue of gay and lesbian versus trans identity, Feinberg writes:

> While oppressions within these two powerful communities are not the same, we face a common enemy. Gender-phobia – like racism, sexism and bigotry against lesbians and gay men – is meant to keep us divided. Unity can only increase our strength. (2013, 206)

Feinberg's language of "gender-phobia" echoes the now more widely used term "transphobia". While we must acknowledge that trans persons may also be gay or lesbian, and that there may be overlap in these communities, Feinberg's point was that the common experience of oppression around gender and sexuality within these groups might be the basis of a shared politics. This idea is reflected today in the acronym LGBTIQ.

Other theorists such as Susan Stryker have suggested that historically there was a need during the 1990s to differentiate between mainstream gay and lesbian politics and the emerging trans politics, given that trans issues

---

Key term: Cisgender

B. Aultman describes a cisgender person as having gender identity that is "on the same side as their birth-assigned sex" (2014, 61). Just as the term "heterosexual" was only coined following that of "homosexual", so too did the term "cisgender" emerge following the development of trans activist discourse around transgender identity in the 1990s.

This reveals that often the unmarked norm is just that: what is considered "normal" and "natural" is not given a referent in language. Introducing the language of "cisgender" has been a way to try and rectify this imbalance, to highlight that trans identity is not more abnormal nor unnatural than any other experience of gender. As transgender studies theorists remind us, "gender is relevant to everyone" (Califia 1997, 6).

The term "cisgenderism" refers to discrimination based on privileging cisgender status over other gender diverse embodiments and identifications. As Erica Lennon and Brian J. Mistler suggest, "The pervasive nature of cisgenderism creates, designates, and enforces a hierarchy by which individuals are expected to conform and are punished if they do not" (2014, 63).

were often sidelined or actively marginalised, within a homonormative political landscape. Stryker describes how trans activists began to use the language of queer for their own purposes, to talk about the radical possibilities opened up by trans ways of being:

> People with trans identities could describe themselves as men and women, too – or resist binary categorization altogether – but in doing either they queered the dominant relationship of sexed body and gendered subject. We drew a distinction between "orientation queers" and "gender queers". Tellingly, *gender queer*, necessary for naming the minoritized/marginalized position of difference within queer cultural formations more generally, has stuck around as a useful term; *orientation queer*, naming queer's unstated norm, has seemed redundant in most contexts and has not survived to the same extent. (Stryker 2008, 147 emphasis in original)

Here Stryker alludes to the fact that trans subjectivity is a challenge to traditional binary accounts of gender. This point sits in contrast to the transphobic accusations of radical feminists since the 1970s, that trans identity reinforces patriarchal notions of gender, as touched on in Chapter 3. For example, trans writer Kate Bornstein describes their own experience of being excluded from the feminist community, and the pain of being defined by others (and not having your own self-identifications recognised) as such: "They said that I'd been socialised as a male, and could never truly be a female; that what I was, in fact, was a castrated male" (1994, 50). These painful exclusionary ideas expressed by some feminists are based on the incorrect assumption that transgender identity necessarily reinforces fixed gender roles.

The rise of transgender studies

The transformative possibilities of imagining gender raised via trans identity meant that trans became a key "example" in some queer theory accounts in the 1990s. However, these theorisations often occurred without acknowledging trans people's lived experiences. As Namaste argued at the time,

> [Queer theory] remains incapable of connecting this research to the everyday lives of people who identify as transgender, drag queen, and/or transsexual. Indeed, queer theory refuses transgender subjectivities even as it looks at them. (1994, 229)

Queer theory in practice: Street Transvestite Action Revolutionaries (STAR)

Sylvia Rivera and Marsha P. Johnson, both activists who played a key role in the Stonewall riots described in Chapter 2, formed the group Street Transvestite Action Revolutionaries (STAR) in New York in 1970.

The aim of STAR was to provide a space and political platform for trans sex workers at risk of homelessness and police violence. An early trans activist group, STAR was connected within a broader context of resistance, including Gay Liberation and anti-racist movements. As Roderick A. Ferguson describes: "STAR attempted to radicalize transgender difference into a social mode that would challenge systemic forms of homophobic and transphobic violence and poverty" (2019, 33–34). STAR clashed with mainstream Gay Liberation organising at the time, particularly given the transphobia expressed by some lesbian feminists within the broader movement.

Today, the Sylvia Rivera Law Project exists in tribute to Rivera, which takes an intersectional approach to legal reform and fights for justice for the gender diverse community, based in New York.

Namaste accuses queer theory of only taking up trans for discussion insofar as "transgender people are only looked at, observed, scrutinised, and spoken about" (Namaste 1996, 196). Here, Butler's discussion of drag in *Gender Trouble* (1999), and trans subjectivity more specifically in her later work (Butler 1993, 2004b), came under a large amount of scrutiny, as discussed in Chapter 5.

Following these critiques, transgender studies has emerged as a field of study in its own right. Stryker suggests that even though the field shares a similar history drawing on feminism and sexuality studies, transgender studies is "queer theory's evil twin" (2004, 212). Transgender studies specifically places experiences of trans identity and embodiment at its centre. Yet, as Stryker describes, the implications of this field are broad:

> Ultimately, it is not just transgender phenomena per se that are of interest, but rather the manner in which these phenomena reveal the operations of systems and institutions that simultaneously produce various possibilities

of viable personhood, and eliminate others. Thus the field of transgender studies, far from being an inconsequentially narrow specialization dealing *only* with a rarified population of transgender individuals ... represents a significant and ongoing critical engagement with some of the most trenchant issues in contemporary humanities, social science and biomedical research. (2006, 3–4 emphasis in original)

Much of this work engages critically with both biologistic essentialist and simple social constructivist accounts of gender. As Julia Serano notes, neither biological nor social constructivist accounts alone do justice to the lived experience of trans life (2007, 234).

However, as the field of transgender studies began to grow, some also questioned the theory of gender informing these discussions. As Lucy Nicholas

---

Queer theory in practice: Serano's *Whipping Girl*

Transgender studies have been crucial for highlighting the limits of feminist and queer theory accounts that preceded the field. One key example of this is Serano's work on experiences of femininity, which she argues has been marginalised in both feminist and queer history:

> [P]eople who are feminine, whether they be female, male, and/or transgender, are almost universally demeaned compared with their masculine counterparts. This scapegoating of those who express femininity can be seen not only in the male-centered mainstream, but in the queer community, where "effeminate" gay men have been accused of holding back the gay rights movement, and where femme dykes have been accused of being the Uncle Toms of the lesbian movement. (2007, 5)

Serano suggests that the emphasis on femininity as always already subordinate to masculinity has marginalised many LGBTIQ people for whom feminine embodiment is a central part of their gender expression. The term "femmephobia" is sometimes used to describe discrimination (Blair and Hoskin 2015). Serano's work has been key in opening up new perspectives on femininity in both LGBTIQ communities and in academic discussions of gender.

argues, a fixed idea of the gender binary – as two distinct genders (male/female) – underpins many discussions of trans identity. Nicholas states:

> [T]he limits of these models tend to be the separation of gender from biological sex, resulting in a fixed category of masculine/feminine gender not continuous with male/ female sex, or the idea of an expansion of gender displays such that this is more variable, but still with a fixed, binary bodily sex ... these accounts tend to assume that these models could be implemented on an individual level, downplaying the weight of social and cultural attribution in sex/gender identity, and overemphasising how voluntaristic this process could be. (2014, 25)

As some trans theorists suggest, articulating trans identity is fraught because while essentialist accounts offer limited visions of the gender binary, they also often allow for greater recognition, access to medical interventions and more. As Sandy Stone remarks, "What is gained is acceptability in society. What is lost is the ability to authentically represent the complexities and ambiguities of lived experience" (1991, 295).

Indeed, a "wrong body" discourse (the idea that trans identity is simply about being born into an incorrect body), emerged in mainstream accounts of trans experience, that has been reiterated in medical gatekeeping around trans identity. J. R. Latham describes this as a "feedback loop" between medicine and how trans people experience their identity, where the self-description necessary to access to medicine and surgery reinforces a narrow range of ways of talking about trans experiences (2018, 4). Legal theorists such as Dean Spade (2003) have also pointed out the double standards applied to trans people

---

Queer theory in practice: The problem of "recognition"

In his examination of contemporary trans politics, Dean Spade (2015) suggests that demands centred on "equality" and "recognition" are limited insofar as they rely on the nation-state as arbiter. Echoing Brown's arguments from the 1990s, Spade argues that reform-focused politics reinforce the existing system. He draws on Critical Race Theory's challenge to biologically essentialist ideas and suggests that a more transformative trans politics or "critical trans analysis" is needed that moves beyond the paradigm of "recognition".

who may wish to seek surgical interventions versus cisgender people who may elect to undergo purely cosmetic procedures such as breast augmentation. While the former requires persons to jump over various legal, psychological, medical and social hurdles to obtain surgery, cisgender women are culturally encouraged and supported to undergo surgery to align with feminine ideals.

Phenomenology and the lived body

The limits of both biologistic and social constructivist accounts in understanding trans identity bring to the fore the importance of phenomenological approaches in transgender studies. Originating in philosophical writing from Maurice Merleau-Ponty (2010) and others in the early twentieth century, phenomenology is useful as it takes into account subjective embodied experience without reliance on essentialist notions. In 1998, Henry S. Rubin first described the usefulness of phenomenology to trans studies. As Rubin defines, "phenomenology takes it as a matter of fact that essences are always already constituted in relationship to embodied subjectivity, hence they are unnatural and malleable" (1998, 267). Phenomenology emphasises experience as it is "lived" (Kruks 2014, 75), and in this way is seen by some as an antidote to the limits of queer theory which often overlooks the question of experience in favour of deconstruction. Prosser, for example, claims that it is the "bodiliness" of some trans experiences that show queer theory's limits (Prosser 1998, 6).

Phenomenology has been taken up by some transgender studies scholars as a dynamic framework for understanding the centrality of embodiment and bodies in many trans accounts. As Rubin further adds: "Phenomenology recognizes the circumscribed agency of embodied subjects who mobilize around their body image to sustain their life projects" (1998, 271). Describing the application of a phenomenological approach to trans subjectivity, Ulrica Engdahl argues that the "wrong body" discourse might be adapted to better account for the complexity of the body as it is "lived":

> Wrong body as lived body expresses the situatedness of trans body experience as wrong, hence relativizing it. Wrong body as trans embodiment expresses subjectively felt bodily meaning interacting with cultural interpretations of bodies, where the subjective and the cultural are not always congruent. This way the gender binary is replaced with gender variance as a frame for understanding gender, offering a more fluid understanding of the trans body. (2014, 269)

Such an approach stresses that bodies are at once socially constituted *and* the site of identity and sense of self. As Sonia Kruks describes, "one's body is also one's mode of 'being-in-the-world': it is the site of both one's lived experience and one's particular style of acting, and of expressing and communicating who one is" (2014, 85). Importantly, this approach to trans subjectivity does not see "lived experience" as diametrically opposed to "theories" of gender – or what Gayle Salamon describes as "[a] call for a return to 'real' gender" (2010, 71). While some theorists such as Prosser have been critiqued for opposing "transgender" to "queer" (Hale 1998, 340), phenomenological accounts help to illuminate the value of subjective embodied experience in theorising gender.

Transnormativity and the issue of representation

Following the language of heteronormativity and homonormativity, "transnormativity" has been proposed to delineate trans identity formations that bolster fixed notions of gender that undermine more transformative understandings. As Austin H. Johnson suggests:

> Transnormativity ... is a hegemonic ideology that structures transgender experience, identification, and narratives into a hierarchy of legitimacy that is dependent upon a binary medical model and its accompanying standards, regardless of individual transgender people's interest in or intention to undertake medical pathways to transition. (2016, 466)

Since the 1990s, awareness of trans identity has become increasingly mainstream, leading the USA's Time magazine to announce in 2014 that "the transgender tipping point" was upon us (Steinmetz 2014). The visibility of some trans celebrities, such as Caitlyn Jenner and Laverne Cox, is often used as evidence of this "tipping point", yet some theorists have warned that conservative figures such as Jenner have been key in promoting transnormative ideas (McIntyre 2018).

Along these lines, there have been critiques of those who wish to "pass" and "fade into the woodwork" rather than become trans activists, for some time (Califia 1997, 225). This debate raises similar concerns to those around homonormativity – are those who seek "normality" (or what others might call "assimilation") a problem? This conundrum raises broader issues around speaking, who can speak on behalf of marginalised groups, and what the value of representation of marginal identities is in the first place. While mainstream media have announced a "transgender tipping point", trans celebrities do not necessarily represent the interests of all transgender people (many of whom do

---

Queer theory in practice: Halberstam's *Female Masculinity*

Halberstam's (1998) *Female Masculinity* is a key text that reimagines the possibilities of untying masculinity (and thus also femininity) from its presumed "biological" basis. Drawing on several popular film and television texts and drag king performance artists, this work was not only an important precursor for many discussions about diverse gendered embodiments and styles, but has also influenced the field of masculinity studies. As Halberstam suggests: "[F]ar from being an imitation of maleness, female masculinity actually affords us a glimpse of how masculinity is constructed as masculinity" (1998, 1).

One example that Halberstam offers of "female masculinity" is the 1953 Hollywood film *Calamity Jane*, that features Doris Day as a "butch cowgirl" (as Halberstam puts it) (1998, 209). Halberstam's reading of Calamity as "butch" suggests a queer reading strategy: through understanding that stylisations of female masculinity rupture gender expectations, we are given a way to "see" queerness where we might not see it before.

---

not share the same values or desires to present/embody their gender in the same ways). Yet, some may rightly point out that these same trans celebrities have helped to raise the profile and awareness of trans issues, and that this representation – albeit limited – matters.

Non-binary identity

Alongside discussions around trans identification, new terminology has come into use to describe different experiences of gender. The use of the term "non-binary" is relatively recent, particularly in academia, with terminology around genderqueerness/genderfluidity preceding it. As Christina Richards, Walter Pierre Bouman and Meg-John Barker note, 2016 saw the first academic conference, PhD thesis and journal special issue dedicated to non-binary (2017, 2). They define non-binary identity as encompassing a wide range of subjectivities:

> In general, non-binary or genderqueer refers to people's identity, rather than physicality at birth; but it does not exclude people who are

intersex ... Whatever the birth physicality, there are non-binary people who identify as a single fixed gender position other than male or
female. There are those who have a fluid gender. There are those who
have no gender. And there are those who disagree with the very idea of
gender. (Richards, Bouman and Barker 2017, 5)

Here we must recall that the gender binary as discussed by Butler and others is a distinctly Western construct, and that there is a long history of
non-Western alternative gender identities. These include hijra (South Asia),
kathoey (Thailand), waria (Indonesia), two-spirit (North America), machi
(Chile and Argentina) and many more terms and identifications. Crucially,
while contemporary Western frameworks separate gender and sexuality, in
many other contexts these distinctions are not so clear. As Ben Vincent and
Ana Manzano suggest, "Gender variance and sexuality are now conceived
separately in a Western context, but historically and cross-culturally they have
been entwined" (2017, 26). Scholars suggest that the binary man/woman is a
relatively recent Western concept, and that Western frameworks cannot simply be used to understand experiences of gender diversity in other contexts
(Richards et al. 2017, 6).

The language of non-binary identities emerged in the West as a result of
growing awareness of trans identity, illustrated in 2014 when social media
corporation Facebook introduced multiple gender options on their platform.
With growing awareness around non-binary conceptions of gender in the
West, many within trans communities have welcomed the terminology to help
describe complex and sometimes ambivalent relationships to existing gender
frameworks. Richards, Bouman and Barker suggest that

[W]hilst relatively few people may identify as non-binary (to the point of
using a non-binary gender label or refusing to tick the "male/female" box
on a form), many more people experience themselves in non-binary ways.
(2017, 6)

Their point here is to suggest that the language of non-binary does not
only articulate an identity position (from which one might make claims,
such as the right to change one's gender to "X" on a passport), it also
describes a way of relating to the gender binary that is broader than this.
As Richards, Bouman and Barker suggest, many people feel removed or
alienated from the strict norms suggested by the binary man/woman and
have "non-binary" experiences of their own gender as it is embodied and
lived.

Queer theory in practice: Waria identity in Indonesia

The language of gender diversity differs worldwide. One example is waria identity in Indonesia, a term which combines the Indonesian words for woman (*wanita*) and man (*pria*). Western scholarship and media frequently represents waria in terms of transgender identity – however, waria cannot simply be collapsed under this language. Research shows that waria-identifying persons often use the language of "transgender" in specific reference to (youthful) periods in their life course which involved moving to cities, where "transgender" was a term used in reference to sex work. For waria, "The distinction over whether one is *transgender* or not boils down to participation in national and transnational sex work" (Hegarty 2017, 74). This use of language reveals the way that gendered terms migrate across borders and are taken up in specific ways.

CONCLUSION: WHERE TO NOW FOR POSTIDENTITY POLITICS?

This chapter has explored some of the tensions that have emerged between queer theory and emerging articulations of sexual and gender diverse identities in the West. While the queer theory critiques of identity politics outlined at the beginning of this chapter pose significant questions to newly proliferated identifications, areas of discussion such as transgender studies offer different ways to think through questions of lived experience and identity.

Theorists such as Puar even suggest that we ought to bring in ideas around materiality and "assemblage theory" to try and deconstruct identities in a way

Key concept: Assemblage

Assemblage is a theoretical term most notably used by Gilles Deleuze and Félix Guattari (1987). The idea of assemblage places emphasis on notions of becoming, process, connection and transformation. As Kennedy et al. describe: "assemblage refers to complex flows, connections and becomings that emerge and disperse relationally between bodies" (Kennedy et al. 2013, 46). While that may sound like a rather obtuse definition, assemblage can be useful for thinking through how things, feelings, objects, events and other ephemera, are both connected and dynamic.

that does not simply reify discrete identity categories. Puar suggests that taking a material assemblage approach might enable us to see:

> There is no entity, no identity, no queer subject to queer, rather queerness coming forth at us from all directions, screaming its defiance, suggesting a move from intersectionality to assemblage, an affective conglomeration that recognizes other contingencies of belonging (melding, fusing, viscosity, bouncing) that might not fall so easily into what is sometimes denoted as reactive community formations – identity politics – by control theorists. (2007, 211)

As Puar highlights here, rather than thinking about identity politics in terms of "identity" (which only reinforces discrete categories), we might instead turn to "assemblage" to help understand the material elements of belonging (the way things feel, embodiment and so forth) that cannot be reduced to identity in any discrete categorical form. As Anzaldúa similarly suggests, "Identity is a river – a process. Contained within the river is identity and it needs to flow, to change to stay a river" (2009, 166). Introducing other frameworks – such as assemblage theory, or phenomenological approaches – offers additional frameworks for extending queer theory's capacity for critique.

Further reading

Jasbir Puar. (2007). *Terrorist Assemblages: Homonationalism in Queer Times*. Durham, NC: Duke University Press.

Puar's germinal work unpacks the construction of the figure of the terrorist in Western society, exploring how this is entangled with homonationalist rhetoric. Drawing on Deleuze and assemblage theory, Puar offers a unique intervention into "identity politics".

Susan Stryker, and Steven Whittle (eds.). (2006). *The Transgender Studies Reader*. New York and London: Routledge.

This is a key collection of early texts in the field of transgender studies that shows the breadth of ideas in the field, and its aspirations for critical intervention.

Christina Richards, Walter Pierre Bouman, and Meg-John Barker (eds.). (2017). *Genderqueer and Non-Binary Genders*. London: Palgrave Macmillan.

This collection provides an invaluable discussion of non-binary identities (and related identities), which have been oft neglected in academic discussions.

QUESTIONS TO CONSIDER

- What are the specific political underpinnings of "homonormativity"? Can you think of anything that is often called "homonormativity" that might not reflect the politics that Duggan was originally referring to?
- What do critiques of "identity politics" look like today? How are these critiques articulated, and whose political agenda do they tend to support (even if accidentally)?
- What challenge do transgender studies pose for queer theory critiques of identity? How might trans accounts extend queer theory?

Recommended films

All About My Mother (**Pedro Almodóvar 1999**). This film explores issues of gender, grief and motherhood, and addresses complex questions about sexuality, trans identity and kinship.

Hedwig and the Angry Inch (**John Cameron Mitchell 2001**). This cult rock comedy-musical follows the life of the queer character Hedwig, born in East Germany. The film explores political issues around Western culture and gender identity, and the complex relationship between drag, performance, trans identity and the lived experience of gender. Stryker describes this film as "[exploring] shift in post-cold war possibilities for gendered embodiment" (2006, 8).

The Miseducation of Cameron Post (**Desiree Akhavan 2018**). Based on the young adult novel of the same name, the film centres on the experiences of a young white woman, Cameron Post, who is sent to a Christian gay conversion therapy centre. The film features a diverse cast and touches on the intersections of sexuality and disability, religion, race and two-spirit identity.

---

7 Negotiating Intersections

KEY TERMS AND CONCEPTS	queer(s) of colour critique, whiteness, disidentification, Quare Theory, geopolitical, diaspora, Indigenous studies, decolonise, Marxism, affect theory, ontology, queer failure, disability studies

THE PROBLEM OF ERASING DIFFERENCE

How have theorists used queer theory in areas beyond the study of sex, gender, sexuality and identity? How have intersections between queer theory and other theoretical frameworks been negotiated? How does contemporary queer theory respond to the idea that subjectivity, identity, privilege and oppression may be constituted through multiple axes? Addressing these questions, in this chapter we consider how queer theory relates to other key theories in gender studies and beyond, including disability studies, postcolonial theory, Indigenous studies, affect theory and more. We also examine critiques of queer theory, which suggest that queer studies reified a universal (white, able-bodied, middle-class, cisgender, male homosexual) subject (see Bérubé 2010). Highlighting the resilience and flexibility of queer theory, we demonstrate how many queer theorists have embraced intersectionality to extend the field. Drawing on a diverse range of theorists, this chapter turns towards a more substantial discussion of places where queer theory meets other frameworks. While this is not an exhaustive list of places that queer theory intersects with other theoretical lenses, it does highlight several significant avenues of contemporary queer thought.

Queer theory, at its best, may resist the conflation of sex, gender and sexuality, normativity and assimilation, rigid binaries and hierarchies of power, and identity categories. However, paradoxically this insistence upon an anti-foundational, anti-identity, anti-normativity ethos, may at its worst result in a tendency to reify a relatively closed-off universal queer subject. As Sullivan notes, both queer theory and queer politics have been accused of being "informed by, and inform[ing], an overly simplistic definition between what or who is deemed to be queer, and what or who is not" (2003, 48). Other

179

critiques argue that queer theory largely deals with middle-class issues from middle-class perspectives, and/or neglects class altogether (Taylor 2018).

As outlined in Chapter 3, we can understand intersectionality theory in the context of the history of feminist theory. We have already noted many of the intersectional critiques of queer theory throughout this book. For example, as discussed in Chapter 2, lesbian feminism takes aim at the foregrounding of gay male experience within queer studies, critiquing queer theory's ability to deal with the specificity of gender. As also discussed in Chapter 6, transgender studies theorists have raised questions about the way that trans bodies are "used" by queer theory without taking trans lived experience into account. Throughout we have noted the largely US-centric origins of queer theory in terms of its articulation, and the issues of race and location that this raises. The relationship between queer theory and the politics of race is particularly fraught given that the categories of sexuality and race are often thought about separately. As we discuss, the problem with some attempts to account for race, gender, class and more in queer theory, has been to segment these dimensions of oppression, rather than understand how these are intimately interconnected, or as Ferguson describes, "forms of struggle and modes of oppression are *necessarily* interlocking" (2018, 3, emphasis in original).

In what would later be known as the "queer(s) of colour critique", academics and activists in the 1990s challenged the separation of race and sexuality, critiquing the implicit whiteness of queer theory and questioning its revolutionary potential within and beyond the academy. Barbara Smith's 1993 essay "Queer Politics: Where's the Revolution?" argues that queer politics and theory had lost the radical and revolutionary potential of earlier movements because it focused only on singular forms of oppression:

> Unlike the early lesbian and gay movement, which had both ideological and practical links to the left, black activism and feminism, today's "queer" politicos seem to operate in a historical and ideological vacuum. "Queer" activists focus on "queer" issues, and racism, sexual oppression and economic exploitation do not qualify, despite the fact that the majority of "queers" are people of color, female or working class ... Building unified, ongoing coalitions that challenge the system and ultimately prepare a way for a revolutionary change simply isn't what "queer" activists have in mind. (Smith 1993, 13–14)

Similarly, in 1994, Sagri Dhairyam challenged the singular focus and implicit whiteness of queer in her essay "Racing the lesbian, dodging white critics", in which she argued that queer theory had coalesced around questions of sexual difference and sexuality at the expense of questions of race. As she writes:

> "Queer Theory" comes increasingly to be reckoned with as a critical discourse, but concomitantly writes a queer whiteness over raced queerness; it domesticates race in its elaboration of sexual difference. (1994, 26)

Ruth Goldman's 1996 essay, "Who is that Queer Queer? Exploring Norms Around Sexuality, Race, and Class in Queer Theory", notes how queer theory produces its own normalising rhetoric which limits what or who is understood as queer. Goldman suggests inconsistencies between the allure of queer theory and its dominant applications in the mid-1990s, writing:

> [W]hen I came across the term "queer theory," I thought I had finally found my academic home, a theoretical space in which my voice would be welcome. Because I understood the term "queer" to represent any number of intersecting anti-normative identities, I expected queer theory to provide an appropriate framework in which to continue my explorations of the intersections between representations of race, sexuality and gender … However, I found that it was very difficult to apply existing queer theory … without collapsing some of the very nuances that I was trying to highlight. (1996, 169)

Academics and activists working through queer theory's critical lens have increasingly turned to intersectionality as a means of addressing some of these problems of erasing difference evident in queer theory's historical articulation.

Key term: Whiteness

Whiteness studies are about analysing and critiquing the dominance of whiteness, an otherwise unmarked norm, and centring this in critique rather than always focusing on a non-white racialised "other". As Damien Riggs explains, the aim is to challenge whiteness as a norm: "To queer whiteness is thus both to speak of it, and in so speaking to remark upon the oddness of the fact that it must be explicitly spoken of in order to be challenged" (2010, 347). Whiteness cannot be simply understood as an individual quality, but rather, a macropolitical issue integral to "operations of empire and colonialism" (Pugliese and Stryker 2009, 4). Critical whiteness studies as a field is concerned with issues of how racism is related to whiteness, white privilege and white supremacy.

Queer theory in practice: Intersectionality applied

Many interpretations of intersectionality have arisen since Crenshaw's original article discussed in Chapter 3. However, as Patricia Hill Collins (2011, 88) describes, there are several shared aspects to the way that intersectionality is often applied. As she outlines, intersectional approaches are concerned with looking at:

1. "how race, class, gender and sexuality constitute intersecting systems of power" – that is, power operates on multiple axes rather than a single axis (e.g., we should not just focus on gender);
2. "how specific social inequalities reflect these power relations from one setting to the next" – that is, different contexts mean different axes may be more or less relevant, producing site-specific inequalities (e.g., a gay man might be disadvantaged among straight men but advantaged among other LGBTIQ persons);
3. "how identities of race, gender, are socially constructed within multiple systems of power" – that is, subjects are produced in relation to these inequalities (e.g., "the Black lesbian");
4. "how social problems and their remedies are similarly constructed within intersecting systems of power" – that is, analysing how power operates on multiple axes also helps us understand how to challenge this system.

These typical aspects of intersectionality theory in application are useful particularly for challenging the ideas that it is a mere "buzzword".

Morphing from its specific use in the field of legal theory to a more general application, intersectionality is now understood as "a method and a disposition, a heuristic and analytic tool" (Carbado et al. 2013, 303). As Hill Collins writes, intersectionality functions as a field of study, a framework for analysis and as "critical praxis" where it is taken up in activism (2015, 3).

INTERSECTIONALITY OR DECONSTRUCTION?

As discussed in Chapter 3, intersectionality theory extended earlier Black feminist critiques and provided a new framework for thinking about how power operates via multiple axes. In 1991, Crenshaw elaborated on her initial definition and use of the term, suggesting it as a means of enhancing the organising principles of community and activist groups. In "Mapping the Margins", she writes, "identity-based politics has been a source of strength, community, and intellectual development" but it is troublesome for the way that "it frequently conflates or ignores intragroup differences" (1991, 1242). Crenshaw's call to extend and complexify identity politics nonetheless relies on the idea of identity-based organising, which has often been a point of contention in queer theorising, as discussed throughout Chapter 6. Here we see a contrast between intersectional and deconstructionist approaches – while the former tends to complexify subjectivity, the latter tends to challenge the notion of a subject altogether.

Crenshaw saw intersectionality not as a tool for deconstructing subject positions, but specifically as a means of addressing the problem of single-identity-based organising, "a way of mediating the tension between assertions of multiple identities and the ongoing necessity of group politics" (1991, 1296). Here, intersectionality is called upon as a means of re-thinking social and political coalitions. Crenshaw also encourages us to re-think or problematise the identities and communities that seem like "home" to us, acknowledging other parts of our identities that may be excluded.

Particularly relevant for thinking about the relationship between intersectionality and queer theory, is Crenshaw's distinction between intersectionality and postmodern anti-essentialism. Crenshaw argued that postmodern approaches often elide the specificity of marginalisation. As an example of this she gestures to the crude anti-essentialist argument that "since all categories are socially constructed there is no such thing as, say, Blacks or women, and thus it makes no sense to continue reproducing those categories by organising around them", but reminds us, "to say that a category such as race or gender is socially constructed is not to say that category has no significance on our world" (Crenshaw 1991, 1296). This is not to misconstrue queer theory as necessarily involving a "social constructivist" position (a characterisation that theorists such as Butler and Sedgwick would reject), but rather to highlight the possible tensions between intersectional and (postmodern) queer theorising.

AN INTERSECTIONAL APPROACH TO QUEER THEORY

Cohen's 1997 essay "Punks, Bulldaggers, and Welfare Queens" was one of the first to take up Crenshaw's articulation of intersectionality to challenge the single-axis approach of queer politics (which, in turn, had implications for queer theorising). Cohen argued that intersectionality was a useful tool for queer politics, which had organised around sexuality for much of the 1990s. As Cohen writes:

> Undoubtedly, within different contexts various characteristics of our total being – for example, race, gender, class, sexuality – are highlighted or called upon to make sense of a particular situation. However, my concern is centered on those individuals who consistently activate only one characteristic of their identity, or a single perspective of consciousness, to organize their politics, rejecting any recognition of the multiple and intersecting systems of power that largely dictate our life chances. (1997, 440)

Queer theory in practice: Intersectionality and queer politics

Cohen argues that queer politics is frequently "coded with class, gender, and race privilege" (1997, 449), and advocates for intersectionality as a means of addressing this. Cohen (1997, 441–446) suggests that an intersectional queer approach might enable:

1. better understanding the limits of political identities that might inadvertently exclude others who stand outside norms (e.g., we need to broaden what "queerness" means);
2. the tools to recognise intersecting oppressions and to understand how these intersections limit or provide access to power (e.g., we need to look at who has easy access to state resources and who does not within queer communities, and the factors that contribute to this);
3. an understanding of how heteronormativity is not separate from institutional racism, patriarchy or class exploitation, but interacts with these forms of oppression (e.g., we should question how people within the queer community experience different forms of interconnected oppression).

In other words, Cohen contends that intersectionality helps us to extend our thinking around identity, power and oppression, to radically transform queer political approaches.

In 1997, around the same time as Cohen's call for queer politics to embrace intersectionality, the journal *Social Text* published a special issue on "Queer Transexions of Race, Nation, and Gender" edited by Phillip Brian Harper, Anne McClintock, José Esteban Muñoz and Trish Rosen. Rather than critiquing the existing field of queer theory, the volume explicitly sought to locate productive interstices of queer theory, critical race theory and postcolonial studies. While not all of its articles explicitly negotiated Crenshaw's version of intersectionality, they all addressed broader intersectional ideas.

Beginning the project of re-thinking queer through intersectionality, they argued that queer theory could move beyond sexuality to also address questions of nationality, gender, race and class. Articles in the volume put queer theory into conversation with questions of "racial identity and diaspora, nationalism and border panic, AIDS and social normativity, drag performance and transsexualism, privacy and public space" (Harper et al. 1997, 1). As Harper, McClintock, Muñoz and Rosen note in their introduction, the volume sought to harness "the critical potential of queer theory" to show how multiple axes of social experience "can cut across or *transect* one another" (Harper et al. 1997, 1). The authors challenged queer theory's seemingly singular focus on sexuality in order to think broadly about social experience.

Nearly a decade later, *Social Text* again took up the question of queer intersectionality as part of a special issue published in 2005. In the introduction, editors David Eng, Halberstam and Muñoz question "what's queer about queer studies now?" Noting that queer theory has historically shied away from broaching wide-ranging social issues, the authors stress the importance of asking questions such as:

> What does queer studies have to say about empire, globalization, neoliberalism, sovereignty, and terrorism? What does queer studies tell us about immigration, citizenship, prisons, welfare, mourning, and human rights? (Eng, Halberstam and Muñoz 2005, 2)

Much like 1997's "Queer Transexions", the authors offer not simply a critique of the field, but rather, attempt to illuminate the potential of queer intersectionality while mapping out some of queer theory's recent intersectional developments. Specifically, the editors argued that an intersectional approach in which queer is employed as "a political metaphor without a fixed referent" (i.e., "queer" ought not solely imply sexuality) (Eng et al. 2005, 2). They suggest that this imagining of queer might offer a means of addressing an array of late twentieth-century global crises. They suggest queer theory as a "subjectless critique", which sits in continuous tension with identity politics:

What might be called the "subjectless" critique of queer studies disallows any positing of a proper subject *of* or object *for* the field by insisting that queer has no fixed political referent ... A subjectless critique establishes ... a focus on a "wide field of normalisation" as the site of social violence. (Eng et al. 2005, 3)

Despite the continuing tensions of the meaning of "identity" within intersectionality and queer theory, intersectional queer approaches promise a move beyond single-axis analysis. However, more than simply adding additional categories of marginality to our existing frameworks, Cho et al. (2013) suggest we could view intersectionality as a *sensibility*:

[W]hat makes an analysis intersectional is not its use of the term "intersectionality," nor its being situated in a familiar genealogy, nor its drawing on lists of standard citations. Rather, what makes an analysis intersectional ... is its adoption of an intersectional way of thinking about the problem of sameness and difference and its relation to power. (Cho et al. 2013, 795)

As Notisha Massaquoi argues, combining queer theory with this intersectional sensibility and vice versa opens up the possibilities for articulating lived experiences of the intersections of gender, race, sexuality and so forth (Massaquoi 2015, 765). Refracted through intersectionality, queer theory might better understand "queer subjects", even as it aims for a "subjectless" critique. From this perspective, intersectionality might ground queer theory in the material conditions and lived experience of difference, while queer theory might deepen intersectionality's critical engagement with subjectivity.

Key debate: A queer critique of intersectionality

Taking an intersectional approach to queer theory today is not uncontested. For Puar, "intersectional identitarian models" are limited "however queer they may be" (2007, 204). She explains why via three interrelated critiques:

Critique 1: Intersectionality centralises white women's experience
Puar describes how intersectionality has been dominantly employed to disrupt the whiteness of feminist discourse. However, she argues that

it has actually had the opposite effect, instead working to centralise the experience of white women. What Puar suggests here is that intersectionality creates a problematic model of subjectivity by focusing on "difference from" rather than "difference within", establishing white womanhood as a norm and othering women of colour (WOC) by defining them via their "difference from" this norm (2012a, 53).

Critique 2: Intersectionality is based on stable and knowable identities

While intersectionality seeks to recognise difference within social groups and categories of identity, queer theory seeks to denaturalise such categorisations. Yet as Puar notes, intersectionality is based not only on recognising difference, but also on fixing it into a stable form. As she writes:

> Intersectionality demands the knowing, naming, and thus stabilizing of identity across space and time, relying on the logic of equivalence and analogy between various axes of identity. (2007, 212)

A similar argument has been put forward by Grosz, who describes intersectionality as "a gridlike model that fails to account for the mutual constitution and indeterminacy of embodied configurations of gender, sexuality, race, class, and nation" (1994, 19).

Critique 3: Intersectionality allows/produces state violence

Similarly to Brown's critique of identity politics discussed in Chapter 6, Puar argues that because intersectionality insists upon a knowable and stable subject it reifies the mechanisms of power that confer subject status in the first place. Intersectional approaches to identity fit comfortably with state operations of surveillance. As Puar writes:

> [I]ntersectionality colludes with the disciplinary apparatus of the state –census, demography, racial profiling, surveillance – in that difference is encased within a structural container that simply wishes the messiness of identity into a formulaic grid. (2007, 212)

Puar suggests that intersectionality's focus on defined and neat categories of difference (or axes) aligns with the understanding of identity that underpins acts of state violence such as racial profiling.

NEW AVENUES FOR QUEER THEORY

Throughout the 2000s, many new applications, reinterpretations and appropriations of queer theory critique emerged. A significant body of work crossed disciplinary boundaries, bringing queer theory into conversation with a range of different social issues. This included a broad range of queer theory reflections on the intersections of gender, class, race and sexuality across issues of identity, nation, citizenship and belonging (see Delany 1999; Eng 2001; Fiol-Matta 2002; Muñoz 1999; Reid-Pharr 2001). In the wake of this, diverse theoretical approaches to queer theory began to proliferate. While the term "intersectionality" refers to an analytical framework to explore the multiple axes of identity, subjectivity and social formation, we can also use the term "intersection" to refer to instances where one theoretical frame meets another. As discussed below, these theoretical trajectories have included work between queer theory and Critical Race Studies which produced Black Queer Studies and queer analyses of race; queer theory's geopolitical turn, focused on issues including migration and diaspora; queer Indigenous studies; queer theory's ontological turn, focused on issues including materiality, affect, and a turn away from representation; intersections between Marxism and queer theory; and deployments of disability studies with queer theory.

Queer theory in practice: Queering the curriculum part 1

There are many intersections of queer theory that emerge where the critical perspectives and analytical frameworks of queer theory have been taken up in other areas of study. Some of these intersections do take on intersectional ideas (in Crenshaw's terms) though they do not always employ intersectionality as an organising principle.

Queer education
Queer theory has been used within the field of education studies to help think about how knowledge is produced. Academics working in this area show how adopting a queer pedagogy might involve undertaking different "reading" practices to uncover what cannot be otherwise known/thought (Britzman 1995).

Queer performance

Academics in performance studies have borrowed significantly from queer theory and have contributed to queer projects (Muñoz 1999). Queer performance can simply refer to LGBTIQ performance art and practice, but it also takes up queer theory's interest in the performative and the political. Queer performance studies focus on destabilising political, social and aesthetic norms of the body, gender and sexuality.

Queer screen

Taking queer theory beyond gender studies, a substantial body of scholarship unites the interests of queer theory with a range of screen theories. This field includes diverse works ranging from historical analyses of LGBTIQ representation (Russo 1987) to closer examinations of individual texts, genres and auteurs to a broader discussion of the aesthetic and narrative possibilities of queer. Queer film theory also seeks to decode film storytelling and write queerness into the history of cinema (Doty 1993, 2000; Dyer 1990; White 1999). Many ideas from queer theory are distilled in New Queer Cinema, a film movement that emerged in the USA in the 1990s. New Queer Cinema moves away from issues of LGBTIQ visibility to reflect queer theory's focus on queer politics and the construction of sex, gender and sexuality (Aaron 2004; Benshoff and Griffin 2004; Gever et al. 1993). As a union of theory and practice, New Queer Cinema is also notable for experimentation with cinematic form to evoke queer as an aesthetic. Other work in this field seeks to explore the aesthetic possibilities of queer in relation to the pleasures and effects of other screen media such as television (Chambers 2009; Davis and Needham 2009; Villarejo 2014) and videogames (Ruberg 2018), while additional writing demonstrates how queerness has been central to the development of global cinema cultures (Schoonover and Galt 2016).

Queer theology

Taking queer ideas to the study and practice of religion, queer theology challenges the assumption that queerness and spirituality are incompatible (see Cheng 2011; Goh 2017). Queer theologians look to religious texts to demonstrate that gender diversity and non-heterosexual desire have always had a place in human cultures and religions. Other avenues of queer theology seek to open religion to the LGBTIQ community.

Queer(s) of colour theory, queering race

Taking up some questions posed within queer(s) of colour critiques, academics in the 2000s explored the intersections of queer theory and Critical Race Studies to interrogate relationships between sexuality, ethnicity, race, racialisation and nation. Out of this developed Black Queer Studies and other queer analyses of race. One tipping point for this was the "Black Queer Studies in the Millennium" conference held at the University of North Carolina in 2000, which sought to interrogate how "current formulations of queer theory either ignore the categories of race and class or theorize their effects in 'discursive' rather than material terms" (Alexander 2000, 1285). This conference set the tone for future work in Black Queer Studies and was later developed into *Black Queer Studies: A Critical Anthology* (Johnson and Henderson 2005). Early Black Queer Studies used intersectionality to pose a set of important questions to queer theory:

> What are the implications of queer theory for the study of gay, bisexual and transgendered people of color? Does "queer," as a term, actually fulfil its promise of inclusivity as it is currently deployed in Queer Theory? (Alexander 2000, 1285)

Building upon these questions, academics have fleshed out the intersections between queer theory and Critical Race Studies. For instance, Sharon Patricia Holland points to the myopia on race evident in some histories of queerness, such as Foucault's *History of Sexuality* which ignores historical events "such as trans-atlantic slavery or Indian removal as if these events bear no mark upon our sexual proclivities" (2012, 11). Similarly, Ferguson develops queer(s) of colour analysis to argue that discourses of race and sexuality have been deeply entwined, linking the "multiplication of racialized discourses of sexuality and gender" in the USA to the "multiplication of labor under capital" (2003, 12). As Ferguson and Grace Kyungwon Hong further suggest, neoliberal forces demanding "upward redistribution" have severely, violently and disproportionately affected minorities (2012, 1058), and thus a critique of neoliberalism must be central to queer(s) of colour critiques. Also working in this area is E. Patrick Johnson, who brings together Butler and Critical Race Studies, to argue that "Blackness" is performatively constituted (Johnson 2003). As we noted in Chapter 5, Butler argues that gender is "an identity instituted through *a stylised repetition of acts*" (1988, 519). Building on this, Johnson argues that Blackness has no essence, but is produced through the repetition of everyday acts.

A similar argument is put forward in Ian Barnard's *Queer Race: Cultural Interventions in the Racial Politics of Queer Theory*. Barnard uses queer theory to draw out some of the social, and cultural and political meanings of "race". Seeing sexuality and race as intersecting axes of subjectivity "that formatively and inherently define each other" Barnard delineates the racial inscription of the "queer" in queer theory, politics and identity, arguing that sexuality is always racially inscribed and race is always sexualised (2004, 2). Barnard highlights the constructedness of race, how race is shaped by sexuality and fundamentally "how queer race is" (2004, 10).

Key concept: Disidentification

Muñoz proposes an approach to identity that rejects both homonormative identity politics and the dismissiveness about identity evident in some queer theory critiques.

In his 1999 work *Disidentifications: Queers of Color and the Performance of Politics* Muñoz explores the potential ways that dominant regimes of identity can be worked through to simultaneously reference and dismantle identity. Focusing particularly on queers of colour doing drag performances, Muñoz describes how their performances at once reference normative and punitive gender, sexual and racial oppression, while at once calling these into question. He suggests:

> Disidentification is meant to be descriptive of the survival strategies the minority subject practices in order to negotiate a phobic majoritarian public sphere that continually elides or punishes the existence of subjects who do not conform to the phantasm of normative citizenship. (1999, 4)

Disidentification is a way to describe the strategy of negotiating fields of identity constituted within the context of oppression, in ways that refer to, but do not harden, those identity positions.

Drawing on the work of Nancy Fraser, Muñoz refers to the "counterpublics" where disidentification is practised. Here, counterpublics refers to those formations outside of the normative public sphere (such as queer bars) where the subordinated can gather together.

Muñoz also takes on the project of queering racial categories, describing the complex experience of not quite identifying with particular aspects of your identity, subject position or culture. His theory of "disidentification" as noted in Chapter 6 refers to the ways that minority groups negotiate identity in a world that erases difference by punishing those who do not fit the normative mould. This is used to describe how queer people of colour negotiate mainstream culture not simply by assimilating into it or rejecting it outright, but rather by transforming it for their own purposes, in effect producing queer counterpublics. Relating race and sexuality to performance theory, Muñoz argues that disidentifications are both "a process of production and a mode of performance ... shuffling back and forth between reception and production" (1999, 25). This theory shows how minority subjects – such as queer people of colour – participate in queer world-making through complex negotiations with dominant ideologies.

Also contributing to this area of queer(s) of colour theory is E. Patrick Johnson, who argues that queer theory is limited in its capacity to "accommodate the issues faced by gays and lesbians of colour who come from 'raced' communities" (Johnson 2001, 3). To deal with this, Johnson developed an approach to queer theory, which he coined "Quare Theory". As he describes, Quare Theory:

> not only speaks across identities, it *articulates* identities as well. "Quare" offers a way to critique stable notions of identity and, at the same time, to locate racialized and class knowledges. (2001, 3)

Johnson's "Quare Theory" takes an intersectional approach to theory, grounding the critical project of "queer" in the material conditions and lived experience of class and race.

Queer theory's geopolitical turn

Academics have taken up queer theory as a critical framework to investigate queerness alongside geopolitical issues, focusing on colonial histories and postcolonial discourses, nationality and nationalism, citizenship, migration and diasporic identities. Viewing the intersectionality of gender and sexuality as "a function of geopolitical formations" (Arondekar 2004, 236), this work is known as queer theory's "geopolitical turn" and has tended to take either a historical or contemporary focus.

On the one hand, a significant area of scholarship looks at colonial archives and historical contexts to think about sexuality and sexual difference (Holden and Ruppel 2003; Fiol-Matta 2002). Several notable projects take on the project of queering colonial archives by correcting historical materials and writing queerness into the colonial past (Arondekar 2005; Arondekar 2009; Vanita 2002). The other key approach to the geopolitics of queer theory focuses on contemporary issues. Building upon what Cantú (2009) refers to as a "queer political economy of migration", scholarship in this area uses a queer framework to reveal "the complex interplay of sexuality, gender, race, politics, economics, and culture in shaping desire and the mobility of different bodies across many different kinds of borders" (Lewis and Naples 2014, 912). As such, this area focuses on migration, globalisation, queer diasporas and homonationalism, much of which critically interrogates US exceptionalism.

As discussed in Chapter 6, homonationalism is a key concept in queer theory's geopolitical turn. Discussing the effects of homonationalism in the specific context of the USA, Puar (2007) examines national stigmas in the aftermath of the World Trade Center September 11 attacks, and how LGBTIQ rights discourses were used by the US state to support imperialist and racist agendas in relation to "other" cultures. Puar shows how in obituaries and media reports, gendered, sexualised and racial codings were used to associate September 11 US hero Mark Bingham with positive attributes such as masculine, white, American, hero, gay patriot, while negative connotations *once* associated with homosexuality were used to racialise and sexualise the figure of the terrorist. The effect of this was to position mainstream "homonationalist" homosexuality as "good", while simultaneously associate "bad" queerness with terrorism and an explicit threat to US values.

Also theorising hegemonic sexual cultures in the context of the USA, Eithne Luibhéid's research locates the US border as a site for controlling, contesting, constructing and renegotiating women's sexual identities (Luibhéid 2002). Her later work on queer migration focuses specifically on queer immigrants of colour, honing in on the experiences of migrants from places such as Mexico, Cuba, El Salvador and the Philippines (Luibhéid and Cantú 2005), and additionally explores the role of heteronormativity in shaping discourse surrounding migration (Luibhéid 2008, 2013).

While much work within the geopolitical turn in queer theory maintains a focus on the USA, Arnaldo Cruz-Malavé and Martin F. Manalansan IV extend queer geopolitics towards a global understanding of queerness (Cruz-Malavé and Manalansan 2002). Cruz-Malavé and Manalansan draw attention to the impact of globalisation on queer cultures and communities. As we have noted in Chapter 2, the global visibility of LGBTIQ issues, queer sexualities and queer cultures has resulted in the commodification of queer, which we discussed through the contemporary pride movement. Yet Cruz-Malavé and Manalansan also suggest that because politics have been equally globalised in the millennial era, the terrain for queer political intervention has also expanded. In other work, Manalansan suggests such issues of globalisation have produced a range of queer identities and subjectivities, arguing that "migration can be an important factor in the creation of a variety of sexual identity categories and practices that do not depend on Western conceptions of selfhood and community" (2006, 229).

Another key focus of the geopolitical turn, which is also reflected on by Cruz-Malavé and Manalansan, is the area of queer diaspora. This includes the analysis of sexuality, LGBTIQ identities and kinships within diasporic communities (see also Fountain-Stokes 2009) and more conceptual projects that focus on queering the notion of diaspora (see Eng 2003; Gopinath 2005). As Gayatri Gopinath argues, diaspora has traditionally relied on a "genealogical,

---

Key term: Diaspora

Diaspora refers to the dispersion of people and communities from their place of origin or homeland. The term has often been used in relation to refugee and immigrant populations as well as other communities experiencing displacement from their homeland, but it has been taken up by cultural studies to refer to more complex cultural interchanges between "home" and elsewhere.

Some queer scholars have sought to understand the experience of LGBTIQ individuals and communities within diasporic cultures. As Richard Mole (2018) suggests, the concept of "queer diaspora" enables us to think differently about "identity, belonging and solidarity among sexual minorities in the context of dispersal and transnational networks" (2018, 1269).

However, for others, queer theory troubles traditional understandings of diaspora as it encourages us to question these narratives of migration and to think critically about the concepts, such as "home" and "origin", that underpin them.

implicitly heteronormative reproductive logic" (2005, 10) that has tended to reinforce ideologies of the nation-state. For Eng, the process of queering diaspora prompts,

> [N]ew ways of contesting traditional family and kinship structures – of reorganizing national and transnational communities based not on origin, filiation, and genetics but on destination, affiliation, and the assumption of a common set of social practices or political commitments. (2003, 4)

Taking a queer approach to diaspora denaturalises traditional narratives of migration, prompting critical reflection on concepts such as "origin", "home" and even "nation". Hence, as Eng et al. suggest, the field of queer diasporas

> investigates what might be gained politically by reconceptualising diaspora not in conventional terms of ethnic dispersion, filiation, and biological traceability, but rather in terms of queerness, affiliation, and social contingency. (2005, 2)

In relation to this question of diaspora and transnational queer studies, many queer theorists continue to note the problems of transposing Western constructions of sexuality to other geopolitical regions and cultural contexts (see Wallace 2003).

Problematically, a Western-focused approach to understanding "queer" has often been re-inscribed in transnational approaches. As Hayes, Higonnet and Spurlin point out:

> While work on queer globalization often attempts to make postcolonial and non-Euro-American forms of queerness more visible, such legibility is often an extension of Western gazes that read non-Western, same-sex desires as queer. (2010, 8)

Importantly, as discussed in Chapter 6, many cultures do not view gender and sexuality in the binary and essentialist ways that have dominated Western discourses, and many other terms circulate for culturally specific non-heterosexual, gender diverse identities. These include hijra (South Asia), waria and bissu (Indonesia), tom and dee (Thailand), kathoey or phuying (Thailand), two-spirit (North America), tomboy and po (China), sistergirl and brotherboy (Australia), and fa'afafine (Samoa). The term "queer" also translates into different forms/is appropriated/has completely new meaning in different cultural contexts, including quare (Ireland), guaitai and ku-er

Queer theory in practice: Heteronormativity and resource access

Working at the intersection of queer theory and feminist political ecology, Rebecca Elmhirst's (2011) work highlights the role that heteronormativity can play in determining resource access. Elmhirst highlights how norms of "conjugal partnership" in Indonesia's province of Lampung play a large role in which land-poor migrants from other areas of south-east Asia are able to access resources.

This work suggests that while race and class factors are important, the intersection of these with gender and sexuality ought not be overlooked in terms of the role they play in constructing "ideal" citizens. Here, the conjugal partnership cemented through marriage and family works to figure migrants as "stable".

As Elmhirst writes, "the negotiation of resource access is simultaneously a process of regulation, discipline and subject-making that cements gender categories and inculcates gendered (and heteronormative) ideologies of the 'ideal citizen'" (2011, 176). Elmhirst concludes that the relationship between the politics of resource access and heteronormativity are mutually reinforcing, and that men are also affected and constrained in such gendered regimes.

(China and Taiwan), kuir (Turkey) and kvar (Serbia). Differences in language, origin and meaning highlight the fluidity of "queer" in a transnational context. Some academics even suggest that "Western-style Queer Theory has a neo-imperialist quality that limits understandings or radical practice" in local contexts (Schoonover and Galt 2016). Rejecting a monolithic understanding of what queer theory is and how it may be used, the geopolitical turn seeks to remedy this, developing queer critiques that are attuned to local and culturally specific understandings of gender, sex, sexuality, politics and identity. These works are concerned with how "We are queer. Locally" (Kulpa et al. 2012, 137).

Queer Indigenous studies

Academics and activists have also brought queer theory together with postcolonial and Indigenous studies, examining the links between heteronormativity and settler colonialism (see Smith 2010; Morgensen 2011),

---

Queer theory in practice: Takatāpui in Aotearoa, New Zealand

Elizabeth Kerekere (2015) describes how the term takatāpui is used in Aotearoa, New Zealand as a broad umbrella term for sexually and gender diverse persons. While the term was originally used to describe persons with "same-sex" attractions", Takatāpui is now used as a term to embrace radical inclusivity, rather than focusing on the individual. Kerekere writes,

> Takatāpui often have to choose between being Māori and prioritising our gender or sexuality. Claiming takatāpui enables us to bring all of the parts of ourselves together – to be all of who we are. While the Western world tends to classify and label identities, takatāpui offers opportunities to discover and change. (2015, 8)

Kerekere also highlights how British colonisation changed sexual practices in Aotearoa, New Zealand, introducing punishment of queer and gender diverse practices and relationships within Indigenous Māori populations. Colonial rule also introduced the marginalisation of Māori women, and the heteronormative ideal of the nuclear family unit.

---

a term used to refer to the displacement of Indigenous populations via invasive settler societies. For instance, tracing a cultural and literary history of Native American representation, Mark Rifkin argues that settler colonialism has sought to "straighten" Indigenous peoples by inserting them into "Anglo-American conceptions of family, home, desire, and personal identity" (2011, 8). As part of this, Indigenous peoples have been cast as a perverse problem to be fixed. At the same time, Rifkin notes a parallel tradition wherein non-native people have claimed Indigenous social structures and customs as expansive and counterhegemonic symbols of resistance to heteronormativity. Within this tradition, Indigenous cultures are viewed as liberating models to be emulated. As Rifkin highlights, both traditions erase Indigenous political autonomy by interpreting "indigenous social dynamics in ways that emphasize their cultural difference from dominant Euramerican ideals as opposed to their role in processes of political self-definition" (2011, 8).

Queer Indigenous studies seek to decolonise Indigenous knowledges about sex, gender and sexuality. As Driskill et al. note, this involves "interruption of colonial authority over knowledge and a recognition of Indigenous people as central to all knowledge claims about themselves" (2011b, 4). In the North American context, the project of queer Indigenous analysis regularly centres on *queer* and *two-spirit* as organising terms.

> *Queer* carries with it an oppositional critique of heteronormativity and an interest in the ambiguity of gender and sexuality. *Two-Spirit* was proposed in Indigenous organizing in Canada and the United States to be inclusive of Indigenous people who identify as GLBTQ or through nationally specific terms from Indigenous languages. When linked, *queer* and *Two-Spirit* invite critiquing heteronormativity as a colonial project, and decolonizing Indigenous knowledges of gender and sexuality as one result of that critique. (2011, 3)

A key scholar taking up this project is Scott Lauria Morgensen, who stages a conversation between Native American Studies and queer theory to investigate sovereignty and nation alongside a historical analysis of two-spirit

---

Queer theory in practice: Fa'afafine in Samoa

Fa'afafine is a term used in Samoa to refer to persons who are assigned male at birth, but adopt feminine identities. As many scholars have discussed, fa'afafine is not synonymous with Western concepts of homosexuality or transgender identity, and must be understood within the specific Samoan cultural context. In her discussion of fa'afafine identity, Johanna Schmidt argues that labour practices and the preference to do "feminine" tasks in the home at an early age has been traditionally understood as a determining factor for being fa'afafine, rather than sexuality.

However, with globalisation, and the increasing influence of Western capitalism and cultural formations, Schmidt argues that there is greater emphasis on individual gender expression for all Samoans, which has changed self-conceptualisations and embodiments of fa'afafine. Schmidt concludes: "Fa'afafine in Samoa seem to walk a fine line between rupture and continuity, often identifying as gay and fa'afafine simultaneously as a means of adopting and adapting to aspects of globalized western cultures while maintaining and enacting identities through processes that are distinctly Samoan" (2003, 429).

activism (Morgensen 2011). Morgensen argues that within settler states such as the USA, queer subjectivities are the result of distinct sovereignties that developed through US colonial settlement.

Andrea Smith also uses queer theory to "unsettle" the phenomenon of settler colonialism as a formative logic (2010, 44). Rather than simply focus on the inclusion of Indigenous peoples in the US context, Smith uses both queer theory and Indigenous studies to advocate for a broader systemic critique attuned to the normalising logics of colonial rule. Indigenous studies programmes and calls for decolonisation of the curriculum have proliferated in universities, with queer Indigenous studies emerging particularly across North America and the Pacific, in locations such as Australia, New Zealand, Canada and Samoa (see Driskill et al. 2011a).

Queer Marxism

As Kevin Floyd (2009) suggests, following the global financial crisis queer theorists have recently been more open to consider the resonance between queer theory and Marxism (e.g., see Crosby et al. 2012). In *Reification of Desire: Toward a Queer Marxism*, Floyd suggests productive ways that key Marxist concepts might be extended by taking a queer approach, and indeed how queer theory might be more open to considering a theoretical genealogy informed by Marxism. As Rosemary Hennessy (2006) argues, the legacy of Marxist feminism on later lesbian and gay studies (and subsequently queer theory) has often been forgotten. Floyd also suggests that the crisis of capital has also encouraged a return to discussions of "utopia", a topic that we discuss further in Chapter 8.

Karl Marx was a German philosopher, born in 1818. He is perhaps most famous for his 1848 work *The Communist Manifesto*, written with Friedrich Engels. Fundamentally, Marx's theory relies on the idea that society under capitalism is fundamentally underpinned by class struggle, namely the agonism between the working class (the "proletariat") and the ruling class (the "bourgeoise"). The ruling class own the means of production (the factories and infrastructure), and extract profit from the working class who provide labour. It is precisely this hierarchal model of power that sits at odds with some queer theory accounts, such as Foucault's idea of power as dispersed, as discussed in Chapter 2.

While queer theory and Marxism have often been perceived at odds from one another, there have been many who have theorised gender and sexual relations using Marxist ideas, though these would not necessarily

Queer theory in practice: Decolonising the curriculum

Since the 2010s there have been growing calls to "decolonise the curriculum" in universities across the world. The term "decolonise" in this context is often used in reference to teaching practices, and the kind of materials and readings that occupy a privileged place (that are canon) in the curriculum. Decolonising the curriculum is about displacing the whiteness and Western civilisation as the centre of all knowledge.

For example, since 2015, students in South Africa have called for their universities to decolonise, often rallying under the hashtag #Rhodesmustfall. This is a reference to a statue of former colonial Prime Minister Cecil Rhodes, which was defaced as part of student protests against white imperialism at the University of Cape Town (Francis and Hardman 2018, 67).

Similarly, in 2017, student Lola Olufemi's open letter to Cambridge University in the UK went viral, as she called on the Literature department to include more women of colour in their syllabus. Commenting on the letter she described, "Decolonising the curriculum … means rethinking what we learn and how we learn it; critically analysing whose voices are given priority in our education and for what reason. It is not an easy process and why should it be?" Olufemi argued for greater interrogation of whose voices were taken as representative of "humanity" and whose were not.

Some scholars have been critical of the use of the term "decolonise" in the context of curricula, given the original political material meaning of the term. As Eve Tuck and K. Wayne Yang argue, decolonisation should not be mistaken for a metaphor. They write:

> Decolonization brings about the repatriation of Indigenous land and life; it is not a metaphor for other things we want to do to improve our societies and schools. The easy adoption of decolonising discourse by educational advocacy and scholarship, evidenced by the increasing number of calls to "decolonise our schools," or use "decolonizing methods," or, "decolonise student thinking," turns decolonization into a metaphor. (2012, 1)

Yet others have proposed that decolonising the curriculum need not be understood as merely metaphorical. As Gurminder K. Bhambra, Dalia

Gebrial and Kerem Nişancıoğlu suggest, though the term is contested, decolonizing approaches are both political and methodological. They argue that these approaches involve bringing focus on "colonialism, empire and racism" to the fore and thus provide a different lens through which to understand and politically respond to the world (2018, 2). As they suggest, given the historic centrality of universities within colonised territories, it is no wonder that there are demands for transformation of these institutions.

be understood as "queer theory" approaches to gender and sexuality. For example, like many Marxist accounts of sexuality, Hannah Dee argues that the oppression of lesbian, gay, bisexual and transgender persons is fundamentally a result of the regime of the economic family unit of the family under capitalism. Dee writes, "LGBT people are seen as a problem because we undermine and disrupt the relationships and roles that the traditional family rests on" (2010, 9). Unlike Foucauldian accounts, Marxist accounts of sexuality do not emphasise that sexuality is *produced* through prohibition, but rather, that *oppression* based on sexuality only exists because of class society.

However, for many queer theorists looking to the intersection with Marxist theory, discussions of sexuality and gender in Marxist theorising have historically been insufficient. Many, such as Ferguson, have attempted to re-think Marxist concepts to better account not just for questions of sexuality, but also race (see Ferguson's discussion in the roundtable Crosby et al. 2012). Similarly, for some Marxist theorists, discussions of capital and class in queer theorising have historically been lacking. As Yvette Taylor suggests, "Theories of identity are increasingly preoccupied with the queer subject of desire, rather than with material needs and constraints" (2018, 201). As Hennessey also argues, queer Marxist theorising understands there is an intimate relationship between class and sexuality, such that the sexuality one can express is determined by class (2006, 129). Petrus Liu (2015) takes this approach to understand queer cultures in Mainland China and Taiwan, focusing on the way many Chinese writers in the postwar period fused Marxism with inquiries into gender and sexuality within their writing. In this analysis, Liu uncovers the Marxist underpinnings of queer thought in China and Taiwan and highlights how certain geopolitical tensions impact the way queerness is both understood and expressed within these contexts.

Some have also taken a queer Marxist analysis to explain the hierarchical system of social difference through which gender, sexuality and race are organised with respect to capitalism. Discussing the relation between capitalism, gender and sexuality, Hennessy notes:

> In positing male and female as distinct and opposite sexes that are naturally attracted to one another, heterosexuality is integral to patriarchy. Woman's position as subordinate other, as (sexual) property, and as exploited laborer depends on a heterosexual matrix in which woman is taken to be man's opposite; his control over social resources, his clear thinking, strength, and sexual prowess depend on her being less able, less rational, and never virile. (2002, 24–25)

However, she also notes that such relations are not fixed and essential but rather historical and differential. This acknowledges that not all experience power and oppression in the same manner. As Holly Lewis (2016) argues, one of the great mistakes made by many queer thinkers has been to assume that there is something inherently radical to queer sexuality, and as such there has been a disproportionate amount of concern about queers who consume/fail to be radical (the "homonormative", as discussed in detail in Chapter 6). Lewis suggests that to move on from this lacuna, and to pay proper attention to theorising sexuality and economy, "Queer Marxists must disengage with queer nationalism. The time spent denouncing upper echelon queers for behaving like upper echelon queers would be better spent fighting the battles it is wrongly assumed they will fight" (2016).

Queering affect, affect-ing queer theory

The intersection between queer theory and affect theory has also become a significant avenue of exploration in queer theorising in recent years, sometimes referred to as the "affective turn". The term "affect" is sometimes used synonymously for emotions or feelings. Others, strongly influenced by Gilles Deleuze's approach, deploy affect to refer to sensations, intensities or impulses and negate the association of affect with emotion (Massumi 2002, 27). That is, some scholars argue that "emotions" already carry the weight of cognitive interpretation, whereas affect refers to feelings that are pre-cognitive.

Queer theory in practice: Affect according to Deleuze

Gilles Deleuze was a French philosopher who worked closely with Félix Guattari, and was heavily influenced by the philosophical work of Friedrich Nietzsche, Baruch Spinoza and Henri Bergson. According to Deleuze, affect is pre-cognitive, and refers to intensities, becomings, changes and reactions. As Felicity J. Colman writes, "Affect is the change, or variation, that occurs when bodies collide, or come into contact" (11). Here "bodies" is broadly conceived not in terms of the human body, but rather, any *thing*, from the smallest animal body to ideas as concepts as bodies. Given his emphasis on bodies many queer and feminist theorists have explored sexuality and gender using Deleuzian ideas of affect as a foundation (e.g., see Grosz 1994).

As Puar (2011, 154) – drawing heavily on Deleuze – defines, affect theory often involves:

- a shift in focus from rational human agency, to ontological perspectives that understand agency as more broadly dispersed;
- a turn towards the sensory and biological without taking up essentialist positions;
- highlighting non-conscious bodily processes rather than conscious or psychological ones.

As Gregory Seigworth and Melissa Gregg identify, there are multiple strands of affect theory, but the definition they offer perhaps most applicable to work in gender studies and queer theory is described as:

[T]he regularly hidden-in-plain-sight politically engaged work – perhaps most often undertaken by feminists, queer theorists, disability activists, and subaltern peoples living under the thumb of a normativizing power – that attends to the hard and fast materialities, as well as the fleeting and flowing ephemera, of the daily and the workaday, of everyday and everynight life, and of "experience" (understood in ways far more collective and "external" rather than individual and interior), where persistent, repetitious practices of power can simultaneously provide a body (or, better, collectivized bodies) with predicaments and potentials for realizing a world that subsists within and exceeds the horizons and boundaries of the norm. (2010, 7)

While this definition is a lot to take in, the key takeaway is an understanding of queer theory's focus on questions of marginalisation and normativity in concert with affect theory's focus on materiality, bodies and potentiality.

Despite many affect theorists tracing trajectories from Deleuze, much of the turn towards theorising affect within queer theory has been inspired by the work of Sedgwick (discussed in Chapter 5), who moved to studies of affect later in her career. Sedgwick's engagement with affect is best reflected in her analyses of psychologist Silvan Tomkins' work on affect theory (Sedgwick 2003). Tomkins argued that humans are born with innate affects, of which shame is central. As Sedgwick and Adam Frank describe, "Tomkins hypothesizes a set of excruciating scenes in which a child is shamed out of expressing his excitement, distress, anger, fear, disgust, and even shame" (1995, 518). Sedgwick takes up this central focus on shame in much of her later work. Her writing on the intersection between affect and queer theory has been influential in discussions of gay shame as discussed in Chapter 4.

Ann Cvetkovich (2003) explores the intersection of affect theory and queer theory, teasing out the connections between sexuality, trauma and the creation of queer public cultures. Focusing on trauma, Cvetkovich

---

Key term: Ontology

Ontology refers to "being", often used in the context of philosophical discussions of the nature of life. The term the "ontological turn" is sometimes referred to in the humanities and social sciences, and refers to the general trend towards thinking about/concern with questions of ontology, often placed in contrast to representation (see Mol 1999). While earlier poststructuralist accounts focused on issues around language and signification, the ontological turn has been an attempt by scholars to grapple with questions of materiality and life beyond, before, or in addition to discourse. As Clare Hemmings remarks, "If poststructuralist epistemology is the problem, it is perhaps not enormously surprising that a post-deconstructivist ontology is offered as the solution" (2005, 557).

argues that so-called negative affects can be the foundation for political solidarity and community formation. Her later work on depression focuses on affects associated with mental illness (Cvetkovich 2012). Cvetkovich suggests we ought to get to the "depression" at the heart of things, that is, not the negativity and negation of life, but more specifically the "negative" feelings that are part and parcel of being in and surviving the world. This work explores how politics are felt on an affective level, and offers a queer analysis of depression as a historical category, a personal experience and a spark for cultural production and political activism. Cvetkovich suggests a dissolution of the binary between the social and the anti-social, the positive and the negative, because while things such as depression can be anti-social (in quite a literal way – through withdrawal), there is also the possibility that a new sociality may form through making these affective states *public*, and indeed, making *publics* around these affects.

Queer theory in practice: Depressed? It might be political

In the early 2000s, Berlant and a group of other scholars and artists formed a group called "Feel Tank Chicago", which came out of earlier feminist organising following the Barnard Conference discussed in detail in Chapter 3. The aim of the feel tank – a play on the idea of a "think tank" – was to explore feelings (which are often understood as very individual, private and frivolous) as historical, political and important.

As Berlant describes, "Comprised of artists and academics, the feel tank is organized around the thought that public spheres are affect worlds at least as much as they are effects of rationality and rationalization" (2004, 450). Here, rather than the notion of "the personal is political", Berlant evokes the idea of "the political is affective", that is, public life is comprised of feelings, and indeed, feelings inform public life.

Rather than understanding this relationship between feelings and the political as merely personal, the aim of Feel Tank Chicago was to unearth and attend to these feelings. Berlant describes how the group held a protest "International Day of the Politically Depressed", as a way to make feelings (such as apathy, depression and anxiety) public. Along these lines she suggests the slogan "Depressed? ... It Might Be Political" (2004, 451).

Love also focuses on negative affect, describing the contemporary queer experience through the metaphor of "feeling backward" (2007, 27). Love argues that feelings associated with social exclusion and the prohibition of same-sex desire, such as shame, despair and regret, have an immense impact on present-day LGBTIQ culture (2007, 4). Love advocates for exploring feelings of backwardness in LGBTIQ history, without simply overlooking "the difficulties of the queer past" (2007, 32).

Key concept: Queer failure

Inspired by Love's work on the connection between loss, "backwardness" and queer life, Halberstam's 2011 book *The Queer Art of Failure* explores failure as a queer mode. Emerging within a specific postfinancial-crisis context, Halberstam not only draws out the resistant possibilities of "failure" but also the link between failure and anti-capitalism. Halberstam (2012) outlines the possibilities of failure in terms of:

1. failure as a space that can be a site for collective mobilisation;
2. the connection between queerness and failure (as non-conformity/non-belonging);
3. how to aesthetically track failure, looking at artists and popular culture to see where failure is being represented and how;
4. that we need to look to the "losers" of the past, not just glorify queer history;
5. how failure can be anti-social but political, and can come from popular-culture sources, not just high-culture.

Children's texts are a key source for Halberstam. In this way Halberstam also demonstrates "failing" at being an appropriate scholar, through engaging with low culture, children's texts. Halberstam takes the very queer approach of reading these texts in terms of the space that they open up for thinking differently. In these texts Halberstam finds hope, as he suggests: "Renton, Johnny Rotten, Ginger, Dory, and Babe, like those athletes who finish fourth, remind us that there is something powerful in being wrong, in losing, in failing, and that all our failures combined might just be enough, if we practice them well, to bring down the winner" (2011, 120). Queer feminist theorist Robyn Wiegman describes Halberstam's approach as "converting loss into heroic loserdom" (2014, 6).

In contrast to exploring negative affects, Sara Ahmed's (2010a, 2010b) work examines the limitations of seemingly positive affects, specifically happiness. Her work draws attention to links between the Western construction of happiness, the ideal of "the good life" and heteronormativity. As we discuss in more detail in Chapter 8, Ahmed critiques regimes of happiness that necessitate assimilation into particular (white, heteronormative) modes of being (2010, 45).

Berlant (2011) also explores the idea of "the good life", and suggests that striving towards this ideal can entail "cruel optimism", a concept that we discuss in more detail in Chapter 8. Cruel optimism refers to labouring under the promise that things will get better, while staying stuck in the toxic conditions of the present. Berlant argues that the culturally constructed image of "the good life" often conflicts with the conditions of everyday experience, and that the (cruel) promise of a better future horizon demoralises and demobilises political action.

Similarly, Puar (2012b) suggests that we might think about how the slogan "It gets better" used in programmes supporting LGBTIQ youth offers a promise – for a particular white, upwardly mobile gay milieu – that homophobia ends after high school. These kinds of slogans confer a sense of inevitable progress, that homophobia is merely a symptom of age, rather than systemic. Following Berlant, and drawing on disability justice activism, Puar turns her attention to the concept of "slow death", or the idea of ongoing ailment endemic to marginalised populations. Like Berlant, Puar is concerned with the link between experiences of daily life and broader economic structures, as she argues, "Debility is profitable to capitalism, but so is the demand to 'recover' from or overcome it" (2012b, 154). Puar advocates for the term "debility" to refer to bodily injury and social exclusions that are brought on by economic and political factors under late capitalism.

Queerness, disability and debility

The intersection of queer theory and disability studies focuses largely on biopolitics, bodies, embodiment, pleasure and identity. Both fields are concerned with unpacking the processes that produce cultural, political and social norms around ability. For instance, one facet of queer disability studies challenges cultural discourses that represent people with disabilities as "incapable or uninterested in sex" (McRuer 2011, 107). Queer disability studies also critiques binaries that frame disability, ability, gender and sexuality as either normative or deviant. These binaries typically associate disability with medical models that frame particular minds and bodies as deviant and in need of treatment.

Robert McRuer's "Crip Theory" takes a radical approach to this, generating a critical framework to challenge not only these binaries, but also the power structures of neoliberal capitalist culture that produce them. Crip Theory questions how some bodies are incorporated into the state, while others are excluded. In doing so, it also exposes "the flexible corporate strategies that currently undergird contemporary economics, politics, and culture" that "invariably produce a world in which disability and queerness are subordinated or eliminated outright" (McRuer 2006, 29). Crip Theory also rejects demands for normativity, tolerance and assimilation, and advocates for access, transgression and systemic critique of ability and "ideal" bodies and minds.

Queer theory in practice: Disability and coming out

Taking a queer approach to disability studies, Ellen Samuels (2003) explores the trope of "coming out" as an analogy for disclosing disability. Samuels suggests that while some scholars have drawn parallels between coming out as LGBTIQ and coming out as having a disability, "coming out" means a multiplicity of things that do not map so neatly onto one another. Importantly, Samuels highlights how many accounts of disclosing disability involve explaining disability to others, rather than a liberatory practice of self-acceptance. Samuels highlights the differential ways that coming out might play out, for example, the scepticism that might be encountered with disclosure of non-visible disabilities.

Samuels also explores the connections between coming out as femme and coming out with a non-visible disability, given the common experience of not being immediately visible. Yet Samuels suggests that the emphasis on visibility within discussions of disability further excludes those who do not present with visible disabilities: "while disability studies has presented profound challenges to dominant cultural conceptions of the body, social identity, and independence, it has not provided the theoretical basis on which to critique and transform the equation of appearance with ability" (2003, 248).

Alison Kafer uses Crip Theory to frame disability through queer politics, arguing that disability is a political, contested and contestable identity (Kafer 2013). This view rejects monolithic or fixed notions of identity and challenges "disability" and "ability" as discrete and self-evident categories. Through this intersection of queer theory and disability studies, Kafer shows how queer frameworks are useful for questioning how "disability", "impairment" and "ability" are culturally produced and understood. Kafer also takes up Crip Theory to reflect on the temporality of the feminist, queer, disabled embodiment, which we discuss further in Chapter 8.

Critiquing Halberstam's *Queer Art of Failure*, Merri Lisa Johnson's "A Crip Feminist Critique of Queer Failure" argues that queer theorists have sometimes failed to adequately engage with questions of disability. Johnson suggests that Halberstam romanticises the concept of craziness, "the conflation of madness with countercultural adventure both reflects and contributes to the cultural trivialization of psychological pain" (253). Halberstam's use of madness as productive for queer theory (rather than a state of mental illness) is also reflected in his later work *Gaga Feminism*, with his emphasis on going "gaga". Johnson argues that in turning towards the "pathological" queer theory can sometimes occlude the experiences of people living with certain conditions, in ways that both cover over and romanticise their reality. Johnson argues that queer theorists need to be careful to avoid fetishisation of disability, and more carefully engage with questions of mental health.

CONCLUSION: QUEER INTERSECTIONS

As we have noted in this chapter, queer theory has undergone dramatic transformation over the last two decades. Queer(s) of colour theory, Crip Theory, postcolonial queer theory and other intersecting theoretical engagements with queer have opened up a vast and dynamic array of queer strands, taking queer theory into new directions. While queer theory always sits in discomfort with intersectionality as it is deployed in identarian ways, the tension between these lenses reminds us of the productive power of uncomfortable relations. To put it simply, when we sit in discomfort, we grow. As queer ideas continue to transgress, infect, pervert, challenge, critique and question – and perhaps most importantly, *be* questioned – queer theory offers a multitude of powerful intersections with other bodies of work.

Queer theory in practice: Queering the curriculum part 2

Queer biology

Drawing on queer theory's focus on "transgressing boundaries" has helped researchers to re-think the categories and linear definitions used in biology to understand sex, bodies and individuals (Hird 2004). Combining queer theory with the biological sciences has enabled scholars to challenge the scientific assumption that opposite-sex sexuality is natural and based on the need for species procreation. Scholars working in queer biology have documented same-sex sexual behaviours across many species, highlighted the prevalence of species that reproduce asexually, and those that change sex during their lifetime (Bagemihl 1999; Roughgarden 2004). More directly responding to human sexuality, other scholarship draws attention to the ideological subjectivity of scientific studies, arguing that what we know about sex, gender and sexuality is actually shaped by politics and biases within the production of scientific knowledge (Fausto-Sterling 2000; Lancaster 2003).

Queer code

Critical perspectives from queer theory have also been applied in the field of computer science, intersecting with analyses and practices of coding, software engineering, algorithms and artificial intelligence. In this intersection, queer theory has been used to expose how gender functions through the conventions of software programming (Stephen 2017) and how algorithms reinforce heteronormativity (Gieseking 2017).

Queer science and technology studies (STS)

Academics have used queer theory to critique the heteronormativity of science and technology studies, which have often reinforced hegemonic points of view (Landström 2007). As it has developed through the 2000s, queer STS examines identity and sexuality in virtual worlds, queer interactions between bodies and technology, and broader relationships between sexuality and technology, which in turn produce diverse critical perspectives on race, class, ethnicity and nation. Queer STS is connected to the ontological turn in theory more broadly (Barad 2007).

Further reading

David L. Eng, J. Halberstam, and José Esteban Muñoz. (2005). "What's Queer About Queer Studies Now?" *Social Text*, 23(3–4 (84–85)): 1–17.

The introduction to this special issue discusses the potential of queer intersectionality while mapping out some of queer theory's recent intersectional developments. The coeditors outline queer theory as a "subjectless critique".

Jasbir K. Puar. (2012). "'I Would Rather be a Cyborg than a Goddess': Becoming-Intersectional in Assemblage Theory." *PhiloSOPHIA*, 2(1): 49–66. State University of New York Press.

Puar's critique of intersectionality is outlined succinctly in this article. She advocates for a theory of queer assemblage to make up for intersectionality's limitations.

Ian Barnard. (2004). *Queer Race: Cultural Interventions in the Racial Politics of Queer Theory*. New York: Peter Lang.

Barnard uses queer theory to draw out some of the social, and cultural and political, meanings of race, demonstrating how race can be queered.

QUESTIONS TO CONSIDER

- In what ways does intersectionality address the risk of queer theory erasing difference altogether?
- What value do you think queer theory has, as a "subjectless critique", for broad-reaching social issues such as globalisation?
- What are some practical ways you might "decolonise" the curriculum? How is this different to "queering" the curriculum?
- What do the "intersections" between queer theory and other fields of ideas (such as affect theory or disability studies) reveal about the limits of queer theory?

Recommended films

Margarita with a Straw **(Shonali Bose 2014).** This is a coming of age film about a teenage girl with cerebral palsy coming to terms with her sexuality. One of only a few narrative feature-length films to foreground the intersectional experience of gender, sexuality, race, nationality and disability.

Futuro Beach **(Karim Aïnouz 2014).** This film follows the story of a difficult relationship between a Brazilian man and his German boyfriend who both live in Berlin. Director Karim Aïnouz aimed to capture the experience of living in queer diaspora in this film.

Moonlight **(Barry Jenkins 2016).** This award-winning drama is also a coming of age story that focuses on issues of class, race and sexuality through three key periods in the life of a young, African-American, gay man growing up in a rough neighborhood of Miami.

8 Temporality and Queer Utopias

KEY TERMS AND CONCEPTS	temporality, chrononormativity, anti-social thesis, orientation, queer time, cruel optimism, utopia, happiness scripts, chronobiopolitics, temporal drag

QUEER THEORY AND TIME: A TEMPORAL TURN

What does queer theory have to say about time and temporality? As we highlight in this chapter, a significant body of contemporary queer theory known as "the temporal turn" raises questions about queerness and time, productivity and what counts as a "good" life. Some theorists have asked where queer theory stands in relation to the past, present and future while others have considered what queer temporalities might look like or how they might be experienced. Navigating queer theory's temporal turn, we explore how theorists have approached these questions of time by debating the relationship between queerness and "the future". Examining key perspectives from opposing anti-social and optimistic theorists, we highlight tensions between positive and negative affects that have been associated with past, present and future orientations. We conclude with the question of queer time and consider how different theorists have imagined the political potential of time through queer theory.

As a re-framing of conversations and debates on sexuality and politics, queer theory's temporal turn has encouraged queer theorists to "rethink the very meaning of queer" by recognising it "as concept that is always entangled with temporality" (Monaghan 2019, 99). In a roundtable discussion on "Theorizing Temporalities", Elizabeth Freeman asked a range of queer theorists, "how and why the rubric of temporality … became important to your thinking as a queer theorist. What scholarly, activist, personal, political, or other concerns motivated the turn toward time for you?" (Dinshaw et al. 2007, 177). For many of the theorists involved, the answer was to pose a critique of historicism and linear narratives of progress, while for others the turn was

Key term: Temporality

In the broadest sense, temporality means time. Philosophers have used the term to refer to the experience of duration, the perception of time passing and relations of past, present and future. Within humanities research, temporality is also used to refer to the social organisation of time through categories such as working hours and leisure time. To describe queer theory as having a "temporal turn" means that the field began to focus on intersections between sex, gender, sexuality, history, power and time.

more personal. Carolyn Dinshaw notes that she had always had a concern with the "relationship of past to present" (Dinshaw et al. 2007, 177), which bloomed into "a queer desire for history" (Dinshaw et al. 2007, 178) in her later work. For Christopher Nealon, who had been researching activism and social movements, the turn towards temporality was motivated by recognition of the queerness of "lesbian and gay writers who lived before the time of a social movement ... dreaming of collectivities, and forms of participation in History-with-a-capital-H, that they might never, themselves experience" (Dinshaw et al. 2007, 179). For Jagose, the temporal came unexpected in her research on figurations of lesbian representation in popular culture, while for Ferguson, temporality was a necessary frame for critiquing narratives of progress in discourses of African-American sexuality and "other geopolitical histories of racialized sexuality" (Dinshaw et al. 2007, 180).

In an introductory essay on queer theory and temporalities, Freeman set out some further ideas for thinking about queerness in relation to time. This work suggested that queer theory and temporality could be united as a critical framework to provide insight into everything from "life narratives to the eight-hour workday, to premature ejaculation, the AIDS crisis, the queer past and future, the lived experience of being an LGBTIQ person" (Monaghan 2019, 97). Freeman's introduction preceded a roundtable "theorizing queer temporalities" where theorists addressed several key questions: Is time part of the history of sexuality and has it shaped Queer Studies? What might queer theory's attention to temporality open up "conceptually, institutionally, politically, or otherwise?" (Dinshaw et al. 2007).

A key text in queer theory's temporal turn that responds to such questions is Carolyn Dinshaw's *Getting Medieval: Sexualities and Communities, Pre and*

Postmodern (1999) in which she seeks to *queer* the history of sexuality. In this book, Dinshaw analyses both pre-modern and postmodern categories of sexuality, focusing on the key question, "how do communities, then and now, form themselves in relation to sex?" (1999, 1). In Dinshaw's work, sex (or the erotic) is "heterogeneous, multiple, and fundamentally indeterminate" (1999, 1), which means that it cannot be traced via linear path from past to present. As such, Dinshaw follows "a queer historical impulse ... making connections across time between, on the one hand, lives, texts, and other cultural phenomena left out of sexual categories back then and, on the other, those left out of current sexual categories now" (1999, 1). By analysing queer sexualities within this historical frame and describing them as "affective relations across time" (Dinshaw 1999, 138), Dinshaw argues for an understanding of queer history as non-linear. Describing queerness in this way, via non-linear forms of connection across time, Dinshaw's early contribution to queer theory's temporal turn "explode[s] the categories of sameness, otherness, present, past, loss, pleasure" (1999, 2).

HETERONORMATIVE TEMPORALITY

Scholarship on queer temporality has tended to fall on either side of opposing anti-social and optimistic perspectives. However, both sides of the debate explore how heterosexual ideology shapes the way we understand and organise the temporality of social life. As we have discussed in Chapter 1, heteronormativity refers to the pervasive and largely invisible heterosexual norms that underpin society (Warner 1991). Within queer theory's temporal turn, heteronormativity is thought of in relation to time with a particular focus on the question of what counts as a "good", happy or successful life. According to queer theorists, heteronormative life narratives are marked by a particular set of celebrated milestones, which include birth, childhood, adolescence, adulthood, marriage, reproduction, parenthood, anniversaries, retirement and death. As Halberstam argues, these are based on "institutions of family, heterosexuality, and reproduction" (2005, 1). We have plotted these along a timeline in Figure 8.1 to show their linearity as they progress from one milestone to the next. In Western culture, a person is thought to have a successful life if they pass through each stage at an appropriate speed. For example, behaviours associated with adolescence (such as recklessness) should be forsaken as the person grows up, gets married to someone of the opposite gender and starts their own family.

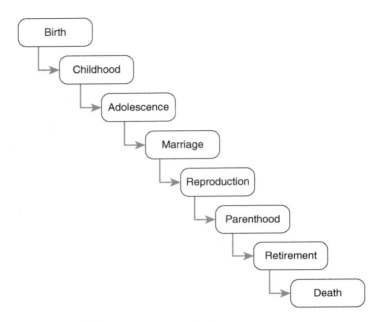

Figure 8.1   The heteronormative timeline

For women, reproductive temporality is ruled by a biological clock; for married heterosexual couples it is ruled by "strict bourgeois rules of respectability and scheduling" (Halberstam 2005, 5). Halberstam identifies family time as referring to the scheduling of daily life, particularly the phrase "early to bed, early to rise" that accompanies the practice of child-rearing. Notions of respectability and normality are also governed by "the time of inheritance" (2005, 5), which refers to a generational time within which "values, wealth, goods, and morals are passed through family ties from one generation to the next" (2005, 5). This also connects family to the historical past and "glances ahead to connect the family to the future of both familial and national stability" (2005, 5).

While not all people keep these times, Halberstam argues that "many and possibly most people believe that the scheduling of repro-time is natural and desirable" (2005, 5). These temporalities have become ingrained into our understandings of how a normal life *should* be lived. However, there are some people or some groups of people who are unable or unwilling to follow these normalised life narratives and there are others who are blatantly rejected and pathologised by them. In contrast to the linear "good" life, queer life narratives in particular are described in ways that conflict with or challenge the heteronormative timeline. As Monaghan argues, "Queer life narratives ... do not fit with these dominant temporal logics. Non-linear in their temporality, they do not follow the same milestones and are often not celebrated" (Monaghan 2016, 14). Halberstam acknowledges that not all LGBTIQ people live their lives in opposition to these heterosexual life narratives, however, he argues that "part of what has made queerness compelling as a form of self-description in the past decade or so has to do with the way it has the potential to open up new life narratives" (2005, 1–2).

Queer theory in practice: Just a phase?

A pervasive trope within popular culture and popular discourse more broadly sees queerness written off as "just a phase" with deviations from heteronormativity often classified as temporary and therefore unthreatening to the heterosexual status quo. This idea is represented through a wide range of cultural forms such as film, television, music and literature within which LGBTIQ identity has been associated with a passing phase of adolescent development.

As Monaghan (2016) highlights, this can occur in television series that introduce an LGBTIQ character for a few episodes, stories where older women nostalgically remember their queer romances of their youth and films where teenage boredom is associated with rebellion against heterosexuality. Within examples like these, cisgender heterosexuality is assumed to be a natural state and must be restored. As a result, binary understandings of gender and sexuality are upheld. Bisexuality, for instance, is erased if we consider same-sex desire only as a temporary departure on the path towards a heterosexual adulthood.

Beyond screen media, these ideas also relate to real-world experiences of gender, sexuality and identity. For example, if you are an adolescent who comes out as an LGBTIQ person you may be met with the attitude that you are just experimenting or that you are too young to know your true identity. Attitudes like this are reflective of the interrelation between heteronormativity and temporality that many contemporary queer theorists are keen to critique.

Mainstreaming of LGBTIQ culture through homonormativity, which we have discussed in Chapter 6, sees queer lives more closely follow the heteronormative timeline. As Duggan defines:

> [Homonormativity] is a politics that does not contest dominant heteronormative assumptions and institutions but upholds and sustains them while promising the possibility of a demobilized gay constituency and a privatized, depoliticized gay culture anchored in domesticity and consumption. (2002, 179)

Viewing the politics of homonormativity through the lens of temporality shows how particular life narratives are upheld as "good" by the association of success with productivity in both a material sense, through consumption, and in a domestic sense through the cultivation of a particular domestic ideal. Following the above timeline, this ideal upholds monogamous long-lasting relationships and child-rearing as the model for a "good", successful or happy life.

THE ANTI-SOCIAL THESIS

Related to the concept of homonormativity, is the queer critique known as the "anti-social" thesis, which emerged through AIDS discourse in the 1980s. As we have discussed in Chapter 4, the AIDS crisis ushered in a wave of academic writing devoted to theorising sexual practice rather than identity. At the peak of the crisis, US literary theorist Leo Bersani published a paper "Is the Rectum a Grave?" (1987), which came to be influential in many later academic accounts of queer theory. In the paper, Bersani explores an association between homosexuality and death that played out in a visceral way through the AIDS crisis (1987, 199). Tracking homophobic responses to AIDS, as well as the relationship between homophobia and misogyny (noting the conflation between femininity and the "passive" position in gay male sex), Bersani advocates strongly for an *embrace* of these subordinate positions to contest and shatter hierarchies of power. Bersani also reflects on the issue of whiteness in prominent AIDS discourse and how the media marked white heterosexual families as those endangered by the epidemic (1987, 203). However, Bersani's focus here is not on the racism of AIDS discourse, but rather, the threat of AIDS to the celebrated (white, heterosexual) reproductive family unit. As Watney – who influenced Bersani's work – writes:

> [T]he spectacle of AIDS operates as a public masque in which we witness the corporeal punishment of the "homosexual body", identified as the

enigmatic and indecent source of an incomprehensible, voluntary resistance to the unquestionable governance of marriage, parenthood, and property. (1987b, 83)

The discursive construction of AIDS as a "homosexual disease" marked homosexuality in opposition to the family unit at the heart of modern capitalist society. Rather than attempt to wash homosexuality of this "failure", Bersani advocates an anti-social thesis, that is: embracing the imagined nihilism of the homosexual position.

Bersani's work ushered in an "anti-social turn" within theories of sexuality, emphasising the negative and productive value of the negative, rather than focusing on positivity, pride or destigmatisation. As legal theorist Janet Halley describes (perhaps tongue-in-cheek), Bersani's essay is a key piece of queer theory work which, "[B]ids to be a sweeping critique of social dominance, of which male dominance of women becomes only one example; and thus to be more feminist than feminism" (2006, 161). Halley describes Bersani as having "willingness to affirm sexuality as carrying an appetite for deep threats to integrated selfhood" (2006, 165). In advocating for an anti-social approach, Bersani's essay also epitomised the turn away from identity politics past: Bersani's point was not to rally around homosexuality as an identity so much as the social *position* of vulnerability.

Bersani continues this argument within his later work, *Homos*, in which he argues that "homo-ness" is inherently anti-social. Questioning whether "a homosexual [should] be a good citizen", Bersani opposes a "rage for respectability … in gay life today", that he locates within the valorisation of marriage and parenting within gay-rights activism, and in the sanitisation of gay sex (Bersani 1996, 113). As Robert Caserio highlights, Bersani's theorising inspired "a decade of explorations of queer unbelonging" (Caserio et al. 2006, 819).

No Future and figure of the Child

One of the most infamous and influential ways that Bersani's anti-social thesis has been taken up in queer theory, is in the work of Lee Edelman, specifically his book *No Future: Queer Theory and the Death Drive* (2004). In this work, Edelman argues that the symbolic figure of "the Child" dominates in politics and culture, operating to eliminate queerness and alternative formations of sexuality and kinship. Pointing out the many ways in which the Child is represented on television, in movies and in other media, Edelman illustrates how the Child functions as a symbol of the future horizon: the

Queer theory in practice: Fake orgasms as resistance

Jagose extends queer theory's focus on sexual practice to develop a theory of orgasm. Jagose builds on Rubin's influential essay "Thinking Sex" in which she juxtaposes common understandings of "good" and "bad" sex, arguing that bad sex "may be homosexual, unmarried, promiscuous, non-procreative, or commercial. It may be masturbatory or take place at orgies, may be casual, may cross generational lines, and may take place in 'public,' or at least in the bushes or the baths. It may involve the use of pornography, fetish objects, sex toys, or unusual roles" (Rubin 1984, 13–14). Within queer theory, certain acts associated with "bad" sex have become privileged as inherently political acts. When queer theorists valorise such acts, they attach political potential to certain forms of queer sexual practice. In doing so, they suggest "it is the queerness of erotic practice that makes it recognizable as political" (Jagose 2013, 182).

Critiquing this, Jagose makes a case for understanding fake orgasm as an ultimate embrace of negativity and thus as a form of resistance to the heteronormative social order. Jagose argues that fake orgasm "brings to visibility the presumptions that underpin claims to the transformative capacities or potentials of some sex acts, some amatory transactional relations or erotic spaces but not others" (Jagose 2013, 178). She suggests that fake orgasm can be thought of as a critique of the "disciplinary imperatives" of sex (Jagose 2013, 197), in a way "hold[ing] open an alternate way of thinking about the political, offering not a future-directed strategy for political transformation but an eloquent figure for political engagement with the conditions of the present" (Jagose 2013, 202).

promise of a better tomorrow, a future firmly rooted in the stability and safety of the heterosexual nuclear family unit. Edelman argues that in contrast to the Child, queer sexuality is understood as a perverse *threat* to the future, via the association with death (as theorised by Bersani) and the reproductive failure of homosexuality. Edelman suggests that even where queer couples attempt to have children of their own, there is a social refusal to acknowledge this as appropriate assimilation, and queer failure persists (2004, 20). As Edelman writes, "[T]he cult of the Child permits no shrines to the queerness of boys and girls, since queerness ... is understood as bringing children and childhood to an end" (2004, 19). Edelman suggests that rather than assimilate, queers ought to reject this regime altogether, writing:

> Fuck the social order and the Child in whose name we're collectively ter-rorized; fuck Annie; fuck the waif from *Les Mis*; fuck the poor, innocent kid on the Net; fuck Laws both with capital ls and with small; fuck the whole network of Symbolic relations and the future that serves as its prop. (2004, 29)

Edelman's theory here not only builds upon earlier work inspired by AIDS discourse, but also heralded a discussion around the question of queer tem-porality and futurity. By proclaiming (and celebrating) the idea of queerness as invested in "no future" and calling for the rejection of future, Edelman proposes a consideration of radical presentism for discussions of queer life. In other words, Edelman offers a clear position in the debate about sexual assimilation – Edelman calls for a rejection of the entire order of sexual moral-ity in the first instance. Edelman's approach, following Bersani, proposes a radically different version of politics around sexuality, one that is not about identity per se. Edelman's political suggestion to "Fuck the social order" suggests that what is needed is not an embrace of identity and unification around this (as seen earlier in Gay Liberation), but rather, a call to shatter social expectations of normative reproduction and thus the "future" of social life altogether: "What is queerest about us, queerest within us, and queerest despite us is this willingness to insist ... that the future stops here" (Edelman 2004, 31).

Negative affect, the critical present and backward orientations

Theorists have responded in a myriad of ways to this anti-social and anti-future paradigm laid out by Bersani and Edelman. Edelman's work in par-ticular has been critiqued by theorists such as Halberstam, who argues that "No future for Edelman means routing our desires around the eternal sun-shine of the spotless child and finding the shady side of political imaginaries in the proudly sterile and antireproductive logics of queer relation" (2008, 148). Yet, Halberstam suggests caution be taken here: he argues that Edelman may be caught in the symbolic to the detriment of the political (2008, 148). As Halberstam also explains of Bersani's theoretical outlook, "Rather than a life-force connecting pleasure to life, survival and futurity, sex, and particu-larly homo-sex and receptive sex, is a death drive that undoes the self, releases

Queer theory in practice: *Play School* and the figure of "the Child"

In May 2004, Australian children's television programme *Play School* sparked a moral panic around the figure of the Child when it aired a segment featuring lesbian parents. The "Through the Windows" segment, which showed short documentary clips of the real world, revealed footage of two girls and two adult women with one of the girls' voiceover narrating, "My mums are taking me and my friend Meryn to an amusement park". The segment caused controversy as it aired shortly after the Australian Prime Minister John Howard had announced a change in legislation to amend the *Marriage Act* to re-define marriage between a man and a woman.

As a result, *Play School* gained a lot of media attention as commentators debated whether it was appropriate to expose young children to lesbian content. The prime minister accused the broadcaster of using its influence to promote a particular agenda among children, invoking the notion of the Child as an impressionable emblem of the future, one in need of protection from the "harmful" threat of queer content. At the time, Howard was quoted as saying, "This is an example of the ABC running an agenda in a children's program. If people want to debate that issue, do it on a (current affairs) program like *Lateline*, but not *Play School*".

the self from the drive for mastery and coherence and resolution" (2008, 140). In his essay "Hope Against Hope", James Bliss poses another critique of the anti-social thesis, challenging the assumed whiteness of the anti-social project. Bliss argues that works such as Edelman's *No Future* fail to account for Black subjectivity and neglects "those modes of reproduction that are not future-oriented, the children who do not register as such, as the 'families' that are not granted the security of nuclear bonds" (Bliss 2015, 86). Bliss offers an alternate conceptualisation of queer negativity as emerging from a tradition of Black feminist theorising.

As we will see in later sections of this chapter, the major counterargument to the anti-social thesis has been an optimistic, future-oriented rendering of queer theory. However, not all theorists have taken up this hopeful orientation. Theorists such as Halberstam, Berlant, Love and Kathryn Bond Stockton demonstrate the tensions between queer theory's past, present and future orientations.

CRITICAL PRESENT-NESS

In his book *In a Queer Time and Place: Transgender Bodies, Subcultural Lives* (2005), Halberstam emphasises the ways in which notions of "respectability" and "the normal" are "upheld by a middle-class logic of reproductive temporality" (2005, 4). He argues that Western cultures "chart the emergence of the adult from the dangerous and unruly period of adolescence as a desired process of maturation" creating "longevity as the most desirable future" while valorising the pursuit of long life at all costs (Halberstam 2005, 4). As we have noted, this normalised schema pathologises modes of living that demonstrate little concern or desire for a life defined by longevity or stability. Like Edelman, Halberstam argues that we should focus on these pathologised modes of living in order to frame queerness through a politics of negativity. Halberstam also argues that queer temporalities allow for lives to be imagined outside of the celebrated milestones of life experience. Thus, in contrast to Edelman, Halberstam suggests that queer uses of time may develop in opposition to logics of normative reproductive temporality. Halberstam suggests that queerness can be detached from sexual identity and considered as a threat to the heteronormative social order when it is thought of as "an outcome of strange temporalities, imaginative life schedules, and eccentric economic practices" (2005, 1).

Queer time is exemplified, according to Halberstam, in writer Mark Doty's memoir about his lover's death from AIDS. Indeed, Halberstam emphasises the AIDS epidemic as one of the sources from which queer time emerges in a dramatic fashion. Of the line "All my life I've lived with a future which constantly diminishes but never vanishes" (Doty 1996, 4), Halberstam notes:

> The constantly diminishing future creates a new emphasis on the here, the present, the now, and while the threat of no future hovers overhead like a storm cloud, the urgency of being also expands the potential of the moment and, as Doty explores, squeezes new possibilities out of the time at hand. (2005, 2)

Halberstam further notes that even as queer time emerges from the AIDS crisis, it is "not only about compression and annihilation" (2005, 2). For Halberstam, queer time allows a shift in focus from the pursuit of a normative future to "the potentiality of a life unscripted by the conventions of family, inheritance, and child-rearing" (2005, 2).

Queer theory in practice: Queer time and the Internet

How might some spaces on the Internet queer time? This is a question that queer digital media scholars have considered: is there something peculiar that happens to time in some social spaces online? How does this impact and shape queer communities?

For example, as Alexander Cho (2015) suggests, the micro-blogging site Tumblr queers time through allowing users to constantly recirculate images and text in ways that keep affects in circulation, "a stubborn persistence of the past" (2015, 44). Or, as Hannah McCann and Clare Southerton suggest in their work on queer fandom on Twitter, the very act of re-circulation of content lays the conditions for a form of queer-ing: "When content is shared, something creative emerges in the new engagements and readings it makes possible" (2019, 60).

Through the constant re-circulation and reverberation of queer content online, the past, present and future are collapsed, affects are intensified and new queer possibilities emerge.

CRUEL OPTIMISM AND THE IMPASSE

As noted in Chapter 7, Berlant also theorises around critical present-ness in her book *Cruel Optimism* (2011) in which she explores frayed fantasies of "the good life" in mass media, literature, television, film and video from 1990 onwards. While Berlant theorises around optimism, her work also aligns with the anti-social thesis as she explores difficult, negative and cruel relations of contemporary social, cultural and political life. Berlant had earlier dealt with the topic of optimism in two key works, where she developed theories of "hegemonic optimism" (Berlant and Warner 1998, 549) and "dubious opti-mism" (Berlant 2001, 129). We could relate Berlant's description of "the good life" to the heteronormative temporal regimes discussed by Edelman, Bersani and Halberstam. Berlant suggests that things once closely related to "the good life", optimistic affect and structural transformation such as meritocracy, "upward mobility, job security, political and social equality, and lively, durable intimacy" (2011, 3) are finding less and less traction in the contemporary neoliberal-capitalist world.

With this in mind, Berlant argues that certain objects and scenarios that once enabled fantasies of "the good life" have dissolved in recent times, giving way to the "kinds of optimistic relation we call 'cruel'" (2011, 3). For Berlant, a cruel relation of optimism is "when something you desire is actually an obstacle to you flourishing" (2011, 1). Taking an approach informed by affect theory (discussed in Chapter 7), Berlant argues that attachments to things, feelings, objects or scenarios are always optimistic because they are based on the idea that "nearness to this thing will help you or a world to become different in just the right way" (2011, 2). However, these optimistic attachments become cruel when they ignite "a sense of possibility [that] actually makes it impossible to attain the expansive transformation for which a person or a people risks striving" (2011, 2). In this case, one's optimistic attachment becomes both the thing that enables them to hope for a better future *and* the prevention of that better future from being attained. Describing this as being stuck at an "impasse", Berlant argues that this cruelly optimistic temporal orientation provides a means of theorising around a critical present-ness.

Berlant describes the present as a "mediated affect", and writes that "the present is what makes itself present to us before it becomes anything else, such as an orchestrated collective event or an epoch on which we can look back" (2011, 4). By this she means that we know we are in the present because, primarily, we feel it. Only in hindsight can we reflect on the moment and describe it as an era, an epoch or a collective event. With this in mind, Berlant suggests that if the present is "a mediated affect" it can also be thought of "as a thing that is sensed and under constant revision" (2011, 4), and up for debate. The present moment is not straightforward if, for instance, one thinks about when "the present" begins and when it ceases. For Berlant, the critical present or the impasse is perceived as a drawn out and elongated present moment. She describes this as:

[A] stretch of time in which one moves around with a sense that the world is at once intensely present and enigmatic, such that the activity of living demands both a wandering absorptive awareness and a hypervigilance that collects material that might help to clarify things, maintain one's sea legs, and coordinate the standard melodramatic crises with those processes that have not yet found their genre of event. (2011, 4)

While it might seem shallow or hedonistic to focus only on the present moment, Berlant's critical present-ness highlights how this orientation allows reflection on "various knowledges and intuitions about what's happening" now (2011, 4), and also enabling a means of thinking about what might follow on from such a reflection. This theory of the impasse provides a means of imagining a better present while simultaneously revealing "what is halting, stuttering, and aching about being in the middle of detaching from a waning fantasy of the good life" (2011, 263). For this reason, Berlant argues that discussions about temporality and temporal orientation are always profoundly political – "they are about what forces should be considered responsible and what crises urgent in our adjudication of survival strategies and conceptions of a better life than what the metric of survival can supply" (2011, 4). However, she argues that any political movement promoting social change that emerges from this present impasse risks becoming stuck in the double bind of cruel optimism, described as thus: "even with an image of a better good life available to sustain your optimism, it is awkward and it is threatening to detach from what is already not working" (Berlant 2011, 263).

QUEER CHILDHOODS

Kathryn Bond Stockton also challenges fantasies of "the good life" and striving towards normative futures. Like Edelman, Bond Stockton argues that childhood is a key site where heteronormativity is played out. However, Bond Stockton directly opposes Edelman's rejection of the Child by centralising childhood, in her theory of queer temporality outlined in *The Queer Child; Or, Growing Sideways in the Twentieth Century* (2009). Bond Stockton highlights that in history, theory, legal texts, literature, cinema and popular culture more broadly, childhood development, "has been relentlessly figured as vertical movement upward (hence 'growing up') toward full stature, marriage, work, reproduction and the loss of childishness" (2009, 4). However, for many LGBTIQ adults, childhood evokes memories of "desperately feeling there was simply nowhere to grow" (2009, 3). Hence, she describes the experience of queer childhood as:

> [A] frightening, heightened sense of growing toward a question mark. Or growing up in a haze. Or hanging in suspense – even wishing time would stop, or just twist sideways, so that one wouldn't have to advance to new or further scenes of trouble. (2009, 3)

For Bond Stockton, these feelings associated with queer childhood are politically useful because they reveal the limits of the heteronormative developmental model. From this perspective, the phrase "growing up" is "a short-sighted, limited rendering of human growth" because it implies that growth ceases "when full stature (or reproduction) is achieved" (2009, 11). By taking a queer approach to analysing childhood, Bond Stockton argues that "there are ways of growing that are not growing up" (2009, 11). Challenging the linear "vertical, forward-motion metaphor of growing up" (2009, 11), she proposes a theory of lateral development and argues that the queer temporality grows sideways. Significantly, Bond Stockton uses this idea of lateral growth to depart from Edelman and the anti-social thesis. That is, by refusing to reject the Child and "the future", this theory of sideways growth "locates energy, pleasure, vitality, and (e)motion in ... back-and-forth connections ... that are not reductive" (2009, 13). She describes these as "moving suspensions and shadows of growth" (2009, 13). By this she means that forms of growth (personal, political and historical change) can be revealed by shifting focus from linear development to lateral connection.

LOOKING FORWARD, FEELING BACKWARD

Love similarly embraces queer negativity in her book *Feeling Backwards: Loss and the Politics of Queer History* (2007). Love's contribution to queer theory's temporal turn focuses on the political potential of being oriented towards the past. By focusing on the loss associated with queer histories, Love explores the contemporary queer experience as a form of past-orientation. From this perspective, queer activism, theory and criticism are founded on a history of "suffering, stigma and violence" (Love 2007, 1), which means that both the present and future will always be bound up in the losses of the past. As Love writes:

> Insofar as the losses of the past motivate us and give meaning to our current experience, we are bound to memorialize them ("We will never forget"). But we are equally bound to overcome the past, to escape its legacy ("We will never go back"). (2007, 1)

Love asserts that the contemporary queer experience is that of "looking forward" while "feeling backward" because we are bound to memorialise the losses of our past while also being "deeply committed to the notion of progress" (2007, 3). Even when embracing queer negativity, "we just cannot stop dreaming of a better life for queer people" (2007, 3). To navigate this contradictory experience of "looking forward" while "feeling backward" Love calls for a criticism that pays particular attention to "feelings tied to the experience of social inclusion and to the historical 'impossibility' of same-sex desire" (2007, 4) such as shame, despair, nostalgia, loneliness and regret.

AFFIRMATION, OPTIMISM AND FUTURE ORIENTATIONS

Responding to queer theory's embrace of negativity, other theorists have developed theories of queerness and time that seek to emphasise affirmation, optimism and utopias. In "Queer Optimism", Michael Snediker calls for a movement away from negativity and "a revaluation of optimism" (Snediker 2006) as queer theory's critical project. It is significant to note that while Snediker considers utopian optimism to be "attached, temporally to a future", he argues that *queer* optimism is "not promissory" (Snediker 2006).

> It doesn't ask that some future time make good on its own hopes. Rather, queer optimism asks that optimism, embedded in its own immanent present, be *interesting*. (Snediker 2006)

Like Berlant, Snediker argues for an understanding of the queerness of present-orientation. However, departing from the anti-social thesis, he "seeks to take positive affects as serious and interesting sites of critical investigation" and critiques what he describes as "queer pessimism" which he sees articulated in the field's attention to negative affect, melancholy, shame, the death drive and shattering (Snediker 2006). For O'Rourke, queer theory has always "been turned toward the future" because it is "a theory permanently open to its own recitation, re-signification and revision" (O'Rourke 2011, 107). He writes:

> in its earliest incarnations as the AIDS activism of ACT UP and Queer Nation, both of which are privileged by utopian political thought that promises an unmasterable future, and the "foundational" theorizations of Eve Kosofksy Sedgwick and Judith Butler (among many others), queer theory has always already been of, for, and promised, given over to, the future. (O'Rourke 2011, 107)

The optimistic side of the temporality debate recognises this and conceptualises a return "to the revolutionary potential of queer studies, and seek[s] to reimagine a hopeful, forward-reaching, world-making queer theory that matters as the future" (O'Rourke 2011, 108). These scholars emphasise the power of the heteronormative temporal order, yet they embrace the queer potential of the future rather than rejecting it outright.

Utopias and the queer future

Directly opposing Edelman's rejection of the future, Muñoz conceptualises a critical hopefulness, relating queerness to utopia and arguing that "the future is queerness's domain" (2009, 1). Muñoz sets up a similar claim to Edelman, using the phrase "straight time" to refer to the temporality associated with both heteronormativity and homonormativity. According to Muñoz, this "self-naturalising" and linear temporality figures *queer* subjects as futureless, telling them "that there is no future but the here and now of ... everyday life" (2009, 22). Hence, like Edelman, Muñoz argues that heteronormative culture views LGBTIQ people as "developmentally stalled, forsaken" and without "the complete life promised by heterosexual temporality" (2009, 98). This temporality "makes queers think that both the past and future do not belong to them" (Muñoz 2009, 112). "All we are allowed to imagine", Muñoz writes, "is barely surviving in the present" (2009, 112).

Here Muñoz departs from queer theory's anti-social paradigm, rejecting the embrace of negativity that characterises the anti-social thesis. Where Edelman and others within the anti-social turn call for queer subjects to refuse the pull of the future and embrace the negativity of this present, Muñoz argues that the present is "not enough", that it is "impoverished and toxic" for those who "do not feel the privilege of majoritarian belonging, normative tastes, and 'rational' expectations" (Muñoz 2009, 27). Explicitly refusing anti-social queer theory's emphasis on the "here and now", Muñoz writes: "what we need to know is that queerness is not yet here but it approaches like a crashing wave of potentiality" (Muñoz 2009, 185). Muñoz positions queer theory as a response to negativity and the "impoverished" temporality of the present, arguing that queerness "should and could be about a desire for another way of being both in the world and in time" (Muñoz 2009, 96). For Muñoz, "queerness is a structuring and educated mode of desiring that allows us to see and feel beyond the quagmire of the present" (2009, 1). As part of this manifesto for the queer future, he writes:

> The here and now is a prison house. We must strive, in the face of the here and now's totalising rendering of reality, to think and feel a *then and there*. Some will say that all we have are the pleasures of this moment, but we must never settle for that minimal transport; we must dream and enact new and better pleasures, other ways of being in the world, and ultimately new worlds. Queerness is the longing that propels us onward, beyond romances of the negative and toiling in the present. Queerness is that thing that lets us feel that this world is not enough. (2009, 1)

Muñoz's theorisation of queer temporality responds to the assertion that there is no future for the figure of the queer and subsequently that both hope and the future are "imbued with and unable to be dislodged from a heteronormative logic" (O'Rourke 2011, 107). Presenting an optimistic side to the debate on queer temporality, Muñoz sees the critical potential of hope and the queer potential of future-orientation.

Queer happiness

Ahmed also challenges the anti-social thesis, with a particular critique against the embrace of negativity, and the association between happiness, the future

---

Queer theory in practice: Barebacking and cruising as queer futurities

Queer futurities are evoked in the subcultures of barebacking and cruising (anal sex without condoms and promiscuous anonymous sex) in Tim Dean's *Unlimited Intimacy: Reflections on the Subculture of Barebacking* (2009). In this work, Dean argues that barebacking "concerns an experience of unfettered intimacy, of overcoming the boundaries between persons" (2009, 2).

While barebacking and cruising are not gay-specific sexual practices, they provide a means of thinking about new forms of queer relationality. Promiscuous sexual activity in particular gives rise to an impersonal ethics where one cares about others "even when one cannot see anything of oneself in them", which in turn gives rise to an "ethics of alterity" (Dean 2009, 25). Therefore, Dean argues that these practices exemplify "a distinctive ethic of openness to alterity and that – irrespective of our view of the morality of barebacking – we all, gay and non-gay, have something to learn from this relational ethic" (2009, 176).

With this in mind, O'Rourke suggests they represent "the queer time and space of the not-yet-here" (2011, 112), shifting from an identitarian focus on lesbian and gay politics to open up a space of *queer* sexualities, future social relations and queer futurities. As Dean suggests, "cruising ... involves not just hunting for sex but opening oneself to the world" (Dean 2009, 25).

and normativity. In doing so, she counters the argument that "if one is to be queer, happiness is ontologically risky and therefore should be refused, given up" (O'Rourke 2011, 111). Her book *The Promise of Happiness* (2010) analyses the ways that happiness is culturally constructed, seeking to understand "how happiness is imagined as being what follows being a certain kind of being" (Ahmed 2010, 2). A key critique posed by Ahmed is against the cultural imperative to "be happy", which she argues is always linked to normativity. Ahmed builds upon feminist, Black and queer scholarship to show how the idea of "happiness" has long been "used to justify oppression" (Ahmed 2010, 2).

Ahmed explores a number of figures that are alienated from the model of normative happiness. One of the most significant of these is the figure of the "unhappy queer". Looking at representations of queer people in literary and media culture, Ahmed contrasts unhappy queer characters against images of happy heterosexuality. She argues that heterosexual love often "becomes about the possibility of a happy ending: about what life is aimed toward, as being what gives life direction or purpose, or as what drives a story" (2010, 90). As a result, Ahmed argues "that it is difficult to separate images of the good life from the historic privileging of heterosexual conduct" (2010, 90). When heterosexuality is aligned with happiness in this way, queerness becomes associated with unhappiness. To explain this, Ahmed examines the phrase "I just want you to be happy" that is often linked to parental grief about children coming out. This grief, she argues, "reminds us that the queer life is already constructed as an unhappy life, as a life without the 'things' that make you happy, or as a life that is depressed as it lacks certain things" (2010, 93).

Key concept: Happiness scripts

In *The Promise of Happiness*, Sara Ahmed describes "happiness scripts" as devices that orient people towards both happiness and heteronormativity. Looking at how happiness is represented in cultural texts, Ahmed argues that happiness "involves a way of being aligned with others, of facing the right way" (Ahmed 2010, 45). Through this alignment, happiness comes to mean "living a certain kind of life, one that reaches certain points and which, in reaching these points, creates happiness for others" (Ahmed 2010, 48). For instance, she describes the ideal happiness script for girls: "you must become a woman by finding your happiness in the happiness of a good man" (Ahmed 2010, 90–91).

However, we must note that Ahmed does not suggest that we should read unhappy queer characters as a literal moral disapproval of LGBTIQ people. She instead argues that "we must consider how unhappiness circulates within and around this archive [of the unhappy queer], and *what it allows us to do*" (2010, 89). Ahmed theorises two models of queer happiness that riff off this figure of the unhappy queer. The first is the "happy queer", a figure who follows normative happiness scripts towards a position of homonormativity. Discussing this, Ahmed writes, "if queers have to approximate signs of happiness in order to be recognised, then they might have to minimize signs of queerness" (2010, 94). This "happy queer" is a familiar figure within popular film and television. It is embodied in the token queer characters that function as background noise in overwhelmingly heterosexual narratives. Happy queer characters are often desexualised characters that have love interests, but are never represented being affectionate with their same-sex partners.

In contrast to the "happy queer", Ahmed locates the "happily queer", a figure who "does not necessarily promote an image of happiness that borrows from the conventional repertoire of images" (2010, 115). The "happily queer", Ahmed argues, refuses to give up their desires, even if these desires take them outside of the parameters of happiness (2010, 117). This figure "still encounters the world that is unhappy with queer love, but refuses to be made unhappy by that encounter" (2010, 117). An example of this occurs in the Swedish teen film *Show Me Love* (1998) in which two teen girl characters fall in love with each other (subverting the conventional happiness script) and live a "happily queer" existence by refusing the unhappiness that their small town associates with queerness. In the film's final scene, they choose to be in a relationship and joyfully drink chocolate milk together while listening to pop music. Other happily queer films include *The Strange One* (Jack Garfein 1957), *The Fox* (Mark Rydell 1967), *That Certain Summer* (Lamont Johnson 1972), *Alexander: The Other Side of Dawn* (John Erman 1977) and *La Cage Aux Folles* (Ennio Morricone 1978).

As Ahmed argues, attention to "happily queer" figures like these offers a means of refusing "to give happiness the power to secure a specific image of what would count as a good life" (2010, 119). This figure also enables queer theory to theorise around happiness without negating the political force of unhappiness which, according to Ahmed, can actually be affirmative because it can "gesture toward another world" (2010, 107). In presenting this figure of the "happily queer", Ahmed takes an optimistic approach to theorising queerness and futurity. More directly responding to Edelman and the anti-social thesis, Ahmed imagines the queer future as "what is kept open as the possibility of things not staying as they are, or being as they stay", and imagines a form of queer potentiality that "would be alive to chance, to chance arrivals, to the perhaps of a happening" (Ahmed 2010, 197–198). As a means of subverting, challenging or simply problematising the scripted, linear temporal logics of heteronormativity, Ahmed argues that queerness could be thought of as "the future of the perhaps" (2010, 198).

An optimistic challenge to chrononormativity

In *Time Binds: Queer Temporalities, Queer Histories* (2010), Elizabeth Freeman coins the terms "chrononormativity" and "chronobiopolitics" to refer to the ways that logics of heteronormativity have coalesced with institutional forces. For Freeman, "chrononormativity" is the means by which schedules, calendars and time zones "come to seem like somatic facts" (2010, 3). She sees this play out in "manipulations of time [that] convert historically specific regimes of asymmetrical power into seemingly ordinary bodily tempos and routines, which in turn organize the value and meaning of time" (2010, 3). For instance, the shift from agricultural to industrial work re-temporalised many bodies that were once in tune with seasonal rhythms. When this process is extended beyond the individual to an entire population, it is referred to as a process of "chronobiopolitics". Freeman describes this as when "the state and other institutions ... link properly temporalized bodies to narratives of movement and change" (2010, 4) such as marriage, reproduction and child-rearing, which we have mapped out in Figure 8.1. Freeman highlights how this heteronormative timeline benefits a nation's economic interests, noting:

> In the United States ... states now license, register, or certify birth (and thus citizenship, eventually encrypted in a Social Security ID for taxpaying purposes), marriage or domestic partnership (which privatizes caretaking and regulates the distribution of privatized property), and death (which terminates the identities linked to state benefits, redistributing these benefits through familial channels), along with sundry privileges like driving (to jobs and commercial venues) and serving in the military (thus incurring state expenditures that often serve corporate interests). In the eyes of the state, this sequence of socioeconomically "productive" moments is what it means to have a life at all. (2010, 4–5)

Queer theory in practice: Queering archives

Where queerness is marked as "Other", history is filled with queer silences. As such delving into archives to recover lost or obscured LGBTIQ voices has been understood as a crucial political activity. Considering queerness via archives raises the question of whose stories are preserved, and whose are yet to be unearthed? As Gemma Killen outlines:

> The aims of queer historians are often similar to feminist historians in that they are attempting to "recover" missing queer voices and produce stories about queer history that resist the medical and legal discourses within which they have traditionally been shrouded. (2017, 60)

As Killen (2017) also suggests, the digital era has heralded an entirely different dimension to archival questions, as queerness is recorded in its everyday forms via social media, blogs and other sites.

The question of archives has become central to many queer theory scholars writing on temporality. As Cvetkovich details in her 2003 work *An Archive of Feelings*, oral histories, ephemera and other community-based records are crucial for understanding the history of everyday queer experiences. Drawing on Cvetkovich, Sara Edenheim differentiates the following (2014, 40):

The queer archive of feelings	The scholar's archive (public research archive)
ephemera	written documents
fragments	linearly structured around canonical events
open and unlimited	closed and limited
everyday events	normative, deviancy excluded
arbitrary	value according to historical or research interests
marginalised and condemned memories and feelings	coherent narratives
"magical" or fictional value	literal value only
material practices	fulfils a scientific need
digital, "non-place"	stagnant
fulfils a psychic/emotional need	
sense of urgency	

However, Edenheim suggests that such a distinction unwittingly positions the queer archive as radical in contrast to the (fantasy) of the non-radical scholarly archive. Edenheim questions what is "queer" about Cvetkovich's archive and calls for queer theorists to do more to interrogate the desire to find queer identities in the archive.

Chrononormativity and chronobiopolitics operate even in zones "not fully reducible to the state" (such as medicine, law and popular culture) because more generally, having a life "entails the ability to narrate it not only in these state-sanctioned terms but also in a novelistic framework: as event-centered, goal-oriented, intentional, and culminating in epiphanies of major transformations" (2010, 5).

Much like other theorists we have engaged with in this chapter, Freeman critiques these logics. Aligning with the optimistic side of the debate, Freeman suggests that an exclusive focus on queer negativity risks losing sight of the potential pleasures of queer theory's unique critical intersection of erotic and body politics. However, she also argues against taking "a purely futural orientation" as she argues that this "depends on forgetting the past" (2010, xvi). Therefore, while her position is situated on the side of optimism, her work is not future-oriented in the same way as Ahmed or Muñoz. Her conception of queer time emphasises detour, delay, deference, asynchrony and stasis as a means of destabilising normative logics of "history 'proper' but also coming out, consummation, development, domesticity, family, foreplay, genealogy, identity, liberation, modernity, [and] the progress of movement" (Freeman 2010, xxii). Hence, she sees the queer potential of "living aslant to dominant forms of object-choice, coupledom, family, marriage, sociability, and self-presentation and thus out of synch with state-sponsored narratives of belonging and becoming" (2010, xv), arguing that queer temporalities can provide models for "moving through and with time, encountering pasts, speculating futures, and interpenetrating the two in ways that counter the common sense of the present tense" (2010, xv).

Key concept: Temporal drag

Building upon Butler's theorising of drag, Freeman coins the term "temporal drag". In *Gender Trouble*, Butler argues that drag is a subversive tool because it demonstrates the mobility of gender identification and highlights certain excesses of gender that allow us to question the gender binary and, more broadly, the heterosexual matrix.

Re-thinking drag through queer theory's temporal turn, Freeman argues that drag might also be thought of as a "*temporal* phenomenon" (2010, 62). By this, she means that drag can be regarded "as a counter-genealogical practice of archiving culture's throwaway objects, including outmoded masculinities from which useable pasts may be extracted" (Freeman 2010, xxiii).

Hence, when we watch drag shows, we see present-day performers raid the history closet for traces of the past: music, popular culture references, gendered behaviours and costume. For Freeman, rather than showing us only excesses of gender, drag represents an excessive and exaggerated performance "of the signifier 'history'" (Freeman 2010, 62).

CONCLUSION: QUEER TIME

As we have explored through this chapter, queer theory has much to say about time and temporality. Drawing attention to this, we have mapped out some of the major contours of the temporal turn, demonstrating how a particular application of Marxist thought has enabled queer theorists to interrogate "the use of time to organize individual human bodies toward maximum productivity" (Freeman 2010, 3). As we have highlighted, the key debate in this area of contemporary queer theory is the question of how queerness should be oriented with regard to the future. While some theorists have advocated for a past- or present-orientation that rejects hope and futurity, others have argued for an affirmative or optimistic perspective that imbues queerness with a hopeful transformative potential. Common across all standpoints is an alignment between queerness and asynchrony – in the sense of being out-of-sync with "chrononormativity" (Freeman 2010), "reproductive futurity" (Edelman 2004), "repro-time" (Halberstam 2005), "straight time" (Muñoz 2009) or "the good life" (Ahmed 2010; Berlant 2011) – and a desire to understand how queer theory could and should respond to this.

Comparing the work of Berlant and Muñoz, for instance, we see that while Berlant offers a critical account of stagnation in the present, Muñoz makes a case for why we should strive towards transformation to an ideal world. Berlant describes how we ultimately desire political transformation, though we sometimes problematically invest this hope in state mechanisms for change. While Berlant focuses on the present saturated in history as the site for the political, in contrast Muñoz critiques the present and focuses on the queer potential of futurity. Arguments such as these, that seek to respond to the temporal logics of heteronormativity, have also enabled theorists to consider what a queer time might look or feel like, or how it might be experienced. Each theorist takes a different perspective on this. For instance, for Edelman and other advocates of the anti-social thesis, a queer time amounts to an embrace of queer negativity and a rejection of hope.

For others, such as Nguyen Tan Hoang, it is the innovative transmission of queer knowledge and experience "from one generation to the next, a process that exceeds ... the heterosexual/kinship reproductive model" (Dinshaw et al. 2007, 183). Halberstam suggests "It is a theory of queerness as a way of being in the world and a critique of the careful social scripts that usher even the most queer among us through major markers of individual development and into normativity" (Dinshaw et al. 2007, 182). Finally, for the optimistic perspective, a queer time is open to the happenstance of the future, a future that has not yet arrived.

Further reading

Carolyn Dinshaw, Lee Edelman, Roderick A. Ferguson, Carla Freccero, Elizabeth Freeman, J Halberstam, Annamarie Jagose, Christopher Nealon, and Nguyen Tan Hoang. (2007). "Theorising Queer Temporalities." *GLQ: A Journal of Lesbian and Gay Studies*, 13(2–3): 177–196.

This roundtable from GLQ's special issue on "Queer Temporalities" features engaging dialogue between prominent queer theorists who each discuss their approach to queer theory's temporal turn. A useful and accessible text that maps out the contours of the debate.

Lee Edelman. (2004). "The Future is Kid Stuff" in *No Future: Queer Theory and the Death Drive*. Durham: Duke University Press, 1–32.

Edelman's theory of reproductive futurity coalescing around the figure of the Child is presented succinctly in this first chapter of his book.

José Esteban Muñoz. (2009). "Queerness as Horizon" in *Utopia: The Then and There of Queer Futurity*. New York: New York University Press, 19–32.

Muñoz lays out his theory of queerness as a horizon of potentiality in this first chapter of his manifesto for the future.

QUESTIONS TO CONSIDER

- Does the Child still function as a symbol of futurity, as Edelman has argued? Where can we see this playing out?
- In what ways might queer life narratives challenge the linear logic of heteronormative temporality?
- Where do you side within the anti-social versus optimistic debate about queerness and the future? Why?

Recommended films

***The Birds* (Alfred Hitchcock 1963).** This canonical Hitchcock horror-thriller about a family traumatised by birds is analysed in Lee Edelman's *No Future: Queer Theory and the Death Drive*. Edelman argues that the birds in *The Birds* are figures of the death drive.

***Butterfly* (Yan Yan Mak 2004).** This coming of age film tells the story of an adult woman remembering a queer encounter in her past. Analysed in Monaghan's *Queer Girls, Temporality and Screen Media: Not 'Just a Phase'* as an example of both Love's theory of "looking forwards, feeling backwards" and Muñoz's approach to queer temporality.

***Show Me Love* (Lukas Moodysson 1998).** This acclaimed queer teen film is about an unpopular teen girl crushing on her popular classmate. The film has a happy ending that aligns well with Ahmed's theory of the "happily queer".

References

Aaron, Michelle. (2004). *New Queer Cinema: A Critical Reader*. New York: Rutgers.

Abelove, Henry, Michèle Aina Barale, and David M. Halperin (eds.). (1993). *The Lesbian and Gay Studies Reader*. New York: Routledge.

Ahmed, Sara. (2010a). *The Promise of Happiness*. London: Duke University Press.

———. (2010b). "Killing Joy: Feminism and the History of Happiness." *Signs: Journal of Women in Culture and Society*, 35(3): 571–594.

———. (2016). "Interview with Judith Butler." *Sexualities*, 19(4): 482–492.

Alcoff, Linda Martín, and Satya P. Mohanty. (2006). "Reconsidering Identity Politics: An Introduction." In *Identity Politics Reconsidered*, Linda Martín Alcoff, Michael Hames-Garcia, Satya P. Mohanty, and Paula M. L. Moya (eds.). New York: Palgrave Macmillan, 1–9.

Alderfer, Hannah, Meryl Altman, Kate Ellis, Beth Jaker, Marybeth Nelson, Esther Newton, Ann Snitow, and Carole S. Vance (eds.). (1981). *Diary of a Conference on Sexuality*. New York. http://www.darkmatterarchives.net/wp-content/uploads/2011/12/Diary-of-a-Conference-on-Sexuality.pdf.

Alexander, Brian Keith. (2000). "Reflections, Riffs and Remembrances: The Black Queer Studies in the Millennium Conference." *Callaloo: A Journal of African-American and African Arts and Letters*, 23(4): 1285–1305.

Allen, T. W. (1994a). *The Invention of the White Race: Volume 1*. Haymarket Series. Verso.

———. (1994b). *The Invention of the White Race: Volume 2*. Haymarket Series. Verso.

Almaguer, T. (1994). *Racial Fault Lines: The Historical Origins of White Supremacy in California*. Berkeley and Los Angeles: University of California Press.

Alonso, Ana, and Maria Teresa Koreck. (1993). "Silences: 'Hispanics', AIDS, and Sexual Practices." In *The Lesbian and Gay Studies Reader*, Henry Abelove, Michèle Aina Barale, and David M. Halperin (eds.). New York and London: Routledge, 110–126.

Altman, Dennis. (1972). *Homosexual: Oppression and Liberation*. Sydney: Angus and Robertson.

———. (2018). "The Growing Gap between Academia and Activism?." *Sexualities*, 21(8): 1251–1255.

Angelides, Steven. (2001). *A History of Bisexuality*. Chicago and London: University of Chicago Press.

Anonymous. 1990. "Queers Read This." http://bilerico.lgbtqnation.com/2010/08/queers_read_this.php.

Anzaldúa, Gloria E. (1987). *Borderlands/La Frontera: The New Mestiza*. San Francisco: Aunt Lute Books.

———. (1991). "To(o) Queer the Writer–Loca Escritoria y Chicana." In *InVersions: Writing by Dykes, Queers and Lesbians*, Betsy Warland (ed.). Vancouver: Press Gang, 249–263.

————. (2009). *The Gloria Anzaldúa Reader.* Durham, NC, and London: Duke University Press.

————. (2013). "The New Mestiza Nation: A Multicultural Movment." In *Feminist Theory Reader: Local and Global Perspectives*, Carole R. McCann and Seung-kyung Kim (eds.). (Third Edition). New York and London: Routledge, 277–284.

Armstrong, E. A. (2002). *Forging Gay Identities: Organizing Sexuality in San Francisco, 1950–1994.* Chicago: University of Chicago Press.

Arondekar, Anjali. (2004). "Geopolitics Alert!." *GLQ: A Journal of Lesbian and Gay Studies*, 10(2): 236–240.

————. (2005). "Without a Trace: Sexuality and the Colonial Archive." *Journal of the History of Sexuality*, 14: 10–27.

————. (2009). *For the Record: On Sexuality and the Colonial Archive in India.* Durham, NC: Duke University Press.

Arroyo, José. (1993). "Death, Desire and Identity: The Political Unconscious of the "New Queer Cinema"." In *Activating Theory: Lesbian, Gay, Bisexual Politics*, Joseph Bristow, Angelia R. Wilson (eds.). London: Lawrence & Wishart, 70–96.

Atkinson, Ti-Grace. (2000). "Radical Feminism." In *Radical Feminism: A Documentary Reader*, Barbara A. Crow (ed.). New York and London: New York University Press, 82–89.

Aultman, B. (2014). "Cisgender." *TSQ: Transgender Studies Quarterly*, 1(1–2): 61–62.

Austin, J. L. (1962). *How to Do Things with Words.* Cambridge, MA: Harvard University Press.

Bagemihl, Bruce. (1999). *Biological Exuberance: Animal Homosexuality and Natural Diversity. Stonewall Inn Editions.* New York: St. Martin's Press.

Barad, Karen. (2007). *Meeting the Universe Halfway.* Durham, NC: Duke University Press.

Barber, Stephen M., and David L. Clark. (2002). "Queer Moments: The Performative Temporalities of Eve Kosofsky Sedgwick." In *Sedgwick: Essays on Queer Culture and Critical Theory*, Stephen M. Barber and David L. Clark (eds.). Durham, NC: Duke University Press, 1–56.

Barker, Meg-John, and Julia Scheele. (2016). *Queer: A Graphic History.* London: Icon Books.

Barnard, Ian. (2004). *Queer Race: Cultural Interventions in the Racial Politics of Queer Theory.* New York: Peter Lang.

Bebbington, Laurie, and Margaret Lyons. (1975). "Why SHOULD We Work with You? Lesbian-Feminists versus Gay Men" *Homosexual Conference Papers* (Melbourne), 26–29.

Beemyn, Brett. (2004). "Bisexuality, Bisexuals, and Bisexual Movements." In *Encyclopedia of Lesbian, Gay, Bisexual and Transgender History in America*, Marc Stein (ed.). Vol. 1. Detroit, MI: Charles Scribner's Sons, 141–145.

Benshoff, Harry M., and Sean Griffin. (2004). *Queer Cinema: The Film Reader.* New York: Routledge.

Berlant, Lauren. (1997). *The Queen of America Goes to Washington City: Essays on Sex and Citizenship.* Durham, NC: Duke University Press.

————. (2001). "The Subject of True Feeling: Pain, Privacy, and Politics." In *Feminist Consequences: Theory for the New Century*, Elisabeth Bronfen and Misha Kavka (eds.). New York: Columbia University Press, 126–160.

————. (2004). "Critical Inquiry, Affirmative Culture." *Critical Inquiry*, 30(2): 445–451.

————. (2011). *Cruel Optimism*. Durham, NC: Duke University Press.

Berlant, Lauren, and Elizabeth Freeman. (1993). "Queer Nationality." In *Fear of a Queer Planet: Queer Politics and Social Theory*, Michael Warner (ed.). Minneapolis and London: University of Minnesota Press, 193–229.

Berlant, Lauren, and Michael Warner. (1995). "What Does Queer Theory Teach Us about X?." *PMLA*, 110(3): 343–349.

————. (1998). "Sex in Public." *Critical Inquiry*, 24(2): 547–566.

Bersani, Leo. (1987). "Is the Rectum a Grave?" *AIDS: Cultural Analysis/Cultural Activism*, 43: 197–222.

————. (1996). *Homos*. London: Harvard University Press.

Bérubé, Allan. (2010). "How Gay Stays White and What Kind of White It Stays." In *Privilege*, Michael S Kimmel and Abby L. Ferber (eds.). Boulder, CO: Westview Press, 197–210.

Bhattacharyya, Gargi. (2002). *Sexuality and Society: An Introduction*. London: Routledge.

Blair, Karen L., and Rhea Ashley Hoskin. (2015). "Experiences of Femme Identity: Coming Out, Invisibility and Femmephobia." *Psychology & Sexuality*, 6(3): 229–244.

Bliss, James. (2015). "Hope against Hope: Queer Negativity, Black Feminist Theorizing, and Reproduction without Futurity." *Mosaic*, 48(1): 83–98.

Block, Andreas De, and Pieter R. Adriaens. (2013). "Pathologizing Sexual Deviance: A History." *Journal of Sex Research*, 50(3–4): 276–298.

Bornstein, Kate. (1994). *Gender Outlaw: On Men, Women and the Rest of Us*. London: Routledge.

Bourdieu, Pierre. (1986). "The Forms of Capital." In *Handbook of Theory of Research for the Sociology of Education*, J. E. Richardson (ed.). Greenwood Press, 241–258.

Brandzel, A. L. (2005). "Queering Citizenship?: Same-Sex Marriage and the State." *GLQ: A Journal of Lesbian and Gay Studies*, 11(2): 171–204.

Britzman, Deborah P. (1995). "Is There a Queer Pedagogy? Or, Stop Reading Straight." *Educational Theory*, 45(2): 151–165.

Brown, Wendy. (1993). "Wounded Attachments." *Political Theory*, 21(3): 390–410.

————. (1995). *States of Injury: Power and Freedom in Late Modernity*. Princeton: Princeton University Press.

Brownmiller, Susan. (1975). *Against Our Will: Men, Women and Rape*. London: Secker and Warburg.

Butler, Judith. (1988). "Performative Acts and Gender Constitution: An Essay in Phenomenology and Feminist Theory." *Theatre Journal*, 40(4): 519–531.

————. (1991). "Imitation and Gender Insubordination." In *Inside/Out: Lesbian Theories, Gay Theories*, Diana Fuss (ed.). New York: Routledge, 13–32.

————. (1993). "Critically Queer." *GLQ: A Journal of Lesbian and Gay Studies*, 1: 17–32.

————. (1994). "Against Proper Objects. Introduction." *Differences: A Journal of Feminist Cultural Studies*, 6(2/3): 1–26.

————. (1999). *Gender Trouble: Feminism and the Subversion of Identity*. New York: Routledge (originally published 1990).

————. (2002). "Is Kinship Always Already Heterosexual?." *Differences: A Journal of Feminist Cultural Studies*, 13(1): 14–44.

————. (2004a). "Imitation and Gender Insubordination." In *The Judith Butler Reader*, Sarah Salih (ed.). Malden, MA: Blackwell Publishing, 119–137.

————. (2004b). *Undoing Gender*. New York: Routledge.

————. (2014). *Bodies that Matter: On the Discursive Limits of "Sex."*. New York: Routledge (originally published 1993).

————. (2016). "Rethinking Vulnerability in Resistance." In *Vulnerability in Resistance*, Judith Butler, Zeynep Gambetti, and Leticia Sabsay (eds.). Durham, NC: Duke University Press, 12–27.

Calhoun, Cheshire. (1994). "Separating Lesbian Theory from Feminist Theory." *Ethics*, 104: 558–581.

Califia, Pat. (1996). "Feminism and Sadomasochism." In *Feminism and Sexuality: A Reader*, Stevi Jackson and Sue Scott (eds.). Edinburgh: Edinburgh University Press, 230–237.

————. (1997). *Sex Changes: The Politics of Transgenderism*. San Francisco: Cleis Press.

Cameron, Deborah, and Ivan Panovic. (2014). *Working with Written Discourse*. Los Angeles: SAGE Publications.

Cantú, Lionel. (2009). "Entre Hombres/Between Men: Latino Masculinities and Homosexualities." In *The Sexuality of Migration: Border Crossings and Mexican Immigrant Men*, Nancy A. Naples and Salvador Vidal-Ortiz (eds.). New York: New York University Press. 143–162.

Capper, Beth, and Arlen Austin. (2018). "'Wages for Housework Means Wages *against* Heterosexuality': On the Archives of Black Women for Wages for Housework and Wages Due Lesbians." *GLQ: A Journal of Lesbian and Gay Studies*, 24(4): 445–466.

Carbado, Devon W., Kimberlé Williams Crenshaw, Vickie M. Mays, and Barbara Tomlinson. (2013). "'INTERSECTIONALITY: Mapping the Movements of a Theory'." *Du Bois Review: Social Science Research on Race*, 2(10): 303–312.

Carbery, Graham. (1995). *A History of the Sydney Gay and Lesbian Mardi Gras*. Parkville, Victoria: Australian Lesbian and Gay Archives.

Carter, David. (2004). *Stonewall: The Riots that Sparked the Gay Revolution*. New York: St Martin's Press.

Caserio, Robert L., Lee Edelman, J. Halberstam, José Esteban Muñoz and Tim Dean. (2006). "PMLA Conference Debate: The Antisocial Thesis in Queer Theory." *Modern Language Association Annual Conference*, 121(3): 819–828.

Cerankowski, Karli June, and Milks, Megan. (2010). "New Orientations: Asexuality and Its Implications for Theory and Practice." *Feminist Studies*, 36(3): 650–664.

Chambers, Samuel A. (2009). *The Queer Politics of Television*. London: I.B Taurus.

————. (1983). "Refugees of a World on Fire: Foreword to the Second." In *This Bridge Called My Back: Writings by Radical Women of Color*, Cherríe Moraga and Gloria Anzaldúa (eds.). New York: Kitchen Table: Women of Color Press, 1–4.

Champagne, John. (1995). *The Ethics of Marginality: A New Approach to Gay Studies*. Minneapolis: University of Minnesota Press.

Cheng, Patrick S. (2011). *Radical Love: An Introduction to Queer Theology*. New York: Seabury Books.

Cho, Alexander. (2015). "Queer Reverb: Tumblr, Affect, Time." In *Networked Affect*, Ken Hillis, Susanna Paasonen, Michael Petit (eds.). London: MIT Press, 43–57.

Cho, Sumi, Kimberlé Williams Crenshaw, and Leslie McCall. (2013). "Toward a Field of Intersectionality Studies: Theory, Applications, and Praxis." *Signs: Journal of Women in Culture and Society*, 38(4): 785–810.

Christiansen, Adrienne E., and Jeremy J. Hanson. (1996). "Comedy as Cure for Tragedy: Act up and the Rhetoric of AIDS." *Quarterly Journal of Speech*, 82(2): 157–170.

Churchill, David S. (2008). "Transnationalism and Homophile Political Culture in the Postwar Decades." *GLQ: A Journal of Lesbian and Gay Studies*, 15(1): 31–66.

Cohen, Cathy J. (1996). "Contested Membership: Black Gay Identities and the Politics of AIDS." In *Queer Theory/Sociology*, Steven Seidman (ed.). Cambridge, MA: Blackwell Publishers, 362–394.

———. (1997). "Punks, Bulldaggers, and Welfare Queens: The Radical Potential of Queer Politics." *GLQ: A Journal of Lesbian and Gay Studies*, 3: 437–465.

Cole, Cheryl L. (1996). "Containing AIDS: Magic Johnson and Post[Reagan] America." In *Queer Theory/Sociology*, Steven Seidman (ed.). Cambridge, MA: Blackwell Publishers, 280–310.

Collins, Patricia Hill. (2011). "Piecing Together a Genealogical Puzzle: Intersectionality and American Pragmatism." *European Journal of Pragmatism and American Philosophy*, 3(2): 88–112.

———. (2015). "Intersectionality's Definitional Dilemmas." *Annual Review of Sociology*, 41(1): 1–20.

Colman, Felicity J. (2010). "Affect." In *The Deleuze Dictionary Revised Edition*, Adrian Parr (ed.). Edinburgh: Edinburgh University Press, 11–13.

The Combahee River Collective. 1977. "The Combahee River Collective Statement." http://circuitous.org/scraps/combahee.html.

Comella, Lyn. (2008). "Looking Backward: Barnard and Its Legacies." *The Communication Review*, 11(3): 202–211.

Cordova, Jeanne. (2000). "Radical Feminism? Dyke Separatism?." In *Radical Feminism: A Documentary Reader*, Barbara A. Crow (ed.). New York: New York University Press, 358–364.

Crenshaw, Kimberlé. (1989). "Demarginalizing the Intersection of Race and Sex: A Black Feminist Critique of Antidiscrimination Doctrine, Feminist Theory and Antiracist Politics." *University of Chicago Legal Forum*, 1(8): 139–168.

———. (1991). "Mapping the Margins: Intersectionality, Identity Politics, and Violence against Women of Color." *Stanford Law Review*, 43(6): 1241–1299.

Crimp, Douglas. (1987). "AIDS: Cultural Analysis/Cultural Activism." *October*, 43: 3–16.

———. (1988). "How to Have Promiscuity in an Epidemic." In *AIDS Cultural Analysis/Cultural Activism*, Douglas Crimp (ed.). Cambridge, MA: MIT Press, 237–271.

———. (1993). "Right On, Girlfriend!." In *Fear of a Queer Planet: Queer Politics and Social Theory*, Michael Warner (ed.). Minneapolis and London: University of Minnesota Press, 300–320.

Crimp, Douglas, and Adam Rolston. (1990). *AIDS Demo Graphics*. Seattle: Bay Press.

Crosby, Christina, Lisa Duggan, Roderick Ferguson, Kevin Floyd, Miranda Joseph, Heather Love, Robert McRuer, Fred Moten, Tavia Nyong'o, Lisa Rofel, Jordana Rosenberg, Gayle Salamon, Dean Spade, and Amy Villarejo. (2012). "Queer Studies, Materialism, and Crisis: A Roundtable Discussion." *GLQ: A Journal of Lesbian and Gay Studies*, 8(1): 127–147.

Cruz-Malavé, Arnaldo, and Martin F. Manalansan (eds.). (2002). *Queer Globalizations: Citizenship and the Afterlife of Colonialism*. New York: New York University Press.

Cvetkovich, Ann. (2003). *An Archive of Feelings: Trauma, Sexuality, and Lesbian Public Cultures*. Durham, NC: Duke University Press.

———. (2012). *Depression: A Public Feeling*. Durham, NC: Duke University Press.

D'Emilio, John. (1998). *Sexual Politics, Sexual Communities: The Making of a Homosexual Minority in the United States, 1940–1970*. Second Edition. Chicago: University of Chicago Press.

Dalton, H L. (1989). "AIDS in Blackface." *Daedalus*, 118(3): 205–227.

Danius, Sara, Jonsson, Stefan and Spivak, Gayatri Chakravorty. (1993). "An Interview with Gayatri Chakravorty Spivak." *Boundary 2*, 20(2): 24–50.

Davis, Glyn, and Gary Needham (eds.). (2009). *Queer TV: Theories, Histories, Politics*. New York: Routledge.

Davis, Lennard J. (2006). "Constructing Normalcy: The Bell Curve, the Novel, and the Invention of the Disabled Body in the Nineteenth Century." In *The Disability Studies Reader*, Lennard J. Davis (ed.). New York: Routledge, 3–16.

De Lauretis, Teresa. (1991). "Queer Theory: Lesbian and Gay Sexualities. An Introduction." *Differences: A Journal of Feminist Cultural Studies*, 3(2): iii–xviii.

Dean, Tim. (2000). *Beyond Sexuality*. Chicago: University of Chicago Press.

———. (2009). *Unlimited Intimacy: Reflections on the Subculture of Barebacking*. Chicago: University of Chicago Press.

Dee, Hannah. (2010). *The Red in the Rainbow: Sexuality, Socialism and LGBT Liberation*. London: Bookmarks.

Deitcher, David. (1995). *The Question of Equality: Lesbian and Gay Politics in America since Stonewall*. New York: Scribner.

Delany, Samuel R. (1999). *Times Square Red, Times Square Blue*. New York: New York University Press.

Deleuze, Gilles, and Felix Guattari. (1987). *A Thousand Plateaus*. Minneapolis: University of Minnesota Press.

Dhairyam, Sagri. (1994). "Racing the Lesbian, Dodging White Critics." In *The Lesbian Postmodern*, Laura Doan (ed.). New York: Columbia University Press, 24–46.

Dilley, Patrick. (1999). "Queer Theory: Under Construction." *International Journal of Qualitative Studies in Education*, 12(5): 457–472.

Dinshaw, Carolyn. (1999). *Getting Medieval: Sexualities and Communities, Pre- and Postmodern*. Durham, NC: Duke University Press.

Dinshaw, Carolyn, Lee Edelman, Roderick A. Ferguson, Carla Freccero, Elizabeth Freeman, J. Halberstam, Annamarie Jagose, Christopher Nealon, and Nguyen Tan Hoang. (2007). "Theorising Queer Temporalities." *GLQ: A Journal of Lesbian and Gay Studies*, 13(2–3): 177–196.

Dolgert, S. (2016). "The Praise of Ressentiment: Or, How I Learned to Stop Worrying and Love Donald Trump." *New Political Science*, 38(3): 354–370.

Doty, Alexander. (1993). *Making Things Perfectly Queer: Interpreting Mass Culture*. Minneapolis: University of Minnesota Press.

———. (2000). *Flaming Classics: Queering the Film Canon*. New York: Routledge.

Doty, Mark. (1996). *Heaven's Coast*. New York: Halperin.

Drescher, Jack. (2001). *Psychoanalytic Therapy and the Gay Man*. New York and London: Routledge.

———. (2015). "Out of DSM: Depathologizing Homosexuality." *Behavioral Sciences*, 5(4): 565–575.

Driskill, Qwo-Li, Chris Finley, Brian Joseph Gilley, and Scott Lauria Morgensen. (2011a). *Queer Indigenous Studies: Critical Interventions in Theory, Politics, and Literature*. Tuscon: The University of Arizona Press.

———. (2011b). "Introduction." In *Queer Indigenous Studies: Critical Interventions in Theory, Politics, and Literature*, Qwo-Li Driskill, Chris Finley, Brian Joseph Gilley, and Scott Lauria Morgensen (eds.). University of Arizona Press, 1–28.

Duberman, Martin. (2013). *The Martin Duberman Reader: The Essential Historical, Biographical, and Autobiographical Writings*. New York: The New Press.

Duggan, Lisa. (1992). "Making It Perfectly Queer." *Art Papers*, 14(4): 10–16.

———. (2002). "The New Homonormativity: The Sexual Politics of Neoliberalism." In *Materializing Democracy: Toward a Revitalized Cultural Politics*, R. Castronovo and D. D. Nelson (eds.). Durham, NC: Duke University Press, 175–194.

———. (1981). *Pornography*. New York: Plume.

Duggan, Lisa, Nan D. Hunter, and Carole S. Vance. (1995). "False Promises: Feminist Antipornography Legislation." In *Sex Wars: Sexual Dissent and Political Culture*, Lisa Duggan and Nan D. Hunter (eds.). New York: Routledge, 43–64 (originally published 1985).

Dunk-West, Priscilla, and Heather Brook. (2015). "Sexuality." In *Introducing Gender & Women's Studies* Fourth Edition, Victoria Robinson and Diane Richardson (eds.). London: Red Globe Press, 150–165.

Dworkin, Andrea. (1985). "Against the Male Flood: Censorship, Pornography, and Equality." *Harvard Women's Law Journal*, 1(30): 1–29.

———. (1997). *Life and Death*. New York: The Free Press.

———. (2007). *Intercourse*. New York: The Free Press.

Dyer, Richard. (1990). *Now You See It: Studies in Lesbian and Gay Film*. New York: Routledge.

Edelman, Lee. (1994). "The Plague of Discourse: Politics, Literary Theory, and AIDS." In *The Postmodern Turn: New Perspectives on Social Theory*, Steven Seidman (ed.). New York: Cambridge University Press, 299–312.

———. (2004). *No Future: Queer Theory and the Death Drive*. Durham, NC: Duke University Press.

Edenheim, Sara. (2014). "Lost and Never Found: The Queer Archive of Feelings and Its Historical Propriety." *Differences: A Journal of Feminist Cultural Studies*, 24(3): 36–62.

Elliot, Beth. 1992. "Holly Near And Yet So Far". In Elizabeth Reba Weise (ed.). *Closer to Home: Bisexuality and Feminism*. Seattle: The Seal Press, 233–254.

Ellis, Havelock. (1927). *Studies in the Psychology of Sex: Volume 2 Sexual Inversion*. Philadelphia: F. A. Davis Co. http://www.gutenberg.org/files/13611/13611-h/13611-h.htm (originally published 1900).

Elmhirst, Rebecca. (2011). "Migrant Pathways to Resource Access in Lampung's Political Forest: Gender, Citizenship and Creative Conjugality." *Geoforum*, 42: 173–183.

Eng, David L. (2001). *Racial Castration: Managing Masculinity in Asian America. Perverse Modernities*. Durham, NC: Duke University Press.

———. (2003). "Transnational Adoption and Queer Diasporas." *Social Text*, 21(3 (76)): 1–37.

Eng, David L., J. Halberstam, and José Esteban Muñoz. (2005). "What's Queer About Queer Studies Now?." *Social Text*, 23(3–4 (84–85)): 1–17.

Engdahl, Ulrica. (2014). "Wrong Body." *TSQ: Transgender Studies Quarterly*, 1(1–2): 267–269.

Eribon, Didier. (2004). *Insult and the Making of the Gay Self*. Durham, NC, and London: Duke University Press.

Erickson-Schroth, Laura, and Jennifer Mitchell. (2009). "Queering Queer Theory, or Why Bisexuality Matters." *Journal of Bisexuality*, 9(3-4): 297–315.

Esterberg, Kristin G. (1994). "From Accommodation to Liberation: A Social Movement Analysis of Lesbians in the Homophile Movement." *Gender and Society*, 8(3): 424–443.

Fausto-Sterling, Anne. (2000). *Sexing the Body: Gender Politics and the Construction of Sexuality*. New York: Basic Books.

Fawaz, Ramzi. (2015). "'I Cherish My Bile Duct as much as Any Other Organ': Political Disgust and the Digestive Life of AIDS in Tony Kushner's *Angels in America*." *GLQ: A Journal of Lesbian and Gay Studies*, 21(1): 121–152.

Federici, Silvia. (2017). "Capitalism and the Struggle against Sexual Work (1975)." In *The New York Wages for Housework Committee, 1972 – 1976: History, Theory, and Documents*, Silvia Federici and Arlen Austin, Brooklyn (eds.). New York: Autonomedia, 144–146.

Feinberg, Leslie. (2013). "Transgender Liberation: A Movement Whose Time Has Come." In *The Transgender Studies Reader*, Susan Stryker and Steven Whittle (eds.). Hoboken: Taylor and Francis, 205–220.

Fejes, Fred. (2002). "Bent Passions: Heterosexual Masculinity, Pornography, and Gay Male Identity." *Sexuality & Culture*, 6(3): 95–113.

Fela, Geraldine. (2018). "Blood Politics: Australian Nurses, HIV and the Battle for Rights on the Wards." *Labour History*, 115: 87–104.

Fela, Geraldine, and Hannah McCann. (2017). "Solidarity Is Possible: Rethinking Gay and Lesbian Activism in 1970s Australia." *Australian Feminist Studies*, 32(93): 325–334.

Ferguson, Roderick A. (2003). *Aberrations in Black: Toward a Queer(s) of Colour Critique*. Minneapolis: University of Minnesota Press.

———. (2018). "Queer(s) of Colour Critique." In *Oxford Research Encyclopedia of Literature*.

———. (2019). *One-Dimensional Queer*. Cambridge: Polity.

Ferguson, Roderick A., and Grace Kyungwon Hong. (2012). "The Sexual and Racial Contradictions of Neoliberalism." *Journal of Homosexuality*, 59: 1057–1064.

Fetner, Tina. (2001). "Working Anita Bryant: The Impact of Christian Anti-Gay Activism on Lesbian and Gay Movement Claims." *Social Problems*, 48(3): 411–428.

Fiol-Matta, Licia. (2002). *A Queer Mother for the Nation: The State and Gabriela Mistral*. Minneapolis: University of Minnesota Press.

Firestone, Shulamith. (1970). *The Dialectic of Sex: The Case for Feminist Revolution*. New York: Bantam Books.

Flore, Jacinthe. (2014). "Mismeasures of Asexual Desires." In *Asexualities: Feminist and Queer Perspectives*, Karli June Cerankowski and Megan Milks (eds.). New York: Routledge, 17–34.

Floyd, Kevin. (2009). *The Reification of Desire: Toward a Queer Marxism*. Minneapolis: University of Minnesota Press.

Forstie, Clare. (2016). "Trigger Warnings." In *Critical Concepts in Queer Studies and Education: An International Guide for the Twenty-First Century*, Edward Rodriguez, Nelson M. Martino, Wayne J. Ingrey, Jennifer C. Brockenbrough (eds.). New York: Palgrave Macmillan, 421–433.

Foucault, Michel. (1972). *The Archaeology of Knowledge and the Discourse on Language*. A. M. Sheridan Smith (Trans.). New York: Pantheon Books.

———. (1978). *The History of Sexuality: Volume 1*. Robert Hurley (Trans.). Penguin History. Victoria: Penguin (originally published in 1976).

Fountain-Stokes, Lawrence Martin La. (2009). *Queer Ricans: Cultures and Sexualities in the Diaspora*. Minneapolis: University of Minnesota Press.

Francis, S., and J. Hardman. (2018). "#Rhodesmustfall: Using Social Media to 'Decolonise' Learning Spaces for South African Higher Education Institutions: A Cultural Historical Activity Theory Approach." *South African Journal of Higher Education*, 32(4): 66–80.

Fraser, Nancy. (1995). "From Redistribution to Recognition? Dilemmas of Justice in a 'Post-Socialist' Age." *New Left Review*, 1(212): 68–93.

———. (2005). "Mapping the Feminist Imagination: From Redistribution to Recognition to Representation." *Constellations*, 12(3): 295–307.

Freeman, Elizabeth. (2010). *Time Binds: Queer Temporalities, Queer Histories*. Durham, NC: Duke University Press.

Freud, Sigmund. (1962). *The Ego and the Id*. J Strachey (ed). New York: Norton.

———. (2001). "Mourning and Melancholia." In *Complete Psychological Works of Sigmund Freud (Volume 14)*, James Strachey (ed.). New York: Random House, 243–258.

Freud, Sigmund, and J. Strachey. (2000). *Three Essays on the Theory of Sexuality*. Basic Books Classics. New York: Perseus Books.

Friedan, Betty. (1963). *The Feminine Mystique*. New York: W. W. Norton & Company.

Fuss, Diana. (1991). "Inside/Out." In *Inside/Out: Lesbian Theories, Gay Theories*, Diana Fuss (ed.). London: Routledge, 1–10.

———. (1995). *Identification Papers*. New York: Routledge.

Gagnon, John H., and William Simon (1973). *Sexual Conduct: The Social Sources of Human Sexuality*. Chicago: Aldine Pub.

Gallo, Marcia M. (2007). *Different Daughters: A History of the Daughters of Bilitis and the Rise of the Lesbian Rights Movement*. New York: Seal Press.

Galvan, Margaret A. (2016). "Archiving the '80s: Feminism, Queer Theory, & Visual Culture." *CUNY Academic Works*. https://academicworks.cuny.edu/gc_etds/1248.

Gamson, Josh. (1989). "Silence Death and the Invisible Enemy: AIDS Activism and Social Movement 'Newness.'." *Social Problems*, 36(4): 351–367.

Gamson, Joshua, and Dawne Moon. (2004). "The Sociology of Sexualities: Queer and Beyond." *Annual Review of Sociology*, 30(1): 47–64.

Garber, Linda. (2006). "On the Evolution of Queer Studies: Lesbian Feminism, Queer Theory and Globalization." In *Intersections between Feminist and Queer Theory*, Diane Richardson, Janice McLaughlin, and Mark E. Casey (eds.). New York: Palgrave, 78–96.

Garber, Marjorie. (2000). *Bisexuality and the Eroticism of Everyday Life*. New York: Routledge.

Gever, Martha, Pratibha Pramar, and John Greyson. (1993). *Queer Looks: Perspectives on Lesbian and Gay Film and Video*. New York: Routledge.

Gieseking, Jen Jack. (2017). "Messing with the Attractiveness Algorithm: A Response to Queering Code/Space." *Gender, Place & Culture*, 24(11): 1659–1665.

Giffney, Noreen. (2018). "Introduction: The 'Q' Word." In *The Ashgate Research Companion to Queer Theory*, Noreen Giffney and Michael O'Rourke (eds.). New York: Routledge, 1–13 (originally published 2009).

Giles, Fiona. (2004). "'Relational, and Strange': A Preliminary Foray into A Project to Queer Breastfeeding." *Australian Feminist Studies*, 19(45): 301–314.

Gill, Rosalind. (2008). "Empowerment/Sexism: Figuring Female Sexual Agency in Contemporary Advertising." *Feminism & Psychology*, 18(1): 35–60.

Gillis, Stacy, and Rebecca Munford. (2004). "Genealogies and Generations: The Politics and Praxis of Third Wave Feminism." *Women's History Review*, 13(2): 165–182.

Glick, Elisa. (2000). "Sex Positive: Feminism, Queer Theory, and the Politics of Transgression." *Feminist Review*, 64: 19–45.

Goh, Joseph N. (2017). *Living Out Sexuality and Faith: Body Admissions of Malaysian Gay and Bisexual Men. Gender, Theology and Spirituality*. London and New York: Routledge.

Goldman, Ruth. (1996). "Who Is that Queer Queer? Exploring Norms around Sexuality, Race, and Class in Queer Theory." In *Queer Studies: A Lesbian, Gay, Bisexual and Transgender Anthology*, Brett Beemyn and Michelle Eliason (eds.). New York: New York University Press, 169–182.

Gopinath, Gayatri. (2005). *Impossible Desires: Queer Diasporas and South Asian Public Cultures. Perverse Modernities*. Durham, NC: Duke University Press.

Gorman-Murray, Andrew. (2017). "Que(e)Rying Homonormativity: The Everyday Politics of Lesbian and Gay Homemaking." In *Sexuality and Gender at Home: Experience, Politics, Transgression*, Brent Pilkey, Rachael M. Scicluna, Ben Campkin, and Barbara Penner (eds.). London: Bloomsbury, 149–162.

Gossett, Che. (2014). "We Will Not Rest in Peace: AIDS Activism, Black Radicalism, Queer And/Or Trans Resistance." In *Queer Necropolitics*, Jin Haritaworn, Adi Kuntsman, and Silvia Posocco (eds.). Oxon: Routledge, 31–50.

Gould, Deborah B. (2009a). *Moving Politics: Emotion and ACT Up's Fight against AIDS*. Chicago and London: University of Chicago Press.

————. (2009b). "The Shame of Gay Pride in Early AIDS Activism." In *Gay Shame*, David M. Halperin and Valerie Traub (eds.). Chicago and London: The University of Chicago Press, 221–255.

Gray, Mary L. (2009). "'Queer Nation Is Dead/Long Live Queer Nation': The Politics and Poetics of Social Movement and Media Representation." *Critical Studies in Media Communication*, 26(3): 212–236.

Green, Adam Isaiah. (2002). "Gay but Not Queer: Toward a Postqueer Study of Sexuality." *Theory and Society*, 31(4): 521–545.

Greer, Germaine. (1970). *The Female Eunuch*. London: MacGibbon & Kee.

Grewal, Inderpal, and Caren Kaplan. (1994). "Introduction: Transnational Feminist Practices and Questions of Postmodernity." In *Scattered Hegemonies: Postmodernity and Transnational Feminist Practices*, Inderpal Grewal and Caren Kaplan (eds.). Minneapolis: University of Minnesota Press, 1–33.

Grosz, Elizabeth. (1989). *Sexual Subversions: Three French Feminists*. St Leonards: Allen & Unwin.

————. (1994). *Volatile Bodies: Toward a Corporeal Feminism*. Bloomington: Indiana University Press.

Grover, Jan Zita. (1987). "AIDS: Keywords." *October*, 43: 17–30.

Gutting, Gary (ed.). (2005). *The Cambridge Companion to Foucault* (Second Edition). New York: Cambridge University Press.

Halberstam, J. (1998). *Female Masculinity*. Durham, NC, and London: Duke University Press.

————. (2003). "Reflections on Queer Studies and Queer Pedagogy." *Journal of Homosexuality*, 45(2–4): 361–364.

————. (2005a). *In a Queer Time and Place: Transgender Bodies, Subcultural Lives*. New York: New York University Press.

————. (2005b). "Shame and White Gay Masculinity." *Social Text*, 8485(23): 3–4.

————. (2008). "The Anti-Social Turn in Queer Studies." *Graduate Journal of Social Science*, 5(2): 140–156.

————. (2011). *The Queer Art of Failure*. Durham, NC: Duke University Press.

————. (2012a). *Gaga Feminism: Sex, Gender, and the End of Normal*. Boston: Beacon Press.

————. (2012b). "Bullybloggers on Failure and the Future of Queer Studies." *BullyBloggers*. https://bullybloggers.wordpress.com/2012/04/02/bullybloggers-on-failure-and-the-future-of-queer-studies/.

————. (2014). "You are Triggering Me! the Neo-Liberal Rhetoric of Harm, Danger and Trauma." *Bully Bloggers*. https://bullybloggers.wordpress.com/2014/07/05/you-are-triggering-me-the-neo-liberal-rhetoric-of-harm-danger-and-trauma/.

————. (2018). *Trans*: A Quick and Quirky Account of Gender Variability*. Oakland: University of California Press.

Halcli, Abigail. (1999). "AIDS, Anger, and Activism: ACT UP as a Social Movement Organization." In *Waves of Protest: Social Movements since the Sixties*, Jo Freeman and Victoria Johnson (eds.). Lanham: Rowman & Littlefield, 135–150.

Hale, C. Jacob. (1998). "Consuming the Living, Dis(Re)Membering the Dead in the Butch/FTM Borderlands." *GLQ: A Journal of Lesbian and Gay Studies*, 4(October 2018): 311–348.

Hall, Donald E. (2003). *Queer Theories*. London: Red Globe Press.

Halley, Janet. (2006). *Split Decisions: How and Why to Take a Break from Feminism*. Princeton and Oxford: Princeton University Press.

Halley, Janet, and Andrew Parker. (2011). "Introduction." In *After Sex? on Writing since Queer Theory*, Janet Halley and Andrew Parker (eds.). Series Q. Durham, NC: Duke University Press, 1–16.

Halperin, David M. (2003). "The Normalisation of Queer Theory." *Journal of Homosexuality*, 45: 339–343.

Hames-García, Michael. (2011a). *Identity Complex: Making the Case for Multiplicity*. Minneapolis and London: University of Minnesota Press.

———. (2011b). "Queer Theory Revisited." In *Gay Latino Studies: A Critical Reader*, Michael Hames-García and Ernesto Javier Martínez (eds.). Durham, NC, and London: Duke University Press, 19–45.

Hammonds, Evelynn. (1987). "Race, Sex, AIDS: The Construction of 'Other.'" *Radical America*, 20(6): 28–36.

Harper, Phillip Brian. (1993). "Eloquence and Epitaph: Black Nationalism and the Homophobic Impulse in Responses to the Death of Max Robinson." In *Fear of a Queer Planet: Queer Politics and Social Theory*, Michael Warner (ed.). Minneapolis and London: University of Minnesota Press, 239–263.

Harper, Phillip Brian, Anne McClintock, José Esteban Muñoz, and Trish Rosen. (1997). "Queer Transexions of Race, Nation, and Gender: An Introduction." *Social Text*, 52/53: 1–4.

Hayes, J., Margaret Higonnet, and R. W. Spurlin. (2010). "Comparing Queerly, Queering Comparison: Theorizing Identities between Cultures, Histories, and Disciplines." In *Comparatively Queer: Interrogating Identities across Time and Cultures*, W. Spurlin, J. Hayes, Margaret R. Higonnet (eds.). New York: Palgrave, 1–19.

Heaney, Emma. (2016). "Women-Identified Women: Trans Women in 1970s Lesbian Feminist Organizing." *TSQ: Transgender Studies Quarterly*, 3(1-2): 137–145.

———. (2002). *Profit and Pleasure: Sexual Identities in Late Capitalism*. New York: Routledge.

Hegarty, Benjamin. (2017). "'When I Was Transgender': Visibility, Subjectivity, and Queer Aging in Indonesia." *Medicine Anthropology Theory*, 4(2): 70–80.

Hemmings, Clare. (2005). "Invoking Affect: Cultural Theory and the Ontological Turn." *Cultural Studies*, 19(5): 548–567.

———. *Why Stories Matter: The Political Grammar of Feminist Theory*. Durham, NC: Duke University Press.

Hennessy, Rosemary. (2006). "The Value of a Second Skin." In *Intersections between Feminist and Queer Theory*, Diane Richardson, Janice McLaughlin and Mark E. Casey (eds.). New York: Palgrave, 116–135.

Hines, Sally. (2015). "Feminist Theories." In *Introducing Gender & Women's Studies* Fourth Edition, Victoria Robinson and Diane Richardson (eds.). London: Red Globe Press, 23–39.

Hird, Myra J. (2004). "Naturally Queer." *Feminist Theory*, 5(1): 85–89.

Holden, Philip, and Richard R. Ruppel (eds.). (2003). *Imperial Desire: Dissident Sexualities and Colonial Literature*. Minneapolis: University of Minnesota Press.

Holland, Sharon Patricia. (2012). *The Erotic Life of Racism*. Durham, NC: Duke University Press.

hooks, bell. (1984). *Feminist Theory: From Margin to Center*. Boston: South End Press.

———. (2015). *Ain't I a Woman: Black Women and Feminism*. New York: Routledge.

Horn, Katrin. (2010). "Camping with the Stars: Queer Performativity, Pop Intertextuality, and Camp in the Pop Art of Lady Gaga." *Current Objectives of Postgraduate American Studies*, 11: 1–16.

Huffer, Lynne. (2010). *Mad for Foucault: Rethinking the Foundations of Queer Theory*. New York: Columbia University Press.

———. (2013). *Are the Lips A Grave? A Queer Feminist Ethics of Sex*. New York: Columbia University Press.

Hunter, Nan D. (2006). "Contextualizing the Sexuality Debates: A Chronology 1966-2005." In *Sex Wars: Sexual Dissent and Political Culture*, Lisa Duggan and Nan D. Hunter (eds.). New York: Routledge, 15–28.

Jackson, Ronald L., and Michael A. Hogg. (2010). "Identity Politics." In *Encyclopedia of Identity*, Ronald L. Jackson and Michael A. Hogg (eds.). Thousand Oaks, California: SAGE Publications, 368–369.

Jackson, Stevi. (2006a). "Heterosexuality, Sexuality and Gender: Re-Thinking the Intersections." In *Intersections between Feminist and Queer Theory*, Diane Richardson, Janice McLaughlin, and Mark E. Casey (eds.). New York: Palgrave, 38–58.

———. (2006b). "Gender, Sexuality and Heterosexuality: The Complexity (And Limits) of Heteronormativity." *Feminist Theory*, 7(1): 105–121.

Jacobson, M. F. (1999). *Whiteness of a Different Color*. Cambridge, MA: Harvard University Press.

Jaggar, Alison. (1983). *Feminist Politics and Human Nature*. Brighton: Rowman & Allanheld.

Jagose, Annamarie. (1996). *Queer Theory: An Introduction*. Carlton: Melbourne University Press.

———. (2009). "Feminism's Queer Theory." *Feminism & Psychology*, 19(2): 157–174.

———. (2010). "Counterfeit Pleasures: Fake Orgasm and Queer Agency." *Textual Practice*, 24(3): 517–539.

———. (2013). *Orgasmology*. Durham, NC: Duke University Press.

———. (2015). "The Trouble with Antinormativity." *Differences: A Journal of Feminist Cultural Studies*, 26(1): 26–47.

Jakobsen, Janet R. (1998). "Queer Is? Queer Does? Normativity and the Problem of Resistance." *GLQ: A Journal of Lesbian and Gay Studies*, 4(4): 511–536.

Jeffreys, Shelia. (1997). "Transgender Activism: A Feminist Perspective." *Journal of Lesbian Studies*, 1(3–4): 55–74.

Johnson, Austin H. (2016). "Transnormativity: A New Concept and Its Validation through Documentary Film about Transgender Men." *Sociological Inquiry*, 86(4): 465–491.

Johnson, Carol. (2003). "Heteronormative Citizenship: The Howard Government's Views on Gay and Lesbian Issues." *Australian Journal of Political Science*, 38(1): 45–62.

Johnson, Patrick E. (2001). "'Quare' Studies, or (Almost) Everything I Know about Queer Studies I Learned from My Grandmother." *Text and Performance Quarterly*, 21(1): 1–25.

———. (2003). *Appropriating Blackness: Performance and the Politics of Authenticity*. Durham, NC: Duke University Press.

Johnson, Patrick E., and Mae G. Henderson. (2005). *Black Queer Studies: A Critical Anthology*. Durham, NC: Duke University Press.

Johnston, Jill. (1974). *Lesbian Nation: The Feminist Solution*. New York: Simon & Schuster.

Kafer, Alison. (2013). *Feminist, Queer, Crip*. Bloomington: Indiana University Press.

Katz, Jonathan. (1992). *Gay American History: Lesbians and Gay Men in the U.S.A.: A Documentary History*. New York: Meridian.

———. (2014). *The Invention of Heterosexuality*. Chicago: University of Chicago Press.

Kennedy, Rosanne, Jonathon Zapasnik, Hannah McCann, and Miranda Bruce. (2013). "All Those Little Machines: Assemblage as Transformative Theory." *Australian Humanities Review*, 55: 45–66.

Kerekere, Elizabeth. (2015). *TakatāPui: Part of the WhāNau*. Auckland: Tīwhanawhana Trust and Mental Health Foundation.

Khan, Ummni. (2014). *Vicarious Kinks: S/M in the Socio-Legal Imaginary*. Toronto: University of Toronto Press.

Killen, Gemma. (2017). "Archiving the Other or Reading Online Photography as Queer Ephemera." *Australian Feminist Studies*, 32(91–92): 58–74.

Kinser, Amber E. (2004). "Negotiating Spaces For/Through Third-Wave Feminism." *NWSA Journal*, 16(3): 124–153.

Kinsey, Alfred C., Wardell B. Pomeroy, Clyde E. Martin, and Paul H. Gebhard. (1998). *Sexual Behaviour in the Human Female*. Bloomington: Indiana University Press.

Kinsey Institute. 2018. *The Kinsey Scale*. https://kinseyinstitute.org/research/publications/kinsey-scale.php.

Koedt, Anne. (1973). "Lesbianism and Feminism." In *Radical Feminism*, Anne Koedt, Ellen Levine, and Anita Rapone (eds.). New York: Quadrangle, 246–258.

Koyama, Emi. (2003). "Transfeminist Manifesto." In *Catching a Wave: Reclaiming Feminism for the Twenty-First Century*, R. Dicker and A. Piepmeier (eds.). Boston: Northeastern University Press, 1–15.

Krieger, Susan. (1996). *The Family Silver: Essays on Relationships among Women*. Berkeley and Los Angeles: University of California Press.

Kruks, Sonia. (2014). "Women's 'Lived Experience': Feminism and Phenomenology from Simone De Beauvoir to the Present." In *The SAGE Handbook of Feminist Theory*, Mary Evans, Clare Hemmings, Marsha Henry, Hazel Johnstone, Sumi Madhok, Ania Plomien, and Sadie Wearing (eds.). Thousand Oaks, CA: SAGE Publication. 75–92.

Kulpa, Robert. (2009). "Lesbian Separatism." In *Encyclopedia of Gender and Society*, Jodi O'Brien (ed.). Thousand Oaks: SAGE Publications, 491.

Kulpa, Robert, Joanna Mizielińska, and Agata Stasińska. (2012). "(Un)Translatable Queer? Or, What Is Lost and Can Be Found in Translation." In *Transport: Queer*

Theory, Queer Critique, and Queer Activism in Motion, Sushila Mesquita, Katharina Wiedlack, and Katrin Lasthofer (eds.). Vienna: Zaglossus, 115–145.

Lancaster, Roger. (2003). *The Trouble with Nature: Sex in Science and Popular Culture*. Berkeley: University of California Press.

Landström, Catharina. (2007). "Queering Feminist Technology Studies." *Feminist Theory*, 8(1): 7–26.

Latham, J. R. (2018). "Axiomatic: Constituting 'Transexuality' and Trans Sexualities in Medicine." *Sexualities*, 22(1–2): 13–30.

Lauritsen, J., and D. Thorstad. (1995). *The Early Homosexual Rights Movement, 1864–1935*. Ojai, CA: Times Change Press.

Lennon, Erica, and Brian J. Mistler. (2014). "Cisgenderism." *TSQ: Transgender Studies Quarterly*, 1(1–2): 63–64.

Leonard, William. (2005). "Queer Occupations: Development of Victoria's Gay, Lesbian, Bisexual, Transgender and Intersex Health and Well Being Action Plan." *Gay & Lesbian Issues and Psychology Review*, 1(3): 92–97.

Lewis, Holly. (2016). *The Politics of Everybody: Feminism, Queer Theory, and Marxism at the Intersection*. London: Zed Books.

Lewis, Rachel A., and Nancy A. Naples. (2014). "Introduction: Queer Migration, Asylum, and Displacement." *Sexualities*, 17(8): 911–918.

Liu, Petras. (2015). *Queer Marxism in Two Chinas*. Durham, NC: Duke University Press.

Lloyd, Moya. (2005). *Beyond Identity Politics: Feminism, Power and Politics*. Thousand Oaks, California: SAGE Publications.

Loftin, Craig M. (2012). *Masked Voices: Gay Men and Lesbians in Cold War America*. New York: SUNY Press.

Lorde, Audre. (1993). "The Uses of the Erotic: The Erotic as Power." In *The Lesbian and Gay Studies Reader*, Henry Abelove (ed.). New York: Routledge, 339–343.

Love, Heather. (2007). *Feeling Backward: Loss and the Politics of Queer History*. Cambridge, MA: Harvard University Press.

———. (2008). "Compulsory Happiness and Queer Existence." *New Formations*, 63: 52–64.

———. (2011). "Queers_____This." In *After Sex? On Writing Since Queer Theory*, Janet Halley and Andrew Parker (eds.). Durham, NC, and London: Duke University Press, 180–191.

Lovelace, Linda. (1980). *Ordeal*. Secaucus: Citadel Press.

Luibhéid, Eithne. (2002). *Entry Denied: Controlling Sexuality at the Border*. E-Libro: University of Minnesota Press.

———. (2008). "Sexuality, Migration, and the Shifting Line between Legal and Illegal Status." *GLQ: A Journal of Lesbian and Gay Studies*, 14(2–3), 289–315.

———. (2013). *Pregnant on Arrival: Making the Illegal Immigrant*. Minneapolis: University of Minnesota Press.

Luibhéid, Eithne, and Lionel Cantú (eds.). (2005). *Queer Migrations: Sexuality, U.S. Citizenship, and Border Crossings*. Minneapolis: University of Minnesota Press.

MacKinnon, Catharine. (1982). "Feminism, Marxism, Method, and the State: An Agenda for Theory." *Signs: Journal of Women in Culture and Society*, 7(3): 515–544.

———. (1987). *Feminism Unmodified: Discourses on Life and Law.* Cambridge, MA: Harvard University Press.

———. (1993). *Only Words.* Cambridge, MA: Harvard University Press.

Manalansan, Martin F. (2006). "Queer Intersections: Sexuality and Gender in Migration Studies." *International Migration Review,* 40(1): 224–249.

———. (2018). "Messing up Sex: The Promises and Possibilities of Queer(s) of Colour Critique." *Sexualities* 21(8): 1287–1290.

Marcus, Sharon. (2005). "Queer Theory for Everyone: A Review Essay." *Signs: Journal of Women in Culture and Society,* 31(1): 191–121.

Marinucci, Mimi. (2010). *Feminism Is Queer: The Intimate Connection between Queer and Feminist Theory.* London: Zed Books.

Martin, Fran. (2003). *Situating Sexualities: Queer Representation in Taiwanese Fiction, Film and Public Culture.* Hong Kong: Hong Kong University Press.

———. (2010). *Backward Glances Contemporary Chinese Cultures and the Female Homoerotic Imaginary.* Asia-Pacific. Durham, NC: Duke University Press.

Massaquoi, Notisha. (2015). "Queer Theory and Intersectionality." In *International Encyclopedia of the Social & Behavioral Sciences: Second Edition,* James D. Wright (ed.). Amsterdam: Elsevier.

Massumi, Brian. (2002). *A Shock to Thought: Expressions after Deleuze and Guattari.* London: Routledge.

McCann, Hannah. (2016). "Epistemology of the Subject: Queer Theory's Challenge to Feminist Sociology." *WSQ: Women's Studies Quarterly,* 44(3–4): 224–243.

———. (2018). *Queering Femininity: Sexuality, Feminism and the Politics of Presentation.* New York: Routledge.

McCann, Hannah, and Clare Southerton. (2019). "Repetitions of Desire: Queering the One Direction Fangirl." *Girlhood Studies,* 12(1): 49–65.

McIntyre, Joanna. (2018). "They're so Normal I Can't Stand It": I Am Jazz, I Am Cait, Transnormativity, and Trans Feminism." In *Orienting Feminism,* C. Dale and R. Overell (eds.). Cham: Palgrave Macmillan, 9–24.

McLaughlin, Janet, Mark E. Casey, and Diane Richardson. (2006). "Introduction: At the Intersection of Feminist and Queer Debates." In *Intersections between Feminist and Queer Theory,* Diane Richardson, Janet McLaughlin and Mark E. Casey (eds.). New York: Palgrave, 1–18.

McLean, Kirsten. (2008). "Inside, Outside, Nowhere: Bisexual Men and Women in the Gay and Lesbian Community." *Journal of Bisexuality,* 8(1–2): 63–80.

McNair, Brian. (1996). *Mediated Sex: Pornography and Postmodern Culture.* London: Arnold.

McRuer, Robert. (2006). *Crip Theory: Cultural Signs of Queerness and Disability.* New York: New York University Press.

———. (2011). "DISABLING SEX: Notes for a Crip Theory of Sexuality." *GLQ: A Journal of Lesbian and Gay Studies,* 17(1): 107–117.

Meeker, Martin. (2001). "Behind the Mask of Respectability: Reconsidering the Mattachine Society and Male Homophile Practice, 1950s and 1960s." *Journal of the History of Sexuality,* 10(1): 78–116.

Mercer, Kobena, and Isaac Julien. (1988). "Race, Sexual Politics, and Black Masculinity: A Dossier." In *Male Order: Unwrapping Masculinity*, Rowena Chapman and Jonathan Rutherford (eds.). London: Lawrence and Wishart, 97–164.

Merleau-Ponty, Maurice. (2010). *Phenomenology of Perception*. New York: Routledge.

Mikulak, Magdalena. (2017). "Godly Homonormativity: Christian LGBT Organizing in Contemporary Poland." *Journal of Homosexuality*, 66(4): 487–509.

Miller, Marshall. (2001). "Ethically Questionable?." *Journal of Bisexuality*, 2(1): 93–112.

Miller, Paul Allen. (1998). "The Classical Roots of Poststructuralism: Lacan, Derrida, and Foucault." *International Journal of the Classical Tradition*, 5(2): 204–225.

Millett, Kate. (2016). *Sexual Politics*. New York: Columbia University Press (originally published 1970).

Mol, Annemarie. (1999). "Ontological Politics. A Word and Some Questions." *The Sociological Review*, 47(1): 74–89.

Mole, Richard. (2018). "Sexualities and Queer Migration Research." *Sexualities*, 21(8): 1268–1270.

Monaghan, Whitney. (2016). *Queer Girls, Temporality and Screen Media: Not "Just a Phase."*. London: Palgrave Macmillan.

———. (2019). "On Time." *GLQ: A Journal of Lesbian and Gay Studies*, 25(1): 97–100.

Moraga, Cherríe. (1996). "Queer Aztlán: The Re-Formation of Chicano Tribe." In *The Material Queer: A LesBiGay Cultural Studies Reader*, Donald E. Morton (ed.). Boulder, CO: Westview Press, 297–304.

Morgan, Robin. (1970). "Introduction: The Women's Revolution." In *Sisterhood Is Powerful: An Anthology of Writings from the Women's Liberation Movement*, Robin Morgan (ed.). New York: Vintage Books, xiii–xl.

———. (1978). *Going Too Far: The Personal Chronicle of a Feminist*. New York: Vintage Books.

Morgensen, Scott Lauria. (2011). *Spaces between Us: Queer Settler Colonialism and Indigenous Decolonization. First Peoples: New Directions in Indigenous Studies*. Minneapolis: University of Minnesota Press.

Muñoz, José Esteban. (1999). *Disidentifications: Queers of Color and the Performance of Politics*. Minneapolis: University of Minnesota Press.

———. (2009). *Cruising Utopia: The Then and There of Queer Futurity*. New York: New York University Press.

Munt, Sally. (2008). *Queer Attachments: The Cultural Politics of Shame*. New York: Routledge.

Murray, Pauli. (1970). "The Liberation of Black Women." In *Voices of the New Feminism*, Mary Lou Thompson (ed.). Boston: Beacom Press, 87–102.

Mykhalovskiy, Eric, and Marsha Rosengarten. (2009). "Editorial: HIV/AIDS in Its Third Decade: Renewed Critique in Social and Cultural Analysis - an Introduction." *Social Theory and Health*, 7(3): 187–195.

Nagle, John. (2018). "Crafting Radical Opposition or Reproducing Homonormativity? Consociationalism and LGBT Rights Activism in Lebanon." *Journal of Human Rights*, 17(1): 75–88.

Namaste, Ki. (1994). "The Politics of Inside/Out: Queer Theory, Poststructuralism, and a Sociological Approach to Sexuality." *Sociological Theory*, 12(2): 220–231.

———. (1996). "'Tragic Misreadings': Queer Theory's Erasure of Transgender Subjectivity'." In *Queer Studies: A Lesbian, Gay, Bisexual, and Transgender Anthology*, Brett Beemyn and Mickey Eliason (eds.). New York and London: New York University Press, 183–203.

Namaste, Viviane K. (2009). "Undoing Theory: The 'Transgender Question' and the Epistemic Violence of Anglo-American Feminist Theory." *Hypatia*, 24(3): 11–32.

Navarre, Max. (1988). "Fighting the Victim Label." In *AIDS Cultural Analysis/Cultural Activism*, Douglas Crimp (ed.). Cambridge, MA: MIT Press, 143–146.

Nelkin, Dorothy. (1991). "AIDS and the News Media." *The Milbank Quarterly*, 69(2): 293–307.

Newton, Esther. (1972). *Mother Camp: Female Impersonators in America*. Chicago: University of Chicago Press.

Ng, Vivien. (1997). "Race Matters." In *Lesbian and Gay Studies: A Critical Reader*, Andy Medhust and Sally Munt (eds.). London: Cassell, 215–231.

Nicholas, Lucy. (2014). *Queer Post-Gender Ethics: The Shape of Selves to Come*. New York: Palgrave Macmillan.

Nicholson, Linda. (2016). "Feminism in 'Waves': Useful Metaphor or Not?." In *Feminist Theory Reader: Local and Global Perspectives*, Carole R. McCann and Seung-kyung Kim (eds.) Fourth Edition. New York and London: Routledge, 43–50.

Nietzsche, Friedrich. (2010). *On the Genealogy of Morals and Ecce Homo*. Walter Kaufmann (ed.). New York: Knopf Doubleday Publishing (originally published 1887).

Nussbaum, Martha. 1999. "The Professor of Parody." *The New Republic*. http://www.tnr.com/index.mhtml.

O'Brien, Jean M. (2010). *Firsting and Lasting: Writing Indians Out of Existence in New England*. Minneapolis: University of Minnesota Press.

O'Rourke, Michael. (2011). "The Afterlives of Queer Theory." *Continent*, 1(2): 102–116.

Oakley, Ann. (1972). *Sex, Gender and Society*. South Melbourne: Sun Books.

Olufemi, Lola. (2017). "Postcolonial Writing Is Not an Afterthought; It Is British Literature." *Varsity*. https://www.varsity.co.uk/comment/13261.

Oosterhuis, H. (1992). "Homosexual Emancipation in Germany before 1933: Two Traditions." In *Homosexuality and Male Bonding in Pre-Nazi Germany: The Youth Movement, the Gay Movement, and Male Bonding before Hitler's Rise: Original Transcripts from Der Eigene, the First Gay Journal in the World*, Hubert Kennedy (ed.). New York: J. Harrington Park Press, 1–28.

Pande, Raksha. (2017). "Strategic Essentialism." In *The International Encyclopedia of Geography: People, the Earth, Environment, and Technology*, Douglas Richardson, Noel Castree, Michael F. Goodchild, Audrey Kobayashi, Weidong Liu, Richard A. Marston (eds.). Chichester: John Wiley & Sons, 1–5.

Patton, Cindy. (1987). "Resistance and the Erotic: Reclaiming History, Setting Strategy as We Face AIDS." *Radical America*, 20(6): 68–78.

———. (1993). "Tremble, Hetero Swine!." In *Fear of a Queer Planet: Queer Politics and Social Theory*, Michael Warner (ed.). Minneapolis and London: University of Minnesota Press, 143–177.

Peacock, Kent W. (2016). "Race, the Homosexual, and the Mattachine Society of Washington, 1961–1970." *Journal of the History of Sexuality*, 25(2): 267–296.

Pearl, Monica. (2004). "AIDS and New Queer Cinema." In *New Queer Cinema: A Critical Reader*, Michele Aaron (ed.). Edinburgh: Edinburgh University Press, 23–35.

Penny, Laurie. 2018. "The Queer Art of Failing Better." *The Baffler*. https://thebaffler.com/latest/the-queer-art-of-failing-better-penny.

Phelan, Shane. 1989. *Identity Politics: Lesbian Feminism and the Limits of Community*. Philadelphia: Temple University Press.

Pilcher, Jane, and Imelda Whelehan. (2017). *Key Concepts in Gender Studies*. (Second Edition). London: SAGE Publications.

Plummer, Ken. (2011). "Critical Humanism and Queer Theory: Living with the Tensions." In *The SAGE Handbook of Qualitative Research*, Norman K. Denzin and Yvonna S. Lincoln (eds.). Los Angeles: SAGE, 195–207.

Ponce, Martin Joseph. (2018). "Queers Read What Now?." *GLQ: A Journal of Lesbian and Gay Studies*, 24(2–3): 315–341.

Probyn, Elspeth. (1993). *Sexing the Self: Gendered Positions in Cultural Studies*. London: Routledge.

———. (1996). *Outside Belongings*. New York: Routledge.

Prosser, Jay. (1998). *Second Skins: The Body Narratives of Transsexuality*. New York: Columbia University Press.

Puar, Jasbir. (2007). *Terrorist Assemblages: Homonationalism in Queer Times*. Durham, NC, and London: Duke University Press.

———. (2011). "CODA: The Cost of Getting Better: Suicide, Sensation, Switchpoints." *GLQ: A Journal of Lesbian and Gay Studies*, 18(1): 149–158.

———. (2012a). "'I Would Rather Be a Cyborg than a Goddess': Becoming-Intersectional in Assemblage Theory." *PhiloSOPHIA*, 2(1): 49–66.

———. (2012b). "Coda: The Cost of Getting Better: Suicide, Sensation, Switchpoints." *GLQ: A Journal of Lesbian and Gay Studies*, 18(1): 149–158.

———. (2013). "Homonationalism As Assemblage: Viral Travels, Affective Sexualities." *Jindal Global Law Review*, 4(2): 23–43.

———. (2017). *The Right to Maim: Debility, Capacity, Disability*. Durham, NC: Duke University Press.

Pugliese, Joseph, and Susan Stryker. (2009). "The Somatechnics of Race and Whiteness." *Social Semiotics*, 19(1): 1–8.

Puri, Jyoti. (2016). *Sexual States: Governance and the Struggle over the Antisodomy Law in India*. London: Duke University Press.

Radicalesbians. (1970). *The Woman Identified Woman*. Pittsburgh: Know, Inc. http://library.duke.edu/digitalcollections/wlmpc_wlmms01011/.

Rand, E. J. (2004). "A Disunited Nation and A Legacy of Contradiction: Queer Nation's Construction of Identity." *Journal of Communication Inquiry*, 28(4): 288–306.

Raymond, Janice. (1980). *The Transsexual Empire*. London: Women's Press.

Reid-Pharr, Robert F. (2001). *Black Gay Man: Essays. Sexual Cultures*. New York: New York University Press.

Rich, Adrienne. (1980). "Compulsory Heterosexuality and Lesbian Existence." *Signs: Journal of Women in Culture and Society*, 5(4): 631–660.

———. (1993). "Compulsory Heterosexuality and Lesbian Existence." In *The Lesbian and Gay Studies Reader*, Henry Abelove, Michele Aina Barale, and David M. Halperin (eds.). New York and London: Routledge, 227–254.

Rich, B. Ruby. (1992). "New Queer Cinema." *Sight and Sound*, 2(5): 30–35.

Richards, Christina, Walter Pierre Bouman, and Meg-John Barker (eds.). (2017). *Genderqueer and Non-Binary Genders*. London: Palgrave Macmillan.

Richardson, Dianne. (2006). "Bordering Theory." In *Intersections between Feminist and Queer Theory*, Diane Richardson, Janice McLaughlin, and Mark E. Casey (eds.). New York: Palgrave, 19–37.

Rifkin, Mark. (2011). *When Did Indians Become Straight?: Kinship, the History of Sexuality, and Native Sovereignty*. Oxford: Oxford University Press.

Riggs, Damien W. (2010). "On Accountability: Towards a White Middle-Class Queer 'Post Identity Politics Identity Politics.'" *Ethnicities*, 10(3): 344–357.

Riley, Denise (1988). *"Am I That Name?" Feminism and the Category of "Women" in History*, Houndmills: Macmillan Press.

———. (2000). *The Words of Selves: Identification, Solidarity, Irony*. Stanford: Stanford University Press.

Robinson, Brandon Andrew. (2016). "Heteronormativity and Homonormativity." In *The Wiley Blackwell Encyclopedia of Gender and Sexuality Studies*, Nancy A. Naples (ed.). Chichester: John Wiley & Sons. 1–3.

Ross, Liz. (2013). *Revolution Is for Us: The Left and Gay Liberation in Australia*. Melbourne: Interventions.

Roughgarden, Joan. (2004). *Evolution's Rainbow: Diversity, Gender, and Sexuality in Nature and People*. Berkeley and Los Angeles: University of California Press.

Ruan, Fang Fu. (1991). *Sex in China: Studies in Sexology in Chinese Culture*. New York: Plenum Press.

Ruberg, Bonnie. (2018). "Queerness and Video Games: Queer Game Studies and New Perspectives through Play." *GLQ: A Journal of Lesbian and Gay Studies*, 24(4): 543–555.

Rubin, Gayle. (1984). "Thinking Sex: Notes for a Radical Theory of the Politics of Sexuality." In *Pleasure and Danger: Exploring Female Sexuality*, Carole S. Vance (ed.). Boston: Routledge and Kegan Paul, 267–319.

———. (2011). "Introduction: Sex, Gender, Politics." In *Deviations*, Gayle Rubin (ed.). Durham, NC, and London: Duke University Press, 1–32.

Rubin, Henry S. (1998). "Phenomenology as Method in Trans Studies." *GLQ: A Journal of Lesbian and Gay Studies*, 4(2): 263–281.

Ruffolo, David. (2009). *Post-Queer Politics. Queer Interventions*. Farnham and Burlington, VT: Ashgate.

Rupp, Leila J. (2011). "The Persistence of Transnational Organizing: The Case of the Homophile Movement." *The American Historical Review*, 116(4): 1014–1039.

Russo, Vito. (1987). *The Celluloid Closet: Homosexuality in the Movies*. New York: Harper and Row.

———. 1988. "Why We Fight." Albany, NY: ACT UP. http://www.actupny.org/documents/whfight.html.

Salamon, Gayle. (2010). *Assuming a Body: Transgender and Rhetorics of Materiality*. New York: Columbia University Press.

Salih, Sarah. (2004). "Introduction." In *The Judith Butler Reader*, Sarah Salih (ed.). Malden, MA: Blackwell Publishing. 1–17.

Samek, Alyssa A. (2016). "Violence and Identity Politics: 1970s Lesbian-Feminist Discourse and Robin Morgan's 1973 West Coast Lesbian Conference Keynote Address." *Communication and Critical/Cultural Studies*, 13(3): 232–249.

Samuels, Ellen. (2003). "My Body, My Closet: Invisible Disability and the Limits of Coming-Out Discourse." *GLQ: A Journal of Lesbian and Gay Studies*, 9(1–2): 233–255.

Sang, Tze-lan D. (2003). *The Emerging Lesbian: Female Same-Sex Desire in Modern China*. Chicago: University of Chicago Press.

Schmidt, Johanna. (2003). "Paradise Lost? Social Change and Fa'afafine in Samoa." *Current Sociology*, 51(3-4): 417–432.

Schoonover, Karl, and Rosalind Galt. (2016). *Queer Cinema in the World*. Durham, NC: Duke University Press.

Sedgwick, Eve Kosofsky. (1991). "How to Bring Your Kids Up Gay." *Social Text*, (29): 18–27.

———. (1992). *Between Men: English Literature and Male Homosocial Desire*. New York: Columbia University Press.

———. (1993). *Tendencies*. Durham, NC: Duke University Press.

———. (2003). *Touching Feeling: Affect, Pedagogy, Performativity*. Durham, NC: Duke University Press.

———. (2008). *Epistemology of the Closet: Updated with a New Preface*. University of California Press.

Sedgwick, Eve Kosofsky, and Adam Frank. (1995). "Shame in the Cybernetic Fold: Reading Silvan Tomkins." *Critical Inquiry*, 21(2): 496–522.

Seidman, Steven. (1996). "Introduction." In *Queer Theory/Sociology*, Steven Seidman (ed.). Cambridge, MA and Oxford: Blackwell Publishers, 1–29.

———. (2002). *Beyond the Closet: The Transformation of Gay and Lesbian Life*. New York: Routledge.

———. (2009). "Critique of Compulsory Heterosexuality." *Sexuality Research and Social Policy*, 6(1): 18–28.

Sender, Katherine. (2006). "Queens for a Day: Queer Eye for the Straight Guy and the Neoliberal Project." *Critical Studies in Media Communication*, 23(2): 131–151.

Serano, Julia. (2007). *Whipping Girl: Transsexual Woman on Sexism and the Scapegoating of Femininity*. Emeryville, CA: Seal Press.

Siegel, Deborah. (2007). *Sisterhood Interrupted: From Radical Women to Grrls Gone Wild.* New York: Palgrave Macmillan.

Simpson, Nicola. (2004). "Coming Attractions: A Comparative History of the Hollywood Studio System and the Porn Business." *Historical Journal of Film, Radio and Television*, 24(4): 635–652.

Slagle, R. Anthony. (1995). "In Defense of Queer Nation: From Identity Politics to a Politics of Difference." *Western Journal of Communication*, 59: 85–102.

Smith, A. (2010). "Queer Theory and Native Studies: The Heteronormativity of Settler Colonialism." *GLQ: A Journal of Lesbian and Gay Studies*, 16(1–2): 41–68.

Smith, Barbara. (1993). "Queer Politics: Where's the Revolution?." *The Nation*, 257(1): 12–16.

Smith, Dinitia. (1998). "'Queer Theory' Is Entering The Literary Mainstream." *The New York Times* https://www.nytimes.com/1998/01/17/books/queer-theory-is-entering-the-literary-mainstream.html.

Snediker, Michael. (2006). "Queer Optimism." *Postmodern Culture*, 16: 3.

Snyder, Claire R. (2008). "What Is Third-Wave Feminism? A New Directions Essay." *Signs: Journal of Women in Culture and Society*, 34(1): 175–196.

Solanas, Valerie. (2004). *SCUM Manifesto.* New York: Verso (originally published 1967).

Somerville, Siobhan B. (2000). *Queering the Color Line: Race and the Invention of Homosexuality in American Culture.* Durham, NC: Duke University Press.

Sontag, Susan. (1982). "Notes on 'Camp.'." In *A Susan Sontag Reader*, Middlesex: Penguin Books, 105–119 (originally published 1964).

———. (1989). *AIDS and Its Metaphors.* New York: Farrar Straus and Giroux.

Spade, Dean. (2003). "Resisting Medicine, Re/Modelling Gender." *Berkeley Women's Law Journal*, 18(15): 15–37.

———. (2015). *Normal Life: Administrative Violence, Critical Trans Politics, and the Limits of the Law.* Durham, NC: Duke University Press.

Spivak, Gayatri Chakravorty. (1996). "Subaltern Studies: Deconstructing Historiography." In *The Spivak Reader: Selected Works of Gayatri Chakravorty Spivak*, Donna Landry and Gerald MacLean (eds.). New York: Routledge, 203–235 (originally published 1985).

Srivastava, Sanjay. (2007). *Passionate Modernity: Sexuality, Class and Consumption in India.* New Delhi: Routledge.

Steakley, James D. (1975). *The Homosexual Emancipation Movement in Germany.* New York: Arno Press.

Stein, Marc. (2019). *The Stonewall Riots: A Documentary History.* New York: New York University Press.

Steinmetz, Katy. 2014. "The Transgender Tipping Point." *Time.* http://time.com/135480/transgender-tipping-point/.

Stephen, Gerald. (2017). "Transcoding Sexuality: Computational Performativity and Queer Code Practices." *QED: A Journal in GLBTQ Worldmaking*, 4(2): 1–25.

Stockdill, Brett C. (1997). "ACT-UP (AIDS Coalition to Unleash Power)." In *Protest, Power, and Change: An Encyclopedia of Nonviolent Action from ACT-UP to Women's Suffrage*, Roger S. Powers and William B. Vogele (eds.). New York and London: Routledge, 9–11.

Stockton, Kathryn Bond. (2009). *The Queer Child; Or, Growing Sideways in the Twentieth Century*. Durham, NC: Duke University Press.

Stoler, Ann Laura. (1995). *Race and the Education of Desire: Foucault's History of Sexuality and the Colonial Order of Things*. Durham, NC: Duke University Press.

Stoltenberg, John. (1990). *Refusing to Be a Man: Essays on Sex and Justice*. New York: Meridian.

Stone, Sandy. (1991). "The Empire Strikes Back: A Posttranssexual Manifesto." In *Body Guards: The Cultural Politics of Gender Ambiguity*, J. Epstein and K. Straub (eds.). New York: Routledge, 280–304.

Stone, Sharon Dale. (1996). "Bisexual Women and the "Threat" to Lesbian Space: Or What if All the Lesbians Leave?"." *Frontiers: A Journal of Women Studies*, 16(1): 101–116.

Strause, Jackie. (2018). "Oscars Devotes Segment to Voices of #Metoo, Time's up Movements." *The Hollywood Reporter*. https://www.hollywoodreporter.com/news/ashley-judd-salma-hayek-honor-diverse-films-metoo-times-up-movements-oscars-2018-1091014.

Stryker, Susan. (2004). "Transgender Studies: Queer Theory's Evil Twin." *GLQ: A Journal of Lesbian and Gay Studies*, 10(2): 212–215.

———. (2006). "(De)Subjugated Knowledges: An Introduction to Transgender Studies." In *The Transgender Studies Reader*, Susan Stryker and Steven Whittle (eds.). New York and London: Routledge, 1–17.

———. (2008). "Transgender History, Homonormativity, and Disciplinarity." *Radical History Review*, 100: 145–157.

———. (2017). *Transgender History: The Roots of Today's Revolution*, Second Edition. New York: Seal Press.

Sullivan, Nikki. (2003). *A Critical Introduction to Queer Theory*. New York: New York University Press.

Sycamore, Mattilda Bernstein. (2008). "Gay Shame: From Queer Autonomous Space to Direct Action Extravaganza." In *That's Revolting: Queer Strategies for Resisting Assimilation*, Mattilda Bernstein Sycamore (ed.). Brooklyn: Soft Skull Press. 268–295.

Taylor, Keeanga-Yamahtta (ed.). (2017). *How We Get Free: Black Feminism and the Combahee River Collective*. Chicago: Haymarket Books.

Taylor, Yvette. (2018). "Queer, but Classless?." In *The Ashgate Research Companion to Queer Theory*, Noreen Giffney and Michael O'Rourke (eds.). New York: Routledge, 199–218 (originally published 2009).

Teal, Donn. (1971). *The Gay Militants*. New York: Stein and Day.

Thomas, Calvin. (2018). "On Being Post-Normal: Heterosexuality after Queer Theory." In *The Ashgate Research Companion to Queer Theory*, Noreen Giffney and Michael O'Rourke (eds.). New York: Routledge, 17–33 (originally published 2009).

Thompson, Debra. (2017). "An Exoneration of Black Rage." *South Atlantic Quarterly*, 116(3): 457–481.

Tomso, Gregory. (2008). "Viral Sex and the Politics of Life." *South Atlantic Quarterly*, 107(2): 265–285.

Treichler, Paula A. (1987). "AIDS, Homophobia, and Biomedical Discourse: An Epidemic of Signification." *AIDS: Cultural Analysis/Cultural Activism*, 43: 31–70.

———. (1999). *How to Have Theory in an Epidemic: Cultural Chronicles of AIDS*. Durham, NC: Duke University Press.

Tuck, Eve, and Yang, K. Wayne. (2012). "Decolonization Is Not a Metaphor." *Decolonization: Indigeneity, Education & Society*, 1(1): 1–40.

Turner, William. (2000). *A Genealogy of Queer Theory*. Philadelphia: Temple University Press.

Valocchi, Stephen. (2016). "Normalisation." In *The Wiley Blackwell Encyclopedia of Gender and Sexuality Studies*, Nancy Naples, Renee C. Hoogland, Maithree Wickramasinghe. Wai Ching Angela Wong (eds.). Malden, MA, and Oxford: Wiley-Blackwell.

Vanita, Ruth. (2002). *Queering India: Same-Sex Love and Eroticism in Indian Culture and Society*. New York: Routledge.

Villarejo, Amy. (2014). *Ethereal Queer: Television, Historicity, Desire*. Durham, NC: Duke University Press.

Vincent, Ben, and Ana Manzano. (2017). "History and Cultural Diversity." In *Genderqueer and Non-Binary Genders*, Christina Richards, Walter Pierre Bouman, and Meg-John Barker (eds.). London: Palgrave Macmillan, 11–30.

Volpp, Leti. (2017). "Feminist, Sexual, and Queer Citizenship." In *The Oxford Handbook of Citizenship*, Ayelet Shachar, Rainer Baubock, Irene Bloemraad, and Maarten Vink (eds.). Oxford: Oxford University Press, 153–177.

Walker, Lisa M. (1993). "How to Recognize a Lesbian: The Cultural Politics of Looking like What You Are." *Signs: Journal of Women in Culture and Society*, 18(4): 866–890.

Wallace, Lee. (2003). *Sexual Encounters: Pacific Texts, Modern Sexualities*. Ithaca, NY: Cornell University Press.

Walters, Suzanna Danuta. (1996). "From Here to Queer: Radical Feminism, Postmodernism, and the Lesbian Menace (Or, Why Can't a Woman Be More like a Fag?)." *Signs: Journal of Women in Culture and Society*, 21(4): 830–869.

———. (2016). "Introduction: The Dangers of a Metaphor — Beyond the Battlefield in the Sex Wars." *Signs: Journal of Women in Culture and Society*, 42(1): 1–9.

Walton, David. (2012). *Doing Cultural Theory*. Los Angeles: SAGE Publications.

Warner, Michael. (1991). "Introduction: Fear of a Queer Planet." *Social Text*, 29: 3–17.

Watney, Simon. (1987a). "The Spectacle of AIDS." *October*, 43: 71–86.

———. (1987b). *Policing Desire: Pornography, AIDS, and the Media*. Minneapolis: University of Minnesota Press.

Weed, Elizabeth. (1997). "Introduction." In *Feminism Meets Queer Theory*, Elizabeth Weed and Naomi Schor (eds.). Bloomington: Indiana University Press, vii–xv.

Weeks, Jeffrey. (1989). *Sex, Politics and Society: The Regulation of Sexuality since 1800*. London: Longman (originally published 1981).

White, Patricia. (1999). *Uninvited: Classical Hollywood Cinema and Lesbian Representability*. Bloomington: Indiana University Press.

Whittle, Steven. (2006). "Foreword." In *The Transgender Studies Reader*, Susan Stryker and Steven Whittle (eds.). New York: Routledge, xi–xvi.

Wiederman, Michael W. (2015). "Sexual Script Theory: Past, Present, and Future." In *Handbook of the Sociology of Sexualities*, J. DeLamater, R.F. Plante (eds.). Cham: Springer, 7–22.

Wiegman, Robyn. (2014). "The Times We're In: Queer Feminist Criticism and the Reparative 'Turn'." *Feminist Theory*, 15(1): 4–25.

———. (2015). "Eve's Triangles, or Queer Studies beside Itself." *Differences A Journal of Feminist Cultural Studies*, 26(1): 48–73.

Willett, Graham. (2000). *Living Out Loud: A History of Gay and Lesbian Activism in Australia*. Melbourne: Allen & Unwin.

———. (2010). "Howard and the Homos." *Social Movement Studies*, 9(2): 187–199.

Williams, Cristan. (2014). "Transgender." *TSQ: Transgender Studies Quarterly*, 1(1–2): 232–234.

Wolf, Sherry. (2009). *Sexuality and Socialism: History, Politics, and Theory of LGBT Liberation*. Chicago: Haymarket Books.

Worth, Dooley, and Ruth Rodriguez. (1987). "Latina Women and AIDS." *Radical America*, 20(6): 63–67.

Yep, Gust A., Karen E. Lovaas, and John P. Elia. (2003). "A Critical Appraisal of Assimilationist and Radical Ideologies Underlying Same-Sex Marriage in LGBT Communities in the United States." *Journal of Homosexuality*, 45(1): 45–64.

Index